Celebrating 100 Years of the Texas Folklore Society, 1909–2009

Celebrating 100 Years of the Texas Folklore Society, 1909–2009

Edited by Kenneth L. Untiedt

Publications of the Texas Folklore Society LXVI

UNT PRESS

University of North Texas Press
Denton, Texas

10 9 8 7 6 5 4 3 2 1

Permissions:
University of North Texas Press
1155 Union Circle #311336
Denton, TX 76203-5017

The paper used in this book meets the minimum requirements of the American National Standard for Permanence of Paper for Printed Library Materials, z39.48.1984. Binding materials have been chosen for durability.

Library of Congress Cataloging-in-Publication Data

Celebrating 100 Years of the Texas Folklore Society, 1909–2009 / edited by Kenneth L. Untiedt.—1st ed.
p. cm. — (Publications of the Texas Folklore Society; 66)
Includes bibliographical references and index.
ISBN 978-1-57441-277-2 (cloth : alk. paper)

1. Texas Folklore Society—History—20th century. 2. Texas Folklore Society—History—21st century. 3. Folklore—Texas. 4. Texas—Social life and customs. I. Untiedt, Kenneth L., 1966 II. Texas Folklore Society. III. Title: Celebrating one hundred years of the Texas Folklore Society, 1909-2009. IV. Series: Publications of the Texas Folklore Society; no. 66.
GR111.T4C45 2009
398.209764--dc22

2009025355

Celebrating 100 Years of the Texas Folklore Society, 1909–2009 is Number LXVI in the Publications of the Texas Folklore Society

CONTENTS

PREFACE

The Texas Folklore Society celebrates its 100th anniversary in 2009, so it wasn't hard to decide on a theme for this year's publication. I didn't want to write Volume IV of the history of the TFS, an undertaking F. E. Abernethy began with the first three volumes that cover the Society's origin and development from 1909–2000. I wanted this book to examine what makes the Texas Folklore Society unique among other scholarly organizations, and thereby sum up why we've lasted so long. I believe the Texas Folklore Society's secret for longevity lies in those things that make it different from other organizations—its publications, its people, and its meetings. Those are the features that have not only kept the Society going for a hundred years, but they have also made it thrive. So, in this book you'll find some articles that provide a critical, analytical view of what the TFS has produced in folklore research, and you'll also find some very personal, reflective articles from members of the memories and friendships they treasure.

In the program for the 1935 annual meeting, J. Frank Dobie summed up the importance of the Texas Folklore Society:

> The Texas Folk-Lore Society is twenty-six years old. It has published nearly 2000 pages of lore pertaining to Texas and the Southwest. It has contributed enormously to such books as Lomax's *American Ballads and Folk Songs*, Sandburg's *The American Song Bag*, Dobie's *Coronado's Children*, and other books. It is by all odds the most important state organization of its kind in America.

That was over seventy years ago, when the Society was practically still in its infancy. We've now published well over 14,000 pages of folklore material, in sixty-six regular publications (including this one). We've also sponsored another thirty-six publications, ranging from pamphlets to full-length books on the cowboy life, the lore of Native Americans, and even traditional oral narratives from Ireland. While most similar organizations publish periodical journals, Publications of the Texas Folklore Society are full-length books that contain a balanced mixture of collected lore and scholarly analysis, as well as many photographs, illustrations, and original artwork from members and nationally renowned artists.

From the beginning, the Society has been filled with people who contributed to the organization and its purpose in significant ways. John Lomax and Leonidas Payne were not only the driving forces behind getting the organization started, but Lomax's fame also attracted other renowned members such as Dorothy Scarborough and Louise Pound. Other influential scholars who presented papers and held offices, or who contributed regularly to the publications include Walter Prescott Webb, J. Mason Brewer, Harry Ransom, C. L. Sonnichsen, and Allen Maxwell. Current active members include James Ward Lee, Joyce Gibson Roach, Robert Flynn, and Elmer Kelton, all of whom bring recognition through their publications and attendance at meetings.

The annual meetings seem more like social events or family reunions than they do formal academic gatherings. Hundreds of members continue to meet each year to fulfill the Society's purpose: to collect, preserve, and share the lore of Texas and the Southwest. We've held meetings in thirty-two different cities, from Arlington to El Paso to San Angelo to Wimberley, but the diversity of locations is only one thing that makes TFS meetings memorable. From the beginning, working anthropologists, photographers, artists, and ranchers have come to share folklore in their fields, as have musicians and storytellers who make their living on the road, keeping their crafts alive through the oral tradition. These members and many other such lay people—secretaries, police officers, farmers, lawyers, journalists, housewives—are all involved in every aspect of the Society's meetings and publications. And members who present papers do so to the entire meeting body, because we hold only one session at a time, something that is unique among organizations these days.

But the papers are only part of the meetings. The hoots are what makes the Society so family-oriented. Many members bring their children (and even their grandchildren), and the kids enjoy taking part in the festivities and performances as much as the adults. In recent years there has been a push to involve more young members, and several college and even high school students have given papers during the regular sessions. Several of our younger members have "grown up" at the annual meetings, attending their first ones while still in diapers. It is those members who will take the Texas Folklore Society into its next one hundred years.

I want to thank the many contributors who wrote articles for this book. I also thank a couple of administrators who have supported the TFS since their arrival at Stephen F. Austin State University: Mark Sanders, the new Chair of the English Department, and Brian Murphy, Dean of the College of Liberal and Applied Arts. As always, I thank all our friends at the UNT Press. I especially thank Janet Simonds, who helps me with nearly every stage of the publication of these books.

This book does not have a specific dedication, but it is for all the people who read papers, contribute articles to publications, serve on the Board, and even those who just come to the meetings and listen to papers. You're what keeps this organization alive.

Kenneth L. Untiedt
Stephen F. Austin State University
Nacogdoches, Texas
Cinco de Mayo, 2009

WHAT'S THE POINT?

WHY THE FOLK COME IN THE FIRST PLACE

"Hooked on Texas" postcard, 1986

HOOKED ON TEXAS

by Clarence Jay Faulkner

[The postcards used as illustrations for this article, as well as those used for "filler pages" and division pages between chapters throughout this book, were collected by Clarence Faulkner and, as he states in his article, donated to the Texas Folklore Society for its archives. We greatly appreciate this contribution, as the postcards display a unique perspective of collectible Texana over the last century.—*Untiedt*]

Being a proud native Texan born in 1949 not far from the confluence of the Brazos and Bosque Rivers, (and raised in east Waco), a survivor of the devastating tornado of May 11, 1953, and a lover of Dr. Pepper and Moon Pie, I remain hooked on Texas even though I am currently far away in the Pacific Northwest.

In recent years, the hook has taken a stronger bite as I've embarked on a serious study of all things Texas. I scan everything for tidbits on Texas and my memberships/subscriptions include the Texas Folklore Society, Sul Ross State's Center for Big Bend Studies, *Texas Observer*, *Texas Monthly*, and Marfa's *Big Bend Sentinel* weekly newspaper. I've even found Texana in the *New Yorker* and *Los Angeles* magazines. One of my neatest and most unpredictable sources of information is from my collecting of old Texas-themed postcards. Let me tell you how that all came about.

About six years ago I was invited to attend a weekly Toastmasters meeting where twenty-five to thirty men gather to practice public speaking and, more so, to shoot the breeze. I decided to attack my lifelong fear of public speaking and took on the challenge of becoming a Competent Toastmaster, with the first-level project of ten speeches to develop basic speaking skills. I began with the introductory "ice breaker" short speech, giving some biographical and personal background, and then moved on to the

"Bosque Bridge. Waco, Texas" postcard, 1914

other projects emphasizing eye contact, gestures, use of props and aids, a convincing speech, and a story/folktale. For the props/ visual aids speech I displayed a variety of Texas postcards I had begun collecting through my new hobby of postcard collecting, more formally known as "deltiology."

It worked so well I decided my story speech would be about a funny event that happened in the early 1950s, when as a kid I often trekked from east Waco to the Brazos River and across the old rickety but now famous Suspension Bridge on Saturdays to attend the weekly movie matinee at the Waco Theater about seven blocks past the river on Austin Avenue. The story was easy to ad-lib, as I simply passed around my postcard of the bridge and told of how when crossing it one Saturday morning with my brother and sister in tow, we looked down into the water and noticed a bunch of half or silver dollars shining in the shallow water. We had been warned not to go down to the water or mess up our clothes, but during the movie I decided that on the way home I would gather my treasure, and I couldn't wait for the western movie to end.

Clarence Jay Faulkner

When we got back across the bridge I hiked down through the Johnson grass and through the stickery brush, getting my clothes messed up and though fearful of quicksand I was committed to wading out to gather the coins. Well, to spare you a long-winded speech, when I reached down and pulled up the first coin I found it to be the end out of a frozen orange juice can. We trudged home and it was no fun facing grandma Pearl Grusendorf disheveled and treasureless.

The men loved the story and I was tagged "Texas Storyteller" and enlisted to speak regularly and to fill in for last minute no-shows. I moved on to tell of the tornado, adventures in "hobo jungle" by Paul Quinn College behind our house in east Waco, my travels and oilfield work in West Texas, and summers on Padre Island.

I never dreamed a few postcards could be such a great personal assistant, garner me new friends, and propel me to aspire to becoming a proficient and interesting Texas storyteller. I obtain mixed lots of Texas-themed postcards from the various postcard eras (pioneer, postcard, white border, linen, chrome, and modern), and especially enjoy those that have been written on and mailed

"San Fernando Cathedral" postcard, 1909

because, aside from the Texas picture, they each preserve a bit of Texas history and record through vignettes of daily life. For example, I recently obtained a card mailed shortly after the turn of the 20th century in San Antonio, and coincidentally about the time of the founding of the Texas Folklore Society. The card was sent by a sixteen-year-old young lady who wrote of moving to the city and working in the dry-goods department at Joske's.

I really enjoy the cards I call "Texas exaggeration," which feature Texas' biggest this or that, and I've donated many to the TFS in hopes they may be preserved and/or used in the annual book. I search for the cards and use them to develop, illustrate, and supplement my repertoire of Texas-themed stories. I think there is a lot of Texas history, folklore, culture, humor, exaggeration, and Texana in general that can be preserved and shared through collecting and preserving Texas postcards.

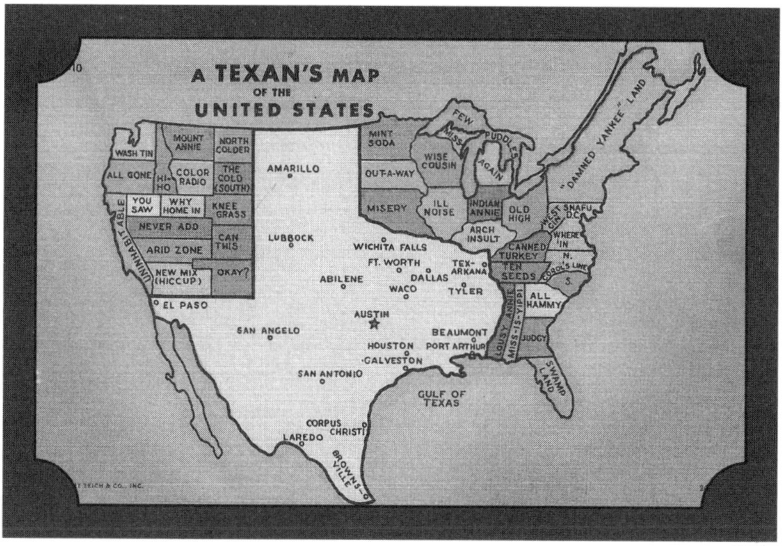

1940s Texas brag postcard

I hope you might consider collecting postcards—or any other items—as a means of preserving bits of Texas history and lore that may otherwise be discarded, and maybe you too will become "hooked on Texas."

One to write home about, Texas postcard from 1954

BUM Ranch Longhorns

BEWARE OF FOLKLORE ADDICTION

by Scott Hill Bumgardner

Texas. Texan. Mentioning either of these words engenders strong reactions regardless of where they might be heard. Throughout the world many people will recall some of our great Texas history from the era of western movies. Many a self-professed civilized urban dweller might stick his nose up in the air and comment about the uncouth rednecks that live here. Surely, some of these same people might make remarks about Texans being gun-toting cowboys. Our neighbors in Louisiana have a much better idea of who we are, but they are likely to sneer at us as a bunch of loud-mouthed braggarts. Even here at home you can find a wide variety of reactions to a question such as, "What defines a Texan?" I believe the best answers are contained in the Texas Folklore Society's publications. But, beware friends—this folklore can be addictive. It may lead you down strange new paths.

Texans are an amazingly diverse group. We have our uncouth rednecks, in the worst sense of the words, as well as our good red-necked hard-working folk. Many of us are armed and ready to protect our realm. No doubt about it, many have embraced the cowboy image, but the real thing is a little harder to find. Do we brag? You bet. The stories of our diverse peoples have been derived from Vietnamese boat people, Mexican peons, healers, oilmen, and more. But for me, the addiction began with the Society's editor, J. Frank Dobie. Dobie brought the history and lore of Texas to life.

Suddenly a new world opened for a Texas boy, stuck in Louisiana. The world of cowboys and Indians from my television and movie-inspired dreams came to life. History that had been terribly dry and boring took on new meaning. Lowly creatures crawled off the pages to take form. Texas Longhorn cattle no longer just ate, fertilized the land, and fed us; they walked the pages to explain the western mystique. The Texan in me sprang up and craved more.

Boots and cowboy hats soon took the place of tennis shoes and ball caps. I now studied on my own to learn more about my land. Drawn as by a magnet, God's land called for me to return. After college I finally escaped Louisiana, the land of yaw-hee, to begin life as a Texas lawman in the land of yee-haw. Working in the big city of Houston was no deterrent to embracing the Texas way. Surrounding myself with Society publications and like-minded friends, I scratched this addiction's itch. Before long my partner and I had even emblazoned our business cards with the phrase, "The law west of Cullen," indicating our patrol area's eastern boundary.

Dobie may have been the key, but the Texas pathway toward my cravings was well paved by a number of other writers and editors, such as Boatright and Abernethy. The addiction led me into the horseman's world, which I guarantee sure required many an extra hour of work to pay for. Twelve hundred pounds of horse flesh rolling around on top of me eventually gave me the leisure time to begin writing my own stories and cowboy poetry. This recuperative leisure time opened new chapters and new doors. Physical recovery was complete, but the addiction to Texas and its stories grew.

Yes friends, as happens with addictions I have now become the pusher. For nineteen years now, I have been pushing this Texas drug to school children and adults alike. Promoting the Houston Livestock Show and Rodeo through their Speakers Committee and later as a professional storyteller, I found the access needed to pass on folklore and original tales to the unwary. The spark I have planted will kindle into a bright flame in a few of the victims of Texas' addictive story.

But life seems to come full circle, and I have recently taken a shot of that earliest of Dobie's drugs, the Texas Longhorn. As my addiction continues to grow to overshadow all of my life, I can sit on the porch and watch my Texas cattle graze. Their horns sweep out, as the Texas sun shines down, sparkling upon those massive horns and illuminating their colorful speckled hides. These cattle represent a strong breed that helped to shape the land and peoples of early Texas.

Scott and storytelling fans at the Hitchcock Public Library

Stories constantly flow though my mind because of the addictive nature of the many resources we have been handed. Our story is often not unique, but the totality of those stories has given our state a unique flavor. Thanks, Texas Folklore Society, for this wonderful addiction.

Vicky Rose with Buddy

McDADE AND ME

by Vicky Rose

The first time I attended a meeting of the Texas Folklore Society, it brought back vivid memories of my hometown. As I sat listening to others talk about different folklore from around the state, I remembered the coolness of Aunt Stell's grape arbor, the sound of gravel crunching under my feet as my sisters and I walked along neglected railroad tracks, and I smelled once again the musty odor of a general store time forgot.

McDade, while I was growing up there, had a population of about 350 people. Situated in Central Texas, thirty-three miles east of Austin, outsiders deemed McDade on the far side of the moon from modern civilization. Most of the people who lived there could be described as either "Dutchmen," meaning those of German extraction, or "Americans," which meant a mongrel race which could be made up of anything, but was mostly Scotch-Irish. Because of their hard work and determination, the Germans were usually wealthier than their American neighbors, owning their own land, building solid houses, and having tidier farms. However, because they were isolated and clannish, they had tended to inbreed, and it caused much more physical and mental defects among them than the healthier Americans.

Although many German Americans fought with valor in both World Wars, there were a few holdouts who still pledged alliance to the fatherland, and this caused friction. Family legend has it that my grandfather, after hearing one man brag about what "the Kaiser's boys" would do to the Americans soldiers, went into the general store and bought an axe handle that he proceeded to take outside and use upon the heretic. By the time I came along, World War II was long gone; the younger generations of "Dutchmen" became sensitive to the problems of marrying family members, and "Americans," like my father, worked hard to escape the poverty of the sharecropper. While relationships in and around the community improved, the rest of the world still looked at us askew.

Paint Creek

Neighbors farming on rich, black gumbo fifteen miles up the road laughed at the deep, infertile sand around McDade. The McDade School only went to the eighth grade, and we had to ride the bus to nearby Elgin to go to high school. Phone calls between the two towns meant long distance rates, putting a deterrent on making friends. McDade had been too small for a band program, so we could not participate in that activity in high school, but because our boys had a reputation as rough hillbillies, the coaches loved them for sports. Two families of Mexicans lived in McDade, and later, two young black students joined our little school when they came to live with their grandparents, the only negroes in McDade. Although we had our prejudices, we got along fairly well, and all of us were dismayed when we began a high school where racial tensions ran high. While most people were kind, we were always aware that we were the outsiders, ultrasensitive at being thought of as poor trash, or as inbred.

These small hills, known as the Yegua Knobs, were used as outlaw hideouts

The thing that saved our dignity was the folklore that surrounded us. Once known as Tie Town because of the railroad ties cut from local lumber, McDade had been a thriving city with saloons, blacksmith stables, and a millinery shop among other businesses. Indians had stopped for generations at nearby Paint Creek to obtain red dirt they used for body painting, camping by the water and burying their dead on a rising hill flanking the creek. For years, men searched for gold supposedly buried by Spaniards just before being attacked by Indians near that creek. Close to McDade, another stream, the Yegua, ran on heavily wooded land from small hills known as "the Knobs." Sam Houston, along with his family, would visit sympathetic friends in the Knobs, often staying for days at a time.

After the Civil War, the Knobs became a hideout for bad men. Gangs like the Notch Cutters robbed and plundered. A deputy sheriff was sent in to investigate, but he was killed and no more

The old rock saloon now houses the McDade Historical Society Museum

dared to come. Men went everywhere armed. As good men continued to be murdered and robbed, a few of them began to take justice into their own hands. After a series of rustlings, hangings, retaliations, and more killings, violence peaked at what became known as the "Christmas Hangings." On Christmas Eve in 1883, men belonging to The League for Law and Order apprehended one outlaw on the streets of McDade, then swept through the old rock saloon and gathered two more. They took them dragging and kicking to a nearby tree and hanged them. Such vigilante justice, although perhaps necessary at the time, caused the other citizens of Bastrop County to further look with distain at wild and wooly McDade. An ancient gnarled post oak stands across the street from the old rock saloon, and in McDade, it became affectionately known as the hanging tree, although old timers insisted that the actual hangings took place a mile out of town on a hickory tree.

We were poor and we were backward, but we knew we were special. We had tales of Indians and Spaniards with fabled gold. We had stories of Sam Houston stomping around our hills, visiting with our people. We had fierce outlaws and gangs of men so bad, they ran off real lawmen and could only be dealt with by the iron-willed men who lived within our community. When old men laugh and tell me my uncles were so rowdy that they had "blood on their hats" from all the fights they got into, I shake my head and grin. The folklore of my town and the folklore of my family have provided me with a rock to cling to when the opinions and abuses of the rest of the world sometimes threaten to overwhelm me.

In the early days, no one came to McDade, or to Texas, because they wanted to. There are better places to live—lands with higher fertility and more moderate climates. They came because trouble and poverty drove them to it. The folklore they surrounded themselves with made what had been forced upon them by circumstances not only bearable, it gave them pride and self-respect.

The Texas Folklore Society continues to do this, providing a rock to stand upon when tribulations try to pull us down. By promoting and preserving a unique part of our heritage, The Texas Folklore Society defines and uplifts all Texans of yesterday, today, and tomorrow. Being a part of it is like coming home.

Lucy Fischer West at age nine in Mexico City, dressed in an outfit bought in the *Zócalo*, the city's main square, where one vendor held up a blanket while another dressed her

MOTHER LODES OF MEXICAN LORE

by Lucy Fischer West

I became acquainted with J. Frank Dobie, Wilson M. Hudson, and Mody Boatright when I worked for James M. Day as a work-study student my first year at Texas Western College. It was James who taught me the tools for historical research. My introduction to the Texas Folklore Society came as I typed and re-typed his TFS articles from the legal-size yellow pads on which he wrote them. My first job for John O. was transcribing tapes of interviews he'd done while on a trip to Mexico he and James had taken, chasing down Pancho Villa stories. When I started attending Texas Folklore Society meetings at the long-ago age of twenty-one, a whole new world opened up. I began discovering to what extent the lore transferred to me through oral tradition had been preserved by folklorists like Jovita Gonzáles, Riley Aiken, Américo Paredes, and others who valued it as I do. In addition to the written word, there were those amazing Hoots brought to life by Hermes Nye, Martha Emmons, Francis E. Abernethy, Jean Schnitz, and the talented Haile family.

By virtue of being married to a bona-fide folklorist, over the years our home became a stopping place for scholars seeking guidance in their projects. Joe Graham's gathering of folk toys purchased at the Juárez market wound up on our front lawn as we catalogued and labeled each piece after eating my Mexican food. Doc Sonnichsen was a frequent visitor to our home, and I listened with rapt attention to his stories, especially the El Paso ghost stories that he told with such gusto and a sparkle in his blue eyes. On one occasion, Doc and Miss Martha shared the piano bench with our very young son John, singing "Go Tell Aunt Rody" while he accompanied them. I wish I'd had the tape recorder going. What an evening that was! In dozens of letters written after he retired from UTEP and moved to Tucson, Doc would relate in great

John O. West

detail the research projects he was in the midst of and insist that I tell him what was going on at the West house, remembering often to send regards to my mother as well. Our nearly weekly letter writing lasted for years, until he could no longer quite position his fingers on the right keys of his Underwood and I'd have to guess what he had written. His greatest gift to me was valuing the seasons and cycles of my life.

One Christmas, James and I surprised John O. with the volumes of Texas Folklore Society Publications missing from his collection. They found a place of honor on our bookshelves. Within these volumes I found parallels to my own folkways, in addition to countless articles about rural ways of which I have no first-hand experience. As I dusted and shelved the collection not too long ago, I perused the tables of contents while I worked and was struck by how seriously the Society has taken its mission to collect and preserve the lore of Texas folk of all our various hyphenated ethnicities. I sat down with *Puro Mexicano* and increased my repertoire of folktales. My dusting task slowed down considerably and contentedly. I re-read the articles that I'd typed for James and for John O. over the years, and reflected on how far back my association with the Society dates. I looked back at decades of scholarship relating to Mexican-American folklore and was both gratified by the manner in which it has been preserved and interested in how what I call "the language of observation" has changed over the years, becoming more respectful as time as progressed.

When John O. was working on his *Mexican-American Folklore*, published by August House and issued as Extra Book-20 of the Texas Folklore Society in 1988, he leaned heavily on my mother's expertise as he wrote. She delighted in explaining in great and glowing details all she knew. He got her to make tamales while he documented her cooking (and mine) on an old Super 8 movie camera, and was fascinated by our Day of the Dead traditions. We took John O. into all our seasonal rituals and he preserved them in print and on film. Mody Boatright says in a 1944 membership brochure that "Folklore is the essence of the cultural inheritance of a people." My attempts to capture the essence of my experiences all begin with my mother Lucina Lara Rey, born in Camargo, Chihuahua in 1910.

I was born into the immeasurable wealth of having a parent whose culture and lore were a source of pride and delight. The pride was passed on to me in mother's milk: the delight I experience in daily snippets of things ingrained in my ways. It was natural that growing up on the Texas-Mexican border I would absorb that which surrounded me. Add to that the visits to my grandmother—my *Mamacita*, born in Aguascalientes in the late 19th century—who lived across the Rio Bravo in Juárez. And yet, on top of that is the fact that my mother valued the instruction of Mexican schooling so dearly she was insistent I begin my formal education across the border and celebrate the traditions that went with every holiday, from *Día de las Madres*, to *Día del Niño*, to *Día del Maestro,* and all the patriotic holidays interspersed throughout the year. My father's German customs didn't stand a chance of seeping into my psyche too deeply, for he was a man of the world who embraced being "American" as soon as he jumped ship in New York harbor that

Lucy on Easter Sunday, Bible in hand, walking in Juárez on the way to see her Mamacita

cold December in 1912. The die thus was cast early that I would value and embrace being "Mexican-American." But if the truth be known, whenever I have to check that ethnicity box on anything set before me, I check Hispanic, both for my maternal genetic roots and the cultural environment that has shaped who I am.

My upbringing was not the norm for a child living in El Paso, for I was not raised Roman Catholic but rather Southern Baptist, a member of the First Mexican Baptist Church, which sat a few blocks from the river on the American side. While the girls I attended school with went to Catechism and Confirmation classes at nearby St. Xavier's, I was going through all the steps to be crowned *Reina Regente en Servicio* ("Queen Regent-in-Service") in

Girls Auxiliary. My culture didn't include that first waltz with my father at my *Quinceañera*. Not only were we too poor to put on such a bash, but Baptists didn't dance—at least those from my church didn't. Dancing was the Devil's pastime. To bring that point home, there was that oft-told "Devil at the Dance" obedience tale which wandered into the conversation any time dancing was brought up. You remember the one—where the recalcitrant girl snuck out at night, met a handsome stranger with the dark, slicked-back hair, cool moves and the rooster foot. None of *my* Baptist girlfriends wanted to wind up lifeless on the floor, their low-cut red dresses in shreds and black patent high-heeled shoes mangled, their bodies scratched beyond recognition. The better the taleteller, the more graphic were the details, and the more obedient we turned out to be. We resigned ourselves to doing without that particular pleasure, and some of us wound up with two left feet. In my upbringing, there was no *Misa de Gallo*—Midnight Mass—followed by an early *menudo* breakfast, but rather a Christmas pageant complete with coat-hanger-haloed angels. We had a "New Year's Eve Watch" potluck supper devoid of those twelve grapes some of my Mexican friends eat at every stroke of midnight for good luck.

Pancho Villa was not *MY* grandmother's folk hero. After all, my grandfather had uprooted her and brought her to the border with whatever they could gather hastily, escaping the burly, dark-skinned, thick-mustachioed, cunning-as-a-fox, gun-toting "Robin Hood" of the 1910 Mexican Revolution. My grandfather had worked hard to acquire his riches in Camargo, Chihuahua, but when life, limb, and treasure were threatened by the increased revolutionary activity, he gathered up his family and traveled north to Cd. Juárez, where, much to his chagrin, the Revolution followed. My *Mamacita* related the tales of Villa's—and his soldiers'—atrocities toward the women who wouldn't cooperate, how citizens would hide the girls in dugouts under houses, or lower them into shallow wells to keep them safe. She told stories of Villa's men, suspecting that girls were indeed hidden, who would set houses on fire or pour kerosene into wells and burn the unfortunate souls alive. While my mother would acknowledge in her history lessons that the Mexican government needed reform, the stories of Villa's ruthlessness made him anything but a hero.

Even if my mother's opinion of Villa was one of contempt, she didn't discount the idea that the scoundrel might indeed have left a path of buried treasure from Camargo to Juárez. And since my childhood house sat on the old river bed, a stone's throw from the Rio Grande, when ghosts showed up, she listened. My *Mamacita* heard the first one, and after one spooky, sleepless night made us take her back home. She described the spine-chilling "scratch-scratch" noises coming from the ceiling, all night long—"scratch-scratch, whimper-whimper, whoo-whooooo." It not only gave her a restless night but scared her no end. She announced in no uncertain terms that that would be *her* last visit if my mother didn't get rid of the night visitor. My sensible mother set herself up where my grandmother had slept, and sure enough, there were noises. So, first thing in the morning she got on a ladder, flashlight in hand, and found a spot where she could look into the space between the roof and the ceiling. She found her ghosts—in broad daylight. One pigeon flew in her face and nearly toppled her off the ladder. She left it to my father to finish the ghost-busting, and we had squab stew for several days after.

The second ghost was the soft-shoe-step variety, the kind who obviously wanted my mother to follow him somewhere, to show her something. It was only a four-room house, so she didn't have far to go. "Shuffle, shuffle, creak" this noisemaker went, all in the direction of the hearth that was the base for a once-operating fireplace. My mother was used to doing all the house repairs herself, so she cracked open the concrete, dug in and around, and after a few days cemented the space back in after finding nothing. You'd think the ghost would've been satisfied, or at least given her better directions. After putting her through all the work with no reward, the ghost took leave of our house, but didn't stay gone for long. The first night it was back, my mother got up from a sound sleep, looked up the chimney, told him in her most authoritarian schoolteacher voice, index finger motioning for emphasis, that if he didn't know where the treasure was and how *she* could get to it, he could just move on. And he did.

Common superstitions were *not* passed down to me by my mother; she saw them as beliefs of the non-analytical, ignorant mind. As the logical thinker in a trio of sisters, she was the exception. What superstitions I have came from my *Tía Toña,* my diminutive aunt who never went out unless she was impeccably dressed, in four-inch heels, perfectly coiffed and made-up. Going anywhere with her always took twice as long as with my mother. If she saw a ladder on the horizon blocking the sidewalk, it wasn't enough to plan a few steps around it; we'd go at least to the next street for safety's sake. We couldn't step on cracks in order to protect our respective mothers' backs. If she saw a black cat even *thinking* of crossing our path within the first few blocks of an outing, we'd have to turn back. Needless to say, we *never, ever* set foot outside the door on *mártes trece*, the Tuesday equivalent of Friday the Thirteenth.

My *Tía Toña* taught me to put the salt shaker down next to whomever was requesting it and under no circumstances to put it in their hand, and if—heaven forbid—I spilled any, to take careful aim throwing that pinch over my left shoulder to make sure I got it in the Devil's eyes. Both of them. A fork or knife dropped while eating lunch at her house meant we'd sit by the window waiting all afternoon for that unexpected visitor. By the way, my other aunt had a reputation for using spells, both good and evil. My mother didn't let me play at her house much.

I was warned not to open an umbrella indoors—by my *Tía Toña* because it was bad luck, by my mother because it was dumb and dangerous and could potentially poke somebody's eye out. About the only "superstition" that I remember coming from my mother's lips was related to our yearly *tamal*-making days: once we started the long work day, nobody left the house, for the opening and closing of the door would surely ruin the endeavor. I secretly think that belief might have been her way of keeping us working steadily until the task was done.

John Martin West with Lucy and her mother making tamales, Christmas 1976

Tamal-making was by far the most time-consuming and exhausting cooking event at our house. There was none of that boisterous "let's get everybody together and split tasks, stay up all night, and tell family stories" atmosphere. I am an only child, my aunts hated to cook, and my father thought cooking was woman's work. Oh, and "in Germany, corn is what we feed the pigs." You can imagine how well that went over. Save for some outside hired help for clean-up, my mother and I executed the whole production, including schlepping the thirty or so pounds of ground *masa* on the local bus from downtown El Paso. My mother taught me well—how to soak and wash the shucks, make the sauce from dried red chilies, cook the pork and save the fat to mix into the dough along with the Snow Cap lard. We split the dough and kneaded it until a dollop dropped in a glass of water floated to the top. The first *tamales* we made were always perfectly balanced with more meat filling than *masa*. Toward the end of the day, we might get a little more generous with the *masa*, as it seemed to multiply like the overflowing porridge pot of nursery rhyme lore. My father did opine that if we added a few more ingredients to the sweet *tamales*, they'd be tastier. Our creations always had not only raisins and pecans and sometimes coconut, but also diced candied fruit, a Mexican *tamal*-German Stollen kind of fusion. If there's anything that brings back the beauty of my mother's homemaking essence, it is duplicating any of her dishes in my own kitchen.

"Custom," as defined by Jan Harold Brunvand, is "a traditional practice—a mode of individual behavior or a habit of social life—that is transmitted by word of mouth or imitation, then ingrained by social pressure, common usage, and parental or other authority."[1] Having been raised by a mother who was born in 1910, and influenced by a grandmother born in the 1880s, both relatively untouched by what I would call a modern watering down of customs, what is ingrained in me goes back perhaps more years than for my contemporaries. However, bear in mind that I had a German father who didn't always cotton to the ways of his Mexican bride. Take the custom of piercing a baby girl's ears shortly after birth. Not only did my father disapprove vehemently about the barbaric mutilation, but there would have been no one up in the hills where they lived who would've pierced my ears. My mother had to wait until she came back to the border from Catskill, New York, where I was born. I have a vision of her arriving in Juárez and within the week seeing to this piercing, so that when my father arrived a month later with the dilapidated truck heaped high with furniture he'd driven down, I'd already have my cute little gold button earrings so common for my generation of babies.

Lucy at age one wearing an outfit knitted by her mother

There was one custom that my mother wasn't able to pull off—the shaving of the baby hair at a year, presumably so that the second crop of hair would grow in thicker and healthier. My mother always said that if my father had just "let her do what she knew to do," I wouldn't have the fine hair that I do. In my year-old picture, I have wispy white-blond hair, as opposed to a shaved head to go with the gold hoop earrings and the frilly dresses customarily picked for the momentous occasion.

The deeply widespread custom of touching a child's head didn't make its full impression on me until our son John came into the picture. All my life I'd seen my mother admire babies at friends' homes, in restaurants, in the market, on the buses we traveled in. She always made it a point to tousle the child's hair or touch his bare skin, usually with a blessing attached to it, spoken to whomever was holding the child. The custom averted the "evil eye," *mal ojo*. Relating that I'd had a *mal ojo* experience for which she'd sought help when I was a baby, she didn't take any chances. With his blue eyes and blond hair, son John attracted as much attention as I had, and if she noticed people around us admiring him, she'd make sure that he got blessed. Any baby who makes eye contact with me wherever I am gets the touch from me; on the border, the parents usually know what I'm doing and the gesture is received with a nod and a smile. Other customs I retain from my Mexican side fall under the universal theme of showing kindness—carrying food to the sick, never returning a dish empty when food has been given in it, making a visit to those who are grieving a loss.

Death and its related rituals were important in my upbringing. In my mother's philosophy, death was as natural to the cycle of life as were the changing seasons. I was accustomed to going to the wakes for my mother's teacher friends, in rooms dim-lit, with black-dressed women, heads veiled in Roman Catholic tradition humming the repetitive prayers. Those long evenings were sprinkled with stories both happy and sad, and mournful songs from the golden age of Mexican classics. Prayers, tears, laughter, and song were the catharsis that helped soothe their losses. We buried them in the harsh, rock-strewn cemetery uphill from where my grandmother lived, frequently walking the long way from the gates to the site of the graves, often in the dust storms that echoed the survivors' grief. One by one, after the prayers were said, we scooped up a handful of dirt and tossed it on the coffin.

Long before my *Mamacita* died while I was in high school, we had visited the Juárez cemetery regularly on *Día de los Muertos* in November. My mother and my *Tía Toña* had different philosophies about these *camposanto* events. My mother hauled the brooms, short and long, the rake, rags, a five-gallon bucket full of flowers she'd picked out of our garden, most notably the yellow-orange and russet zinnias of the season. She bought marigolds and mums from the vendors if she needed more color. My mother was there to make sure that the family plot looked like somebody cared. As a toddler, I vividly remember being put in charge of

Boys carrying water for cleaning headstones

using the whiskbroom to clean a year's worth of dust off the gravestones so we could read my grandfather's name and the dates he'd lived. The decorative "Jesus in the Garden of Gethsemane" tiles had to be polished, old flowers put on the garbage pile. My mother raked the rocks smooth around the large slab. Even though there were lots of kids running around looking to assist for a little pocket change, my mother did most of the hard work herself. Meanwhile, my *Tía*, rosary beads in hand, prayed. I was always reminded of Martha and Mary with this scene. Once everything was spic and span, after most of the fresh flowers were arranged in the urns, my aunt would stop reciting and do the finishing touches, sobbing as she went. My mother's sorrow kept its silence. Once we were done, she would do a quiet sweep of the marker with her hand, hold it still at her father's name, and bid farewell.

Like generations before her, my mother had been expected to learn the art of making a home. Our house was filled with artifacts, folk art creations from my mother's hand. You couldn't turn in any direction without encountering something made by her. Coffee tables were topped with starched crocheted doilies, there were

Lucy's mother passing on *Día de los Muertos* traditions to John Martin West in the Tepeyác cemetery in Juárez

antimacassars on the backs of every chair, cross-stitch-embellished sheets and pillowcases covered our beds, and cat-themed embroidered cuptowels told us which day to do what task. Geometrically designed *deshilados* (which I have no idea how to translate) served as placemats. She was renowned in her teaching community for her *manos maravillosas*—her marvelous, talented hands. Her embroidery was elaborate and creative, her crocheting stitches relaxed and even, her knitting precise and perfect.

To her credit, as antsy as I was about holding still, she did manage to pass on to me enough crocheting skills to make son John a baby blanket, but if it hadn't been for her, he would've gone bootie-less, and the cedar chest would not be full of the handmade treasured goods she made for him. I did learn to be a fairly good seamstress. She passed that art on to me one step at a time, from positioning darts to basting to sewing straight seams, turning collars and properly pressing at each step. When she was sewing something special, she swore by her cast irons heated on the gas stove. I never did quite master that art of not leaving the iron's imprint on my sewing, so I rely on more modern contrivances. As for advice in daily living, I am, however, guided by words repeated by generations of kitchen-table sages like my mother.

I tried taking a rhetoric class several years ago and was overwhelmed by the sheer number of words I was wading through. It was so dizzying, I threw in the towel. With all due respect to the great philosophers, and to my father, whose greatest joy was to read hours on end and contemplate what he termed "the eternal verities," I am much more capable of digesting the richly distilled wisdom of the folk that lies in the *dichos* and proverbs learned in my childhood. They are like simmered, reduced sauces whose complexities are intensified in the taste buds of tongue and palate. "*Dime con quien te juntas y te dire quien eres.*" Roughly, "You are known by the company you keep." Tell me that's not a profound statement, especially when used in regard to parenting. "*Almuerza bien, come más, cena poco y viviras.*" How many grants have funded research whose outcome has been that a good breakfast, substantial lunch, and light supper are healthy? This one serves me well: "*Cuando en duda, consúltalo con tu almohada.*" My pillow and a good night's sleep are indeed good counselors. As in many other languages and cultures, there is at least one proverb to fit every occasion. Hardly a day goes by that an appropriate one doesn't surface—at least silently.

I continue to be fascinated by the universal nature of the lore of the folk—across the world speaking in a language I wouldn't understand, and closer to home across the state, there are mothers like mine who teach children obedience through folk tales and profound wisdom through proverbs. They instill the idea that stories are worth keeping and repeating. They stand up to ghosts and leave the legacy that—whatever our roots may be—customs and traditions are what bind us one to another. To the Texas Folklore Society's mission to collect and preserve the many facets of our heritage I am deeply indebted. The list of articles that follows bears witness to our members' passions and projects that have enriched the scholarship of Mexican-American folklore. In my personal journey of discovery that I too had a family saga worth preserving, Francis E. Abernethy, Joyce Gibson Roach, and Lou Rodenberger have been my mentors in the truest sense of the word. Their encouragement has meant the world to me. *Mil Gracias.*

Endnote

1. Jan Harold Brunvand. *The Study of American Folklore: An Introduction.* 4th ed. New York: W. W. Norton & Company, 1998. 406.

Lucy (on right) at the Galveston TFS meeting in 2006, with Joyce Roach and Lou Rodenberger

BIBLIOGRAPHY OF MEXICAN-AMERICAN FOLKLORE ARTICLES

By Lucy Fischer West

Round the Levee, PTFS I, 1916.
"A Mexican Border Ballad." Ben D. Wood.

Coffee in the Gourd, PTFS II, 1923.
"Customs and Superstitions among Texas Mexicans." Florence Johnson Scott.
"Pedro and Pancho." Mary A. Sutherland.
"Weather Wisdom of the Texas-Mexican Border." J. Frank Dobie.

Legends of Texas, PTFS III, 1924.
"The Treasure Cannon of the Neches." Roscoe Martin.
"Steinheimer's Millions.' L. D. Bertillion.
"The Cave of Montezuma." J. Leeper Gay.

Happy Hunting Ground, PTFS IV, 1925.
"A Mexican Popular Ballad (With Music)." W. A. Whatley.
"Spanish Songs of New Mexico (With Music)." F. S. Curtis, Jr.
"Versos of the Texas Vaqueros (With Music)." J. Frank Dobie.

Rainbow in the Morning, PTFS V, 1926.
"A Texas Border Ballad." Mattie Austin Hatcher.
"Reptiles of the South and Southwest in Folk-Lore." John K. Strecker.
"Superstitions of Bexar County." E. R. Bogusch.

Texas and Southwestern Lore, PTFS VI, 1927.
"Folk-Lore of the Texas-Mexican Vaquero." Jovita González.
"Lore of the Llano Estacado." J. Evetts Haley.

Foller de Drinkin' Gou'd, PTFS VII, 1928.
"Folk-Lore Relating to Texas Birds." John K. Strecker.

Man, Bird, and Beast, PTFS VIII, 1930.
"Ranch Remedios." Frost Woodhull (with illustrations by Will James).
"Tales and Songs of the Texas Mexicans." Jovita González.

Southwestern Lore, PTFS IX, 1931.
"Folk-Lore of the King Ranch Mexicans." Frank Goodwyn.
"The Mexican Pastor." Edgar B. Kincaid.
"Folk-Foods of the Rio Grande Valley." John G. Bourke.
"Songs the Vaqueros Sing." Joaquin Mora.

Tone the Bell Easy, PTFS X, 1932.
"New Mexico Witch Tales." Ruth Laughlin Barker.
"Folk-Curing Among the Mexicans." Ruth Dodson.
"Among My People." Jovita González.

Spur-of-the-Cock, PTFS XI, 1932.
"El Niño Perdido." Mary R. Van Stone and E. R. Sims.

Puro Mexicano, PTFS XII, 1935.
"A Pack Load of Mexican Tales." Riley Aiken.
"The Wonderful Chirrionera." Dan Storm.
"Br'er Coyote." Sarah S. McKellar.
"The Bullet-Swallower." Jovita González.
"Tales from San Elizario." Josefina Escajeda.
"The Metamorphosis of a Folk Tale." Elizabeth W. DeHuff.
"How the Tehuana Women Became Handsome." H. M. Taylor.
"The Flaming Flower." Catherine J. Stoker.
"Juan Garcia Goes to Heaven." Frost Woodhull.
"The Eagle Lover." Bertha McKee Dobie.
"Legends from Durango." Everardo Gámiz (Translation by Bertha McKee Dobie).
"Holy Ghost Canyon." Maude McFie Bloom.
"Old-Time New Mexican Usages." Alice M. Crook.
"Sons of the Devil." Joe Storm.
"Catorce." J. Frank Dobie.
"The Little White Dog." Hugh McGehee Taylor.
"Ranchero Sayings of the Border." Howard D. Wesley.
"Songs of the Mexican Migration." Paul S. Taylor.
"The Echanted City of Monte Albán." E. R. Sims.

Straight Texas, PTFS XIII, 1937.
"The Lobo Girl of Devil's River." L. D. Bertillion.
"Mexican Spooks from El Paso." C. L. Sonnichsen.
"'Old Obadiah' and 'My Juanita.'" Alice Atkinson Neighbors.

Coyote Wisdom, PTFS XIV, 1938.
"The Little Animals of Mexico." Dan Storm.
"The Coyote: Animal and Folk-Character." Lillian Elizabeth Barclay.
"Mexican Folk-Escapades and Tales." Malnor Shumard, Jr.
"Cuerpo sin Alma" (Note by A. L. Campa). Mildred Cohen.

In the Shadow of History, PTFS XV, 1939.
"Inventing Stories About the Alamo." W. P. Zuber to Charlie Jeffries.
"Folk Characters of the Sheep Industry." Winnifred Kupper.
"The *Pastor* and the Serpent." Dan Storm.
"The Mexican Folk Version of King Midas." W. A. Whatley.

"Tortilla Making." Ruth Dodson.
"The Roadrunner in Fact and Folk-Lore." J. Frank Dobie.

Mustangs and Cow Horses, PTFS XVI, 1940.
"Mustangs and Mustanging in Southwest Texas." G. C. Robinson.
"From Mustangs to Mules." Thomas W. Dwyer.
"The Deathless Pacing White Stallion." J. Frank Dobie.
"Horse Lore of the Conquest." Robert M. Denhardt.
"Mexican Color Terms for Horses." W. A. Whatley.
"Texas-Mexican Horse-Breaking." Ruth Dodson.
"Ballad of Manuel Rodriguez." Frank Goodwyn.
"Canelo, A True War Horse." Helen Michaelis.
"Horse Sense." L. A. Guajardo.
"Death Comes at a Trot." Riley Aiken.
"The Mescal-Drinking Horse." Jovita González de Mireles.

Texian Stomping Grounds, PTFS XVII, 1941.
"Frijoles." Roy Holt.
"Rancho Buena Vista." Fermina Guerra.
"How the Burro Tricked the Buzzard." Genoveva Barrera.
"Will-o'-the-Wisp of the Esperanza." John W. Blackwell.

Backwoods to Border, PTFS XVIII, 1943.
"Grave Decoration." Dorothy Jean Michael.
"The Ghost Nun." Ruth Dodson.
"Riddles of Texas Mexican Children." J. A. Rickard.
"Mexican Animal Tales." Fermina Guerra.

From Hell to Breakfast, PTFS XIX, 1944.
"Mexican Münchausen." W. A. Whatley.
"Some Odd Mexican Customs." Oran Warder Nolen.
"Legend of the Tengo Frío Bird." Henry Yelvington.

Mexican Border Ballads and Other Lore, PTFS XXI, 1946.
"Corridos of the Mexican Border." Brownie McNeil.
"The Envious and the Envied Compadres." Wilson M. Hudson.

The Sky Is My Tipi, PTFS XXII, 1948.
"The Yellow Flower of Death," Hortense Warner Ward.

The Healer of Los Olmos and Other Mexican Lore (with illustrations by José Cisneros), PTFS XXIV, 1951.
"Charm in Mexican Folktales." J. Frank Dobie.
"Don Pedrito Jaramillo: The Curandero of Los Olmos." Ruth Dodson.
"Mexican Folklore from Austin, Texas." Soledad Pérez.

"To Whom God Wishes to Give He Will Give." Wilson M. Hudson.
"The Fisherman and the Snake of Many Colors." Wilson M. Hudson.

Folk Travelers: Ballads, Tales, and Talk, PTFS XXV, 1953.
"The Love Tragedy in Texas-Mexican Balladry." Américo Paredes.
"Come Buy, Come Buy." Elizabeth Hurley.
"Black and White Magic on the Texas-Mexican Border." Gabriel Córdova.
"The Devil in the Big Bend." Elton R. Miles.

Texas Folk and Folklore, PTFS XXVI, 1954.
"Stories of My People." Jovita González.
"A Pack Load of Mexican Tales." Riley Aiken.
"The Little Animals." Dan Storm.
"To Whom God Wishes to Give He Will Give." Wilson M. Hudson.
"Ratoncito Pérez." Soledad Pérez.
"The Deathless Pacing White Stallion." J. Frank Dobie.
"Mexican Ghosts from El Paso." Charles L. Sonnichsen.
"The Ghost Nun." Ruth Dodson.
"The Weeping Woman." Soledad Pérez.
"Versos de los Bandidos." J. Frank Dobie.
"El Toro Moro." Frank Goodwyn.
"Corrido de Kansas." Brownie McNeil.
"El Contrabando del Paso." Brownie McNeil.
"Deportados." Paul S. Taylor.
"*Dichos* from Austin." Soledad Pérez.
"The Curandero of Los Olmos." Ruth Dodson.
"Susto." Soledad Pérez.

Mesquite and Willow, PTFS XXVII, 1956.
"The Legend of Gregorio Cortez." Américo Paredes.
"Six Tales from Mexico." Riley Aiken.
"The Twelve Truths in the Spanish Southwest." Wilson M. Hudson.
"To Whom God Wishes to Give: A Tale of Old Mexico in English Ballad Stanzas." Joseph W. Hendren.

Madstones and Twisters, PTFS XXVIII, 1957.
"The Mexican *Corrido*: Its Rise and Fall." Américo Paredes.
"Chisos Ghosts." Elton Miles.
"More Chisos Ghosts." Riley Aiken.
"Around the Fire with My Abuelitos." Guadalupe Duarte.

"With a Pistol in His Hand": A Border Ballad and Its Hero. Américo Paredes. Extra Book-9, 1958.

and horns on the toads, PTFS XXIX, 1959.
"*Curanderos* of South Texas." Brownie McNeil.
"The Bury-Me-Not Theme in the Southwest." Américo Paredes.
"The Personification of Animals in the *Relación* of Mexico." Donald M. Lance.
"Rails Below the Rio Grande." John T. Smith.
"I Heard It on the Border." Meredith Hale.
"Speak of the Devil." Artell Dorman.
"South Texas Sketches." Ruth Dodson.
Singers and Storytellers, PTFS XXX, 1960.
"Some Forms of the Mexican *Canción*." Vicente T. Mendoza (Translated by Américo Paredes).
"Folklore and History." Américo Paredes.
"Owl-Bewitchment in the Lower Rio Grande Valley." Humberto Garza.
"Tales of the Paisanos." Miriam W. Hiester.
"The Origin of the Word *Gringo*." Robert H. Fuson.
"On *Gringo, Greaser*, and Other Neighborly Names." Américo Paredes.

The Golden Log, PTFS XXXI, 1961.
"Don Juan Zurumbete." Riley Aiken.
"Work and Play on a Border Ranch." Rosalinda Gonzalez.
"Cuentos de Susto." Baldemar A. Jiménez.

A Good Tale and a Bonnie Tune, PTFS XXXII, 1962.
"Fifteen Mexican Tales." Riley Aiken.
"Two Treasure Tales." J. Frank Dobie.

Hunters and Healers, PTFS XXXV, 1969.
"The *Huapango*: A Dithyrambic Festival." Henry Schmidt.

Diamond Bessie & The Shepherds, PTFS XXXVI, 1971.
"Julia Nott Waugh on *Los Pastores*." John Igo.
"The Decoration of Graves in Central Texas with Seashells." Sara Clark.

The Folklore of Texan Cultures, PTFS XXXVIII, 1973.
"The Cultures of Texas." R. Henderson Shuffler.
"Vaquero: Genesis of the Texas Cowboy." William D. Wittliff and Joe B. Frantz.
"Charro Jiro Afamado." Arnulfo Castillo (Translation and commentary by Inez Cardozo-Freeman).
"Scratches on the Bedpost: Vestiges of the Lechuza." Ann Carpenter.
"Violeta and the Owls." Alonzo M. Perales.
"Mal Ojo." John O. West.
"Don José and Don Pedrito." H. C. Arbuckle, III.

Some Still Do: Essays on Texas Customs, PTFS XXIX, 1975.
"Tradition and the Candelilla Wax Industry." Joe S. Graham.

Paisanos: A Folklore Miscellany, PTFS XLI, 1978.
"Maime Tobar's Tales of Treasure." As told by Gertrude Bluntzer to Ruth G. Wright.

Built in Texas, PTFS XLII, 1979.
"Adobe: Earth, Straw, and Water." John O. West and Roberto Gonzalez.

Mexican Folktales of the Borderlands. Riley Aiken. Extra Book-17, 1980.

Legendary Ladies of Texas, PTFS XLIII, 1981.
"The Weeping Woman: *La Llorona*." John O. West.

T for Texas: A State Full of Folklore, PTFS XLIV, 1982.
"How to Have, to Hold, or Free Oneself of a Lover." Dolores L. Latorre.

Folk Art in Texas, PTFS XLV, 1984.
"Folk Grave Decoration Along the Rio Grande." John O. West.
"El Paso Murals." Jacquelyn Spier.
"Art Among the Lowriders." Bill Gradante.

Sonovagun Stew, PTFS XLVI, 1985.
"Three *Corridos* of the Big Bend." Elton Miles.

Hoein' the Short Rows, PTFS XLVII, 1987.
"Celebrations of the Dead: Merging Traditions in the Spanish Southwest." John O. West.
"Mexican-American Lime Kilns in West Texas: The Limits of Folk Technology." Joe S. Graham.

Mexican-American Folklore. John O. West. Extra Book-20, 1988.

Texas Toys and Games, PTFS XLVIII, 1989.
"Folk Games of Texas Children." Martha Hartzog.

The Bounty of Texas, PTFS XLIX, 1990.
"Brush Country, Vaqueros, and Hamlet's Ghost." Paul Clois Stone.

Hecho en Tejas: Texas-Mexican Folk Arts and Crafts, PTFS L, 1991.
"*Hecho a Mano en Tejas*." Joe S. Graham.
"Art Among Us/*Arte Entre Nosotros*: Mexican-American Folk Art in San Antonio." Pat Jasper and Kay Turner.

"The Mexican-American Quilting Traditions of Laredo, San Ygnacio and Zapata." Norma Cantú and Ofelia Zapata Vela.
"*Vaquero* Folk Arts and Crafts in South Texas." Joe S. Graham.
"Costume as Cultural Resistance and Affirmation: The Case of a South Texas Community." Norma Cantú.
"*Coronas para los Muertos*: The Fine Art of Making Paper Flowers." Curtis Tunnell and Enrique Madrid.
"Homages in Clay: The Figural Ceramics of José Varela." Suzanne Seriff.
"Miguel Acosta, *Instrumentista*." James C. McNutt.
"The Piñata-Making Tradition in Laredo." Esperanza Gallegos.
"Tejano Saddlemakers and the Running W Saddle Shop." Joe S. Graham.
"Texas-Mexican Religious Folk Art in Robstown, Texas." Cynthia L. Vidaurri.
"Mexican-American Yard Art in Kingsville." Eric Ramos.
"*Grutas* in the Spanish Southwest." John O. West.
"Mexican-American Roadside Crosses in Starr County." Alberto Barrera.
"The *Jacal* in South Texas: The Origins and Form of a Folk House." Joe S. Graham.
"Randado: The Built Environment of a Texas-Mexican Ranch." Mary Anna Casstevens.

Corners of Texas, PTFS LII, 1993.
"The Boat Called '*El Pato*.'" Fernando Garza Quirós.
"Longino Guerrero's Corrido on J. Frank Dobie." F. E. Abernethy.

Between the Cracks of History: Essays on Teaching and Illustrating Folklore, PTFS LV, 1997.
"Tex-Mex Dialect or Gidget Goes to Acuna." Rebecca Cornell.

Features and Fillers, PTFS LVI, 1999.
"The Weeping Woman" (from *The Fort Worth Star-Telegram*). John O. West.
"*El Ojo* and Other Folk Beliefs" (from *The Fort Worth Star-Telegram*). Joe Graham.
"Alfonso's Yearly Routine" (from the *Eagle-News*). T. Lindsay Baker

2001: A Texas Folklore Odyssey, PTFS LVIII, 2001.
"La Quinceañera: A Hispanic Folk Custom." Phyllis Bridges.
"Homemade Religion: Miraculous Images of Jesus and the Virgin Mary in South Texas." J. Rhett Rushing.

Charreada: Mexican Rodeo in Texas, PTFS LVIX, 2002.
"Charrería: From Spain to Texas." Francis Edward Abernethy.
"Charro Regalia." Julia Hambric.

"La Vida del Charro." Brian Woolley.
"The Events in the Charreada." Julia Hambric.
"La Escaramuza." Julia Hambric.

The Family Saga: A Collection of Texas Family Legends, PTFS LX, 2003.
"Villa Raid." Jesse Thompson as told to Austin T. King.
"Thanks to a Psychic in Shanghai." Lucy Fischer West.

Both Sides of the Border: A Scattering of Texas Folklore, PTFS LXI, 2004.
"Growing Up on Both Sides of the Border." Lucy Fischer West.
"Welito: A Mexican-American Family in Southwest Texas." Bertha Dominguez.
"Folklore of a San Antonio Midwife." Alicia Zavala Galván.
"Religion, Supersitions, and Remedios in the Mexican-American Culture." Gloria Duarte.
"Pepe's Panaderia: Bread Folklore." Kenneth W. Davis.
"A Tortilla is Never 'Just' a Tortilla." Lucy Fischer West.

Folklore: In All of Us, In All We Do, PTFS LXIII, 2006.
"La Llorona's Ancestry: Crossing Cultural Boundaries." Gloria Duarte.
"*Mi Fronteridad* in the Classroom: The Power of Writing and Sharing Stories." Meredith E. Abarca.

Folklore in Motion: Texas Travel Lore, PTFS LXIV, 2007.
"The Passage of Scotland's Four: *El Pasaje de los Cuatro de Escocia.*" Consuelo L. Samarripa.

Death Lore: Texas Rituals, Superstitions, and Legends of the Hereafter, PTFS LV, 2008.
"Origins and Celebrations of *El Día de los Muertos.*" J. Rhett Rushing.
"Chipita Rodriguez: The Only Woman Hanged in Texas *During* the Civil War." Carolyn Arrington.
"The Yellow Flower of Death." Hortense Warner Ward.

Tim Tingle

DOBIE'S DISCIPLES AND THE CHOCTAW FIVE

by Tim Tingle

Buck Wade died on Christmas Eve 2008, yesterday. So instead of enjoying a peaceful evening at home on Christmas night, I packed a suitcase and loaded my dog Duke and my best friend Doc onto a mini-van, drove a few hundred miles, and am now staying at a small motel in Hillsboro with a six o'clock wake-up call, on my way to my friend's funeral in a small country graveyard a few miles south of McAlester, Oklahoma. Buck was the last of the Choctaw Five, my own designation for four men and one strong woman who altered my life in ways I am only now beginning to understand. I had been wrestling with how to narrow the focus of an article on the importance of the Texas Folklore Society in my life, and this seems about as good a place to start as any.

Buck was a quiet man with a wry sense of humor, a Choctaw in his mid-seventies who never seemed to mind that his quips went unnoticed by many. He was tall by Choctaw standards, over six feet, with a growing paunch and thick eyeglasses. I met Buck seven years ago at the Choctaw Storytelling Festival in Eufala, Oklahoma, an event whose primary purpose is the recording of elders' memories.

In the first thirty minutes of our initial encounter, Buck told me of his grandfather, a preacher who made his living selling moonshine whiskey after church, a respectable means of livelihood during Depression days. But Buck's granddad had other skills as well. According to Buck:

> I once saw him say a prayer, pick up an ax, and split a tornado in two. Saw him do it more than once. He'd hide himself in a thicket, call out a powerful prayer, and come out swinging his ax slow and thoughtful-like, looking for just the right tree.

> When the funnel got close and he lined it up with the tree, he'd draw back and bury the blade of his ax deep in the tree trunk. Nobody, no matter how strong the tornado was, ever went running for cover, not when grand-dad was around, 'cause nobody wanted to miss seeing it half itself and flitter away like a dust bunny.

Buck also told of once saving himself and two hunting buddies, "Just like I saw grand-dad do," by praying and ax-splitting a tornado. His description of tornado-splitting, which I later found to be a not uncommon occurrence among Choctaw elders, inspired the pivotal scene in the short story "Brothers," included in my first book, *Walking the Choctaw Road.*

Buck also talked of Bigfoot creatures in the Kiamichi Mountains, the power of lightning-struck trees, and walking graveyard spirits. He was the best partner for graveyard prowling I ever met. Now that I think of it, Buck and I probably have our best graveyard prowling days ahead of us. I have seen ghosts in old Choctaw cemeteries before—one little girl in particular in the old cemetery at the Choctaw capitol grounds near Tushkahoma, whom half a dozen fellow Choctaws accompanying me actually thought *was* a small girl 'til we later compared notes of her doings—but I have never seen the ghost of someone I knew. (Okay, other than my father, when the floodwaters were creeping up on our home on Canyon Lake, but that's beyond the scope of this article. And my stepfather Larry, dead by gunshot years before his time. And my brother Danny, drowned when his kayak flipped over a few miles from his home in Clear Creek. Which leads me back to the scope of this article.)

Without the friendship of a man I was never privileged to meet, I would never have considered researching lore—ghostly, Choctaw, or otherwise. I would never have written a single book, never have reshaped vacations around sites of folkloric and historic interest. In fact, I more than likely would have dismissed the aforementioned

J. Frank Dobie, who brought many to the TFS through his writings

happenings as the result of too little sleep or too much Edgar Allan Poe and Alfred Hitchcock as a child. I would still be making and marketing New Canaan Farms jellies and jams from our little factory in Dripping Springs, Texas, the best I could do with an English literature major and a history minor from the University of Texas at Austin. Without the influence of this man and his compadres.

J. Frank Dobie. He was the man. I first heard of Dobie in 1971, from Dr. Wilson Hudson, while taking his survey course at UT, "The European Novel." I later found out Dr. Hudson had been Secretary-Editor of the Texas Folklore Society, and though that meant little to me at the time, he did encourage me to read Dobie. Though Hudson was far too old for an emerging hippie to normally trust on matters of reading, I had to admit he'd been right about Balzac and Dostoyevsky.

I was soon deep into Dobie's TFS books, including *I'll Tell You a Tale*, *Tone the Bell Easy*, and *Coffee in the Gourd*. Besides being astounded that anyone would consider Texas legends as a subject for serious study, I was inspired by Dobie's method of collecting narratives: right from the source. I was unfamiliar with techniques employed by folklorists in the field and had never heard of the American Folklore Society. For the next fifteen years I spent my free reading time on Bedichek, John Graves, and virtually every TFS edition I could afford. My worktime was spent saving enough money to build a log cabin twenty miles from any dirt with a name, near the Pedernales River in the hills southwest of Dripping Springs.

I took on the task of learning Spanish, the real and spoken kind, and spent several summer months in Cuernavaca and Morelia, living with Spanish-speaking-only Mexican families and gathering ghost stories in my free time. At the time, I was convinced I had found my true calling, and at an early age for a liberal arts grad. I was barely forty.

In retrospect, the most impactful aspect of this four-year period was not the new language I acquired, nor even the stories, although several did make their way into a ghost story collection co-authored with Doc Moore; rather, it was the method I developed of moving quietly and respectfully as a foreigner, a technique of listening with no judgments or preconceptions, the wisdom of self-aware idiocy; the awe of Dobie on the doorstep.

By 1990, my road appeared to be two-pronged, south to Mexico and north to Oklahoma Choctaw country. I had initiated a phone call relationship with Charley Jones, our tribal historian, who aided my translation of several Bible passages from English to Choctaw. In the blazing hot summer of 1992, I joined Charley and a thousand other Choctaws on a twenty-one-mile re-enactment of the Trail of Tears, a walk ending at Eagletown, a tiny community tucked away in the piney woods of southeast Oklahoma.

For the first half mile, we were a mass of enthusiastic walkers, but soon we sprawled across several miles of backcountry roads. I found Charley walking all by himself and sidled up to him. After a brief introduction, Charley and I walked without speaking for at least a mile. As I now write, I am realizing this mile to be the most important mile of my life. With no pretense or purpose, I offered to Mister Jones the understanding that I was in his presence to *listen* to him. Not to question. Not to evoke. Not to manipulate the conversation to fulfill a design of my making. I was there, walking with him in the 110 degree heat, simply to listen.

He sighed before he spoke, and I like to think his sigh was a way of saying, "Well, you took your time getting here." Charley spoke first about the Trail and what the old people had to endure just to stay alive. His voice soon took on a melodious monotony, a lulling quality of almost sound tracking the scenes he laid out before us, scenes more experienced than heard. We crossed a creek bridge and he eased into a story of the Choctaw law or custom of executing anyone who had taken the life of another. He talked of an old man who made the choice to face his death rather than violate this most sacred of Choctaw promises.

For the remainder of his life, Charley Jones was my Choctaw father, my teacher and friend. When I received the call that he had died and I made plans to attend the service, I noted that I already had plans for the day. My first book, which included the story of the old man's execution—dedicated to Charley was nominated for the Oklahoma Book Award, and I had accepted the invitation to attend the awards banquet in Oklahoma City, several hours' drive from Idabel, Charley's hometown.

Of course, I attended Charley's funeral service, and I only mention the day for what happened following the service. As a newcomer to awards banquets, I feared walking in late, and immediately after the closing of the coffin, I hit the road at a sweet eighty miles an hour, sobbing and shaking at the remembered sight of Charley in his grey suit with the choir singing old Choctaw hymns he had taught me, singing right over his skinny body. My mind recrossed the creek and I heard his voice tell the story, jumping again when the shot rang out through the woods and pierced the heart of a good Choctaw grandpa.

Then I saw the whirling red and blue lights of an Oklahoma highway patrolman in my rearview mirror. He was a big man. He wore those silvery shades that hid his eyes.

"Do you know how fast you were driving?" Quite a conversation starter, though he didn't wait for me to answer. "A little over eighty, according to my radar." He flipped open his ticket book and started writing.

"I'll need your drivers license." When he saw that I was crying, he peered into the car and took off his shades. "What is going on?"

"I'm sorry, officer. I just came from the funeral of my teacher, an old Choctaw man," I told him, still sobbing. He stood up slowly and closed his book.

"That old fellow from Idabel?" I nodded *Yes.*

"Well, son. Only one thing would be more tragic than that old man being buried today." I looked up and stopped crying, stifling the joy of getting away with it. "That'd be two folks dying 'cause you were speeding! So I'm gonna help you stay alive and write you this ticket."

He had his laugh and I drove away, slowly, and slid a cassette into my tape player, one Charley had given me a year earlier, a recording of him singing Choctaw hymns. I listened and sang along for maybe three hours, and as I neared the city—as Okies refer to Oklahoma City—I tried to pop the tape out, but it refused. On my way home from the banquet, it still refused. And the next day. Charley just kept on singing. Even today, two hundred thousand miles later, if I want to listen to a CD, no problem, but if I turn on my cassette player, it's Charley or nobody. He won't go away.

I now know those hymns by heart.

Following my initial meeting with Charley in 1992, I continued my forays into Tex-Mex culture, still avoiding a commitment to Choctaw lore, until Dr. John Davis of the Institute of Texan Cultures gave me the final nudge. I first performed on the storytelling stage at the Texas Folklife Festival in 1993, a venue managed by John and Rosemary Davis. Most of my stories were of

Texas and south of the border ghosts. I had done very little research of my Choctaw heritage, other than family stories I was convinced would be of no interest to anyone.

After a story relating the Choctaw experience on the Trail of Tears, inspired by Charley, Dr. John complimented me, saying, "Those stories are worth researching." He also said something along the lines of, "I'll bet some of those old Choctaws are still alive." They were, and I knew where to find them: Philadelphia, Mississippi, original homeland of the Choctaws and current stomping grounds of the Mississippi Band of Choctaw Indians.

Within the month I was driving a friend's camper van across the Mississippi Choctaw reservation, armed with a Radio Shack tape recorder and my Oklahoma Choctaw citizenship. I began ferreting out elders too old or good-natured to avoid me, a citybull among the shards of culture. For several afternoons I hung in, out, and around the Choctaw Museum and Culture Center, until Martha Ferguson, museum director, told me to "wait 'til closing time." She led me to Estelline Tubby, a Choctaw storyteller whose grandmother was *alikchi*, a Choctaw woman who knew herbal cures and had a Bohpoli friend and advisor. Bohpolis are Choctaw Little People who select healers and share their old medicine ways.

Estelline and I sat, just the two of us, in her living room, and she began by telling me she had had a dream three months ago of my coming. I had only decided a few weeks previous that I would go to Mississippi. The moment she began speaking, everything I had brought with me, every attitude, every shred of knowledge, ceased to exist. She spoke of modern cancer healings, of owlmen who preyed on the innocent, of alligators as executioners in racially charged times, all the while rocking and singsonging her way through three hours of story, a single story of Choctaw being.

Estelline Tubby and Charley Jones, two Choctaw elders who had never met, nonetheless shared the same mystery, dipped in the same deep waters. I knew this, and I longed for the source of these waters.

The next day I met Archie Mingo. Archie lived on the far fringes of reservation land, and it was ten p.m. when I stumbled on his backyard seventieth birthday celebration. He was surrounded by several hundred well-wishers, all circling a bonfire and fifty gallon pot of *pashofa*, our Choctaw hominy soup. To the amusement of everyone, Archie stuck an old caneback chair into the fire and burned all but two chairlegs, which he broke off and began using as chant sticks, singing and entertaining us all with old Choctaw vocables. He made sure I had a bowl of *pashofa* and, probably seeing my sleepy fire-nodding, asked me to come back in the morning.

Archie lived differently than Estelline. When I arrived at his home shortly after sunrise the next day, nobody answered the door. I walked around back and was surprised to see most of the people still there, huddled and sleeping, families clinging together beneath blankets, single men and women leaning against tree trunks and logs, but everybody sound asleep. The back door was open and I found Archie slumped over in his living room chair. *Pashofa* was perhaps his first choice of beverages, but the dozen or so bottles around his feet told me he had another as well. I had uncles and a dad who'd fit right in with this old man, I thought, and smiled at the familiarity of the morning. It's always good to remember that holy days come in all shapes and sizes, and holy people, too.

At Archie's request, we drove the twenty miles to Nanih Waiyah, the Choctaw origin mound. We climbed the wooden steps to the top and he allowed me to record him singing many of the songs from the night before, standing high above the pastures and pinewoods of ancient Choctaw country. On the drive home, Mingo pointed out a pile of stones in the woods fifty yards from the road.

"That's all that remains of an old fireplace," he said. "Folks that lived there dug a basement and hid out slaves. Escaping slaves. There was some kinda secret way, no bridges or boats, nothing like that. A secret way they had of gettin' 'em 'cross the river. Those old people risked they lives doing that. They'd of been shot, slaves and Indians all, if anybody caught 'em doing it."

From this conversation, and others in the next six years before his death, Mingo opened my eyes, and my thinking, to the friendships between Choctaws and slaves in the Old South. Freedmen became much more than *products* of inter-racial marriages; they became a living testament to a striving for life over death, a bone-deep caring by the old folks, my old folks. And when wine was not available, and it never seemed to be, I am proud to say Archie Mingo and I shared the sacraments in the backwoods way. My dad, Archie Tingle, would have been proud of me.

I never shared anything but coffee with Tony Byars, but Tony has the distinction of being the only one of the Choctaw Five to seek me out. In 1997, he found me telling old tribal stories at a Borders Bookstore in Austin, and invited me to his nearby home. I never knew, until after his death a year later, that Byars was dying of cancer. In all the shivering honesty of his boarding school recollections, his allowing me—even encouraging me—to record accounts of abuses of every nature heaped upon young Indian boys, stories of tragic heroes and stout-hearted victims, he never told me he was dying of cancer.

But he did tell me of four young men, on separate occasions, who came to him during the Korean War and told him they would be killed the next day. Tony was an officer in the Marine Corps, not a priest. "They chose to tell me, and all four of them made me promise not to try to get them out of the battle. They knew it was their time. They were ready. They only wanted me to let their families know they still loved them." Maybe this was Tony's way of letting me know.

Now Buck Wade, the last of my Choctaw Five, has died. I am grateful beyond any words that I knew them. I know I have often let them down in straying from the path of relating their stories. I will now, this New Year's Eve, rewind my lifeclock to their purpose, my purpose, ***our*** purpose as members of the Texas Folklore Society. Below is the briefest listing of my gifts from the Choctaw Five.

- From Estelline Tubby, "The Beating of Wings," a short story in *Walking the Choctaw Road.*
- From Charley Jones, "The Choctaw Way," a short story in *Walking the Choctaw Road*, and *When Turtle Grew Feathers*, a children's book.
- From Tony Byars, a boarding school story in *Walking the Choctaw Road,* "Tony Byars," and *Rolling Way the Rock*, the story of a Choctaw boy at Alcatraz.
- From Buck Wade, "Brothers," a short story in *Walking the Choctaw Road.*
- From Archie Mingo, "Crossing Bok Chitto," a short story in *Walking the Choctaw Road* and a children's book of the same title.
- From J. Frank Dobie and the Choctaw Five, a life filled with awe, real and imagined.

So, why does any of this matter? What are we TSFers really trying to achieve?

Maybe we are trying to defy death, delay the inevitable. Maybe we are honoring the lives of those who paved the way for our work. Maybe we are striving to create something that will be remembered after we pass on. Maybe we are struggling with meaning. Maybe pine-scented sunsets and Gulf waves are not enough anymore; we want evidenced eternity, tombstones that talk, real voices in the almost-heard whisperings, so we know that we the listeners can someday become we the whisperers. Or, maybe graveyards are more of birthings than of dyings.

I think this is it: graveyards giving birth, revisiting old tombs as age wraps its corrosive fingers around our thin-skinned musings. So, maybe the next time I visit Chambers Cemetery in McAlester, Oklahoma, I can poke around Buck Wade's grave and know that he understands my gratitude, accepts the limited nature of our current relationship, and anticipates, as I do, my someday crossing into a new land with him as my guide, just as he and Estelline and Charley and Archie and Tony were my guides into the living and breathing world of Choctaw eternity before they headed home. And now Buck Wade has joined them.

How has the Texas Folklore Society affected my life? What did Dobie, his contemporaries, and his modern-day disciples do to change my way of seeing? Made the word become flesh, that's what they did, nothing more, nothing less. Made the word become flesh.

J. Frank Dobie sitting at the water trough on the Dobie Ranch, 1951. Photo courtesy of Jimmy Jackson

THE TEXAS FOLKLORE SOCIETY WAS PART OF MY LIFE, LONG BEFORE I KNEW IT

by Jean Granberry Schnitz

I didn't join the Texas Folklore Society until 1990, but I now realize some of its members were part of my life before I ever even knew about the organization. The first person I knew of from the Texas Folklore Society was J. Frank Dobie, though I never met him in person. I remember reading some of his books when I was young, when we lived in Raymondville in the 1940s. My favorite place to read at that time was in a big mesquite tree in our yard. There was a place high on the deep, shady side of that tree that was shaped exactly right for me to lean against while holding and reading a book. *That* was where I discovered J. Frank Dobie—through his writings.

J. Frank Dobie was born September 26, 1888, near Lagarto in Live Oak County, on Ramirena Creek near where the present Lake Corpus Christi is located. The house in which he was born sits on part of the "Dobie Ranch" property that comprised 4,162 acres of land, which was purchased in 1951 and 1952 by a group of six men, five of them from Houston, and Ralph Semmes Jackson of Beeville.[1] In the process of the negotiations, Jackson showed his notes and writings about the Jackson family history in Chambers County to Dobie, who strongly urged him to write a book. Mr. Dobie wrote in the Introduction to Jackson's book:

> Land has been personal to me from the time I began having feelings. Certain live oaks, certain patches of grass, certain bends in Ramirenia [sic] Creek, certain mustang grapevines draping trees along the bank, certain hills on the ranch where I was born and reared remain more vivid to me and are more a part of me than numbers of people I knew while I was putting down roots into that plot

> of earth. One time when I came home (several years after the family had moved from the ranch to Beeville) and, a few hours later was setting out for the ranch, my mother said, "Why, Son, you think more of the ranch than of your own people." Whatever in the land pulled me, it was not property values. They were meager anyhow.
>
> But after my mother died in 1948 and the ranch was inherited by six brothers and sisters, it had to become property. My sister Fannie and I were executors. In 1951 we sold it to Ralph Jackson and five other men associated with him. He was the leader. From the minute I looked at his features of cultivated intelligence and heard his gentle voice, I was satisfied with the inevitable transference of deeds to the land. I had strong feelings on who should possess the deeds and would not have transferred them at any price to a certain individual who came trying to buy.[2]

Dobie summarizes in the Introduction how Jackson came to write an account relating his life experiences to the land in which they occurred. Dobie says, "The writer is a part of the parcel of land about which he writes . . ."[3] Both of these men felt strongly about that land, and I eventually came to appreciate just how much through my involvement in the Texas Folklore Society.

My connection to the former leader of the Texas Folklore Society is through Ralph S. Jackson and his family. I remember Mr. Jackson quite well. His sons Jimmy and Ralph, Jr. (called "Brother" and now deceased) have been my good friends for more than fifty years. His daughter, Dauris Ann Jackson is married to my brother, Bill Granberry. Bill and Dauris owned a ranch in Live Oak County they called "The Huisache" that had a camp house or two. Back in about 1978, we visited the Huisache and drove down a dirt road to the Dobie birthplace to have a look around. There was not much left of the back part of the house, which had apparently been built of stone

Ralph S. Jackson at the Huisache Ranch.
Photo courtesy of Jimmy Jackson

and bricks. The wooden portion was still standing. After visiting the area a time or two and re-reading some of Dobie's stories, it became apparent that some of the scenes he so eloquently described were right there! Ramirenia Creek, which is dry much of the time, looks like a "wash" or "gully" through which a car—or horse, or person on foot—had to cross in order to reach parts of the Dobie Ranch. That scene is one of several from the ranch that are described many times in Dobie's writings.

When I went off to college in Kingsville, I heard of Brownie McNeil, who was President of the Texas Folklore Society from 1946–1949, and is sometimes credited with holding the group together during World War II. He was a popular performer in South Texas at various sorts of programs, and his "specialty" was singing the Mexican corridos, and writing about them. I heard him sing for programs several times and was very much impressed with his abilities. My professor, Dr. Orlan Sawey, was another President of the Texas Folklore Society that I knew rather well, at least during the early 1950s when I was taking American Literature under his tutelage. At the time I didn't know a thing about the Texas Folklore Society, but it was apparent to everyone that Dr. Sawey had an intense interest in folklore. I remember him well! Twenty years after I was in his class, he became a President of the Texas Folklore Society.

In 1981, I was invited to play my Great-grandfather Columbus Addison Lee's hammered dulcimer at the Texas Folklife Festival in San Antonio. The tunes I played were taught to me by my grandmother, Dora Belle Lee Scudder, who learned them from C. A. Lee. This was folklore in action—and very close to home. Subsequently, I played more than twenty-five years at the TFF. In fact, at last count, it was twenty-seven years as of 2008. I first appeared on the Irish stage where I played and sang some of the songs I learned from Grandmama that were Irish in origin. I also performed on the storytelling stage, sometimes both in the same day, and both when the temperature was 104 in the shade. I'm not sure I could still do that today. I might melt!

I met some interesting people at the Texas Folklife Festival, including a group from East Texas with a string band, featuring a skinny fellow named Ab playing the bass fiddle. I met a young family named Haile, who had a toddler girl and a baby on a pallet on the ground in the booth of old-time toys they were demonstrating. Paul Patterson and Lora B. Garrison were telling stories. The list goes on and on. At the time, I never even thought about whether they were members of the Texas Folklore Society, but it later became apparent that they were among many participants of the TFF who were also part of the TFS.

A fellow who was the emcee at the Storytelling Stage at the Texas Folklife Festival for several years turned out to be Al Lowman, who told me, "I want you to write your story about your hammered dulcimer and the music your grandmother taught you and present it at the Texas Folklore Society." Good idea, I thought, but I didn't get around to it. Finally, after more urging by

Al, I joined TFS and presented my first paper entitled, "Hammered Dulcimers and Folk Songs—The Musical Legacy of the C. A. Lee Family" at the TFS meeting in Kingsville, Texas, in 1990. Al was President of the TFS that year.

So, you could say that it was Al Lowman who was guilty of getting me involved with the TFS. I don't know whether to BLAME him or CREDIT him, but I will be eternally grateful to him for bringing me into one of the most interesting groups of people I have ever encountered. Yes, the TFS meetings are enjoyable because the subject matter is interesting, but essentially, it is the *people* who are responsible for making the TFS so special to me. It was after I joined the TFS that I started thinking more about that ranch property once owned by J. Frank Dobie, and eventually recognized the connection between me, Dobie, and Texas folklore.

J. Frank Dobie's name appears multiple times in *The Texas Folklore Society, Volume I.* For many Texans, his name is probably better known than any other one person in connection with the Texas Folklore Society, even though he was not one of the founders. As stated by F. E. Abernethy in his well-researched history, "When J. Frank Dobie picked up the Society in 1921, his motive was to use the Society as a base in his own collecting and publishing of legends and folk tales."[4] Obviously, he did a superb job of accomplishing this motive. Dobie was an active participant in every meeting for more than two decades. He also served as Secretary-Treasurer-Editor from 1922 to 1943. According to Abernethy, "Dobie's energy and enthusiasm gave the Society the strength to survive."[5] Though he never served as President, he was an able leader.

Much has been written about Dobie's career, which was unquestionably influenced a great deal by his early years at home with his family on the ranch in Live Oak County where he spent his first years. He lived in what has been called the "Nueces Strip," which he describes in *Coronado's Children* this way:

> Human tracks and human blood will not wash out of a soil, although cement may hide them. The region between the Nueces and the Rio Grande is

> not cemented over; comparatively little of it will ever be cemented over; it will always be a land with a past. . . .
>
> Counterclaims by the republic of Texas and Mexico made the strip a kind of no man's land. Long after the claim of Texas was established, the Nueces was called "the dead line for sheriffs." Below it bandits of two languages raided and rendezvoused, and the sparse ranchers who survived to possess the land, where it was possessed at all, were as hardy a breed as ever justified the law of the fittest. . . .[6]

J. Frank Dobie was an extraordinary storyteller!

Perhaps he developed that skill by listening to his parents read and tell stories to their children. He dedicated *Coronado's Children* to his mother, "who has so often delighted me with conversational sketches of such characters as enter this book...."[7] He learned stories about lost treasure and other folklore of the Southwest by living in an area where such stories abound. According to the *Handbook of Texas Online*, "His fundamentalist father read the Bible to Frank and the other five children, and his mother read them *Ivanhoe* and introduced them to *The Scottish Chiefs, Pilgrim's Progress,* and *Swiss Family Robinson.*"[8] In *Backwoods to Border*, Dobie explains his interest in folklore because of its connection to the land on which he was raised:

Folklore has interested me to the extent that life and life's romance, vitality, flavor, humanity, humor, gusto, drama, songs with tunes and tales without ends, cowchips and stretching rawhide, Bowie knives and quilt patterns and hundreds of other factors of the land I belong to are inherent in it. Folklore to me is an expression of folks, the essence of a cultural inheritance. My idea as an editor has been to favor the folky part of it, and to interest folks in the features of their own inheritances and environments.[9]

Any doubt that Dobie drew strongly on the experiences of his childhood is removed many times in his writings. For example, in *I'll Tell You a Tale*, he writes, "Any ranch in the southern half of Texas might be taken as the setting, but to please my own memories, I shall particularize one—of modest dimensions—on Ramirena Creek in Live Oak County, about the season when wild turkeys begin chasing grasshoppers through the green of grass and weeds and mustang grapes are getting big and hard enough for bullets."[10] His stories repeatedly bear out his statement in his invitation letter to the 1942 meeting of the Texas Folklore Society, in which he says, "A man can no more cut himself off from the past than he can be born without a mother."[11]

James Frank Dobie was the eldest of the five children born to Richard Dobie and Ella Byler Dobie.[12] Since his uncle was already named "James" and was called "Jim," the name "Frank" or sometimes "Pancho" was what friends and family usually called him. He was "officially" known as "J. Frank Dobie," but he occasionally signed his letters and other documents simply as "Frank Dobie."

The real estate records in the Live Oak County Courthouse at George West reveal that the Dobie name first appeared in that county in about 1875. At that time the courthouse was located in the little town of Oakville, and remained there until the county seat was moved to George West in 1919 after the railroad by-passed Oakville. At one time the Dobie family owned some 7,000 acres, more or less, in Live Oak County. The property was located about nine miles Southeast of George West nearer the little towns of Dinero and Lagarto, on Ramirena Creek near what was called "Long Hollow." None of those communities ever grew very large, with most having only a few structures comprising the entire town. When the railroad by-passed the area, the communities dwindled away to a house or two in Dinero, and only a few more buildings that remain in Lagarto.

The Dobie Ranch property is located between Interstate 37 and Highway 281, which runs south from George West. The ranch is south and west of Dinero, not quite adjoining the upper parts of Lake Corpus Christi, which was formed by the Wesley E. Seale Dam on the Nueces River near Mathis, Texas. In the 1940s a smaller dam was at that location, and the lake was called "Lake Mathis." Ramirena Creek, which fed the Nueces River, was the primary water source for the ranch.[13] There is more relief on the Dobie Ranch than was typical of the brush country surrounding it. There were high places, and the creek wound through the low places in a serpentine fashion. The Nueces River and Ramirena Creek would typically run low during the hot and dry months of the summer, but flooding was common when there were big rains either upstream or locally. After seasons with adequate rainfall, the water levels in the creek remained high enough to provide water holes for the cattle and wildlife.

When the Dobie family lived there, there was a garden area near the ranch house, to be used as a source of food. There were some outbuildings that were used as barns for a milk cow or two. The family more than likely had chickens, which might have been housed in a smaller building with roosts to protect them from

Billy Granberry's hat

roaming coyotes that were in the area. Deer, quail, doves, and wild turkeys were plentiful during the years when the Dobie family lived there. The area is a prolific hunting area now, also.

Swinney Switch did not exist until after Dobie had moved away from the area. To visit the area today, the shortest route is to exit the Interstate at a small sign that says, "Swinney Switch," and go a couple of miles to Dinero, then on to a dirt road that leads to the ranch gate. Dobie speaks of the little town of Ramirenia, which no longer exists. It was located about fourteen miles southeast of George West in Live Oak County. As late as 1901, the town was one of only five communities in Live Oak County shown on post office maps. It had a store, church and school.[14] In his book *Cow People*, Dobie wrote:

> For a while we got our mail at Dinero, and I rode horseback once or twice a week to get it. I knew certain places where I'd seen deer cross the road. I always remembered where I'd seen deer cross the road. I always remembered them. I knew two glades where quail—bobwhites—plentiful. I knew a hollow live oak tree off the road a bit where buzzards annually nested and the little buzzards could not fly away until they had turned from whiteness to blackness. . . . I knew where I was almost sure to see a paisano running down the road, though I might see one anywhere. If it had rained, I could expect a certain caliche hill covered with ceniza bushes to be turned by their sudden flowers from ashen grey to almost solid lavender. [15]

Lagarto was once a thriving community called "Roughtown" but the name was changed after the saloons were closed. The current name is said to be Spanish for "alligator."[16] There was a school building at Lagarto, and probably one at Dinero, but the Dobie children went to school in a one-room school building that was built on the Dobie Ranch. A dirt road provided a short-cut from the ranch house to the town of Lagarto, but now fences require a much longer route.

Mike Cox wrote in *Texas Monthly*:

> The land schooled Dobie, literally and figuratively. His father and some of his neighbors built a one-room school on the ranch. Dobie went to class there until he was sixteen, when the family sent him to Alice to attend high school. By that time, he knew Shakespeare as well as he knew which end of a cow gets up first. "That land," he wrote, "my stalwart parents, and the English literature on which they nurtured me have been the chief influences of my life."[17]

When he reached high school age, Dobie was sent to Alice to live with his Dubose relatives while he attended school there. The road to Alice was via a little town called Orange Grove. The roads were of caliche, sand, and dirt, so he probably didn't visit the family many times during the year. The trip from the Dobie home to Alice now takes about an hour by paved Farm to Market roads, but by Dobie's description one hundred years ago, the same trip took more than seven hours.[18]

I am fairly familiar with the area since my family lived in Alice during the 1940s and in Beeville during the 1950s. Alice is approximately forty miles south and west of the Dobie Ranch, and Beeville is (according to Dobie's own description) twenty-seven miles to the east and slightly north. I can tell you that winters were cold at times, and summer days were long and hot in that area of South Texas. Summer sometimes seemed to last most of the year. Electricity did not come to the area until the mid-thirties at the earliest, so at the time when Dobie was a child living on the ranch, there would have been no electricity in the house and no running water. Jimmy Jackson, who still (in 2009) owns a portion of the original Dobie Ranch, explained to me that there were two wells near the Dobie house. One was a cistern that was not useful as a water well, so at

Sarah Granberry and Carl Schnitz at Dobie's water well, 1978

some point it was used to dump trash items. The other was a "dug well" that later had a windmill installed to allow water to be pumped to a nearby cattle water trough and to the house.[19]

I visited the Dobie Ranch on December 2, 2008, with Jimmy Jackson and Bill and Dauris Granberry, and realized the Ranch today is almost as isolated as it was during the years Dobie lived there. Bill Granberry described it as "past the end of the road from Dinero that ends between Long Hollow and Ramirena Creek."[20] The paved road ends a long way from the ranch gate. There is one locked gate and another protected by a gate guard. None of the ranch roads are paved. The only thing we could find at Dinero to take a picture of was the remains of the old store that once stood there.

In 2008, there were pieces of the windmill blades on the ground, but the windmill tower was still in existence. Not far from the windmill is the house in which J. Frank Dobie was born. The years have taken their toll on the house. The large tree near the house has since fallen. A large limb still lies draped over the edge of the roof. Early pictures show the house before the stone part fell. Two chimneys were visible; one would have been in the living area of the house and the other in the kitchen area. Additional heat would have been provided by a wood stove in the kitchen. As a practical matter, there were no chimneys in the wooden part of the house, to reduce the fire hazard. Jimmy Jackson described it this way:

> The house was originally an "L" shaped house with three rooms. Part of the house was built of wood planks and the rock part was not adobe, but was built with stone blocks about two feet by one-and one half feet. These blocks were proba-

Old Dinero store where Dobie picked up the mail

> bly cut from nearby caliche deposits. There was no re-bar used in the construction. The rock absorbed water until it finally disintegrated and fell in about 1970.[21]

At one corner of the front porch there are some lilies that faithfully grow each and every year since they were planted there. They didn't look very good in December of 2008, but Jimmy Jackson expects that they will come out again in the spring!

No one knows how many shade trees were near the house some one hundred years ago. The house was surrounded by live oak, mesquite, and huisache trees—the same as others commonly found in the area. There are several areas where large oak trees still stood in 2008. One was described by Jimmy Jackson as the "Dobie Oak," which Dobie always visited when he came to the ranch.[22] Through the years some of the massive limbs have fallen, leaving it not as impressive as it once was.

Back of Dobie birthplace after rocks fell in 1962.
Photo courtesy of Jimmy Jackson

According to a book by Jean Darby entitled *Alice: A Centennial History 1888–1988*:

> In 1905 the Board of Trustees . . . had a brick school (value $15,000) built on the Southeast corner of Reynolds and Center (now called Third Street) and the new building was named Alice High School. The first class to graduate was 1905–1906 led by Curren Benton as valedictorian and J. Frank Dobie as Salutatorian.
>
> J. Frank Dobie attended Alice High School and was one of first to graduate from the new brick Alice High School. As evidence of his academic excellence, Dobie was salutatorian of the class. Following graduation, he left Alice but his love for the Southwest never waned. Two of his nicknames were "Maverick" and "Pancho" and he liked them both. The picture of the Paisano or Roadrunner was his "trademark."[23]

There were seven other members of the class. The buildings where Dobie and I went to school are gone now, but I walked across the street from the library and stood on the spot where they had been—now the parking lot of the Alice U. S. Post Office.

After Dobie graduated from high school in Alice, he went on to college, and the rest is documented in many biographies. His career took him to several universities in the United States and abroad, but his love for Texas was never lost. In *Corners of Texas*, a copy of his handwritten will from August 27, 1937, reads in part:

> I don't want to be buried in any damned memorial park and I hope that friends instead of undertaker hirelings will throw dirt in on me. I would not mind being buried in the State Cemetery, somewhere in the vicinity of Bigfoot Wallace.

> Otherwise, I'd just as soon have my body burned and the ashes scattered among the live oaks and mesquites on my old ranch home, to which almost every day of my life I have returned in memory, in Live Oak County.[24]

My years as a member of the Texas Folklore Society have been very worthwhile and interesting. Numerous other descriptive phrases would be required to entirely explain the experience. The annual meetings are wonderful opportunities to learn and enjoy hearing about the many "faces of folklore" in Texas. The people who attend the meetings are friendly, intelligent, and enthusiastic, and we find ourselves feeling like we are members of a family instead of an academic organization. I never met J. Frank Dobie personally, but through his writings and through visiting the ranch and the brush country that he loved so dearly, I have come to think of him as a cherished member of my TFS family.

I suggest that you re-read the writings of J. Frank Dobie, savoring the way he put words together to spin tales of old-time Texas. Not only did he tell tales, but he also put songs, ballads, and Mexican corridos into writing. His stories, books and papers comprise a body of work which will likely never be surpassed. He was what could be called "one of a kind"—by his own description a maverick—but he left a legacy for the Texas Folklore Society and for each of us.

ENDNOTES

1. Jimmy Jackson. Email correspondence dated December 10, 2008.
2. J. Frank Dobie. Introduction to Ralph Semmes Jackson's *Home on the Double Bayou: Memories of an East Texas Ranch.* Austin: University of Texas Press, 1961. xv.
3. Ibid. xv.
4. Francis Edward Abernethy. *The Texas Folklore Society, Volume I, 1909–1943.* Denton, Texas: University of North Texas Press. Publication of the Texas Folklore Society LI, 1992. 9.
5. Ibid. 109.
6. J. Frank Dobie. *Coronado's Children: Tales of Lost Mines and Buried Treasures of the Southwest.* Austin: University of Texas Press. 1930. 2nd printing, 1984. 84.
7. Ibid. Dedication page.
8. Francis E. Abernethy. *Handbook of Texas Online*, s.v. "DOBIE, JAMES FRANK." http://www.tshaonline.org/handbook/online/articles/DD/fdo2.html. (Accessed 11/6/2008.)
9. Mody C. Boatright and Donald Day, Editors. *Backwoods to Border.* Dallas: Southern Methodist University Press. Publications of the Texas Folklore Society XVIII, 1943. viii.
10. J. Frank Dobie. "Bulls at a Waterhole on the Ramirena." *I'll Tell You a Tale.* 38.
11. qtd. in *Texas Folklore Society, Volume I, 1909–1943*, F. E. Abernethy, editor. 268.
12. Francis E. Abernethy. *Handbook of Texas Online*, s.v. "DOBIE, JAMES FRANK." http://www.tshaonline.org/handbook/online/articles/DD/fdo2.html. (Accessed 11/6/2008.)
13. "Ramirena" ("Ram-uh-ray-nuh") Creek is the present-day spelling and pronunciation, but most sources, maps, and Dobie himself always spelled it "Ramirena" or Remirenia," pronounced "Ram-uh-ray-nee-yuh." *Handbook of Texas Online*, s.v. "RAMIRENA, TX." http://www.tshaonline.org/handbook/online/articles/RR/hrrqg.html. *Handbook of Texas Online.* (Accessed 12/8/2008.)
14. Ibid.
15. J. Frank Dobie. *Cow People.* Boston: Little, Brown and Company, 1964. Chapter 14, "The Right Tempo." 194.
16. *Texas Escapes Online Magazine.* s.v. "Lagarto, Texas." http:www.texasescapes.com/SouthTexasTowns/Lagarto-Texas.htm. (Accessed 10/15/2008.)

17. Mike Cox. "J. Frank Dobie, Storyteller of the Southwest." *Texas Highways*. May 2003. 52.
18. J. Frank Dobie. *Some Part of Myself*. Austin: University of Texas Press. First Printing 1980. Reprinted by arrangement with Little, Brown and Company, Inc. 118–121.
19. Jimmy Jackson. Personal interview. December 2, 2008.
20. Bill Granberry email.
21. Jimmy Jackson. Email correspondence dated December 10, 2008.
22. Ibid.
23. Jean Darby. *Alice: A Centennial History: 1888–1988*. 32.
24. Holland, Richard A. "A Corner Forever Texas: The Southwestern Writers Collection," in *Corners of Texas*. F. E. Abernethy, editor. Denton: University of North Texas Press. Publication of the Texas Folklore Society LII. 1993. 27.

Members of all ages attend Texas Folklore Society meetings

THE FAMILY NATURE OF THE TEXAS FOLKLORE SOCIETY

by Kenneth L. Untiedt

The first paper I ever presented at an academic conference was at a meeting of the Popular Culture Association. The second was at the 79th annual meeting of the Texas Folklore Society in Fort Worth in 1995. I have since given conference papers for numerous academic organizations, at the state, regional, and even national levels. I realized early on in my scholarly career that there is a difference between the Texas Folklore Society and all other similar organizations. Whole families attend the meetings. I see children of all ages attending the sessions, listening to papers, and joining in the activities such as the Hootenanny and tours of local attractions. This is an organization that *promotes* a family atmosphere, and that's one of the reasons the TFS has lasted so long.

The Texas Folklore Society is a family-oriented organization. It always has been. At the very first annual meeting in 1911, not only was John A. Lomax listed as Secretary, but Mrs. John A. Lomax presented the paper "The Ballad of the Boll Weevil" in the afternoon session. For years after that, Bess Brown Lomax read her husband's papers when he was unable to attend meetings.[1] The paisano seen on our letterhead and many other TFS documents was drawn by Betty Boatright, Mody Boatright's wife. We've had many such husband-and-wife teams who have been active in the Society in various ways, from serving as officers or board members to presenting papers or contributing in other creative ways. Among them is none other than Ab and Hazel Abernethy.

The importance of the family element in our organization, and in folklore in general, is no secret. Back in 1958, Mody Boatright introduced the term "family saga" in his article "The Family Saga as a Form of Folklore." He defines the term as "lore that tends to cluster around families . . . which is preserved and modified by oral transmission, and which is believed to be true."[2] Boatright suggests that collections of family stories "never form a connected history,"[3] probably because a history, much like a work of fiction, is more inclined to have a definitive time frame or scope, not to mention a motive. Boatright is speaking about loosely organized stories of a familial group, told in the oral tradition, with the expected variations included to add an emotional interest. This, he claims, is what really distinguishes a family saga from an historical text.[4]

F. E. Abernethy later used that article as a starting point for the 60th PTFS, *The Family Saga: A Collection of Texas Family Legends*, a work devoted entirely to the preservation of individual stories about families. However, even before that publication, we as a group had been putting the idea in practice all along. Our own family saga is evident at every annual meeting. Attendees meet not just with colleagues who happen to share an interest in a particular academic field. We visit with members who've become *family*. We have our own customs, such as the Hootenanny and the banquet, as well as a particular order and certain ways of doing things, although nothing is set in stone, as our meetings vary from year to year. We also have a common bloodline, and we have an ongoing history to tell. Any of the stories that follow would fit perfectly in the *Family Saga* chapter that includes stories on Courtship & Marriage—or the chapter titled "Family Characters: Heroes, Black Sheep, and Eccentrics," for that matter.

The idea for this paper, appropriately enough, came to me while someone was telling me a story. It wasn't just anyone telling me any story, but a member of the Texas Folklore Society was telling me a story about other members. I was at a meeting of the East Texas Historical Association in San Augustine, and I found myself waiting in line at a banquet with Sarah Greene. She told me how she and her friend Janell had made a habit of attending TFS meetings together. At one meeting, Sarah was looking for Janell, but she couldn't find her. They had agreed to check into the hotel and meet up downstairs, but when Sarah finally located her, Janell was talking with a man named Tom Chesnut. Well, Sarah couldn't get them apart. She had to get used to it. Tom was still married at the time, but he and

Janell began corresponding, and he later got divorced. Tom and Janell eventually got married, and now *they* attend the meetings together. The story struck me as interesting at the time, and it kept popping into my mind when I would think about other TFS business or people. Eventually, I started to associate it with similar stories.

I made a mental note at that banquet in San Augustine, because I thought Sarah's account was a good idea for a paper. However, I thought the details of how Tom and Janell had gotten together sounded familiar. Actually, the more I thought about it the more I thought it sounded *very* familiar, as if someone had just told that story to me a couple of years earlier. In fact, someone had. I remembered that it was in the January 2001 TFS Newsletter that I had read a notice about a wedding. It told about another couple, Debra and Dow Cox, who had gotten married after meeting each other through the Society. They were married on December 28, 2000, in the chapel at Millard's Crossing historic village, which we toured as part of the meeting when we gathered in Nacogdoches just several months earlier. Though I hardly knew them at that time, I have gotten to know them much better in the past few years. I decided to call them and learn more about the background of this very interesting relationship.[5]

Dow told me that he had been going to meetings with his family since he was six. He met Debra Dean at the TFS meeting in Wimberley in 1970, when he was fourteen and she was fifteen. He said he and his brother Jim were out walking around the Holiday Hills resort when he saw the most beautiful girl he'd ever seen. He wanted to get to know her, but he had never seen her at a meeting and thought she was just a guest at the hotel, probably visiting from somewhere far out of state. He saw her later inside, when they were listening to Sid Cox, Dow's father, give an encore presentation of his paper, "The Home Place," and he was able to make his move.

Debra's father, R. G. Dean, actually gives a more dramatic, detailed rendering of this account, telling about how Dow came around a corner and saw Debra standing on a footpath bridge. R. G. and Ouida had told their children, Debra and Keith, that they could go exploring instead of listening to papers, but after hearing

Sid's paper and learning that he was going to read it again, they told the kids that they would have to listen to just this one paper. Debra says she resisted at the time, but she is glad for the experience now. They had never been to the Hill Country, and she was excited to meet the Cox boys. She says her family didn't go very many places when she was younger; they didn't have car trips or take many vacations, and she now views the Texas Folklore Society meetings as widening their horizons. Debra stayed to hear more papers after Sid's, including Joe Lomax's paper, "Yellow Submarine: 1969 Style," which she says was very fortuitous. As they were leaving, Debra asked, "Where is the meeting going to be next year?"

Dow says he can't remember where the meeting was the next year, but the year after that it was in College Station, and he says that was the first time he ever kissed Debra. It wasn't just about the romance, though. Dow remembers that the younger kids have always "formed their own pack" at meetings. He says that Ab and Hazel's kids were part of their group, and going to see all the other kids was a great part of the annual meetings. Dow believes kids like folklore because they get a chance to be treated like real people, whereas many places, like public school, aren't that interested in them. Paul Patterson, George Ewing, Ab and many others like Martha Emmons and Hermes Nye took the time to share stories with them. Dow says he always looked forward to seeing and hearing Hermes play and sing. Debra notes that the old form of folklore was all oral, which facilitates the storytelling tradition, and kids are still into it. She believes this is nothing new: kids have always been a part of it because they have a ready-made group with something in common.

True, they especially like the Hoots, but she emphasizes that for them it wasn't so much about what they did, but that they were getting together. The year the meeting was in College Station, they heard there was supposed to be a great pool. When they arrived, the pool was drained and being sandblasted and painted. So, they just hung out in the empty pool. Dow admits that there occasionally was some mischief. For instance, if you rearrange the letters for "Welcome Texas Folklore Society" on a hotel marquis,

Many young members attend TFS meetings and hear the papers along with their parents

he tells me, it can spell "Welcome Sex at Folklore Society." Kids will be kids, but for the most part, they're generally quite well behaved, especially for adolescents attending what people typically consider an adult-only event.

Debra and Dow dated off and on during their twenties, but she went to Hawaii for eleven years to teach; Dow married his first wife and they had Dylan, who regularly attends TFS meetings, along with his brother Lane. Debra and Dow always kept in touch, though, visiting once or twice a year. Their friendship finally brought them together when they were married in December of 2000. Many TFS members were in attendance, which is exactly what they wanted. They had considered getting married at one of the annual meetings, but they did not want to have a conflict of interest, making it more about their wedding than the meeting.

Although I did not attend the wedding, I did see the video. Jerry Self, their minister, began the ceremony by referring to the way in which Debra and Dow's relationship had started at a Folklore Society meeting, and had developed as they grew to know each other at the yearly events. He said, "The beautiful girl on the bridge of some time ago has accepted the proposal of the stalwart and eager young folklorist . . . Let's have a wedding."[6] R. G. Dean, the proud father of the bride, spoke of a friendship that had, over thirty years' time, become a kinship that had already bonded the two families. The minister concluded by explaining that the wedding was a "storytelling time . . . an event . . . an opportunity to tell family stories . . . and to make them . . . to hear tales and live them . . . to create legends, fashion traditions."[7] He said—before the term was common—that Debra and Dow's wedding was "ground zero" for *their* story.

More recently, Keith Dean has taken a page from Dow and Debra's book of "looking for love in unexpected places." He and Lou Ann Cunningham (formerly Herda) were married at Millard's Crossing in April of 2005. I first met Lou Ann in 2002, when she had attended the meeting in Victoria, according to her, merely to find out if the Headless Horseman tale was true. I invited her to have lunch with my family, and she quickly became part of our little group, partly because her son Taylor was close to our oldest daughter's age (they were born only one week apart). It wasn't until the 2004 meeting that she knew for sure that she was becoming part of the TFS family in a more serious way. It was there that she met Keith. As had become our custom, we had lunch with the Deans and Hailes and some others after the meeting. I recall noticing that Lou Ann and Keith were spending a lot of time together. The next thing I remember is getting a telephone call one night from Lou Ann. They had moved to the "Oldest Town in Texas," and she wanted to know if my family could help unpack the truck. We did.

I visited with them one day at the A-frame house in Nat, a little community northwest of Nacogdoches, where they had moved at least temporarily while looking for work.[8] Luckily, the rain had held off, and we talked for an hour or two about their first memories of the Texas Folklore Society, and meeting each other. Keith told me that Jimmie Sniffin had been a big part of his family getting involved in folklore. He recalled many of the same stories that

Debra and Dow had shared, including one about a young member from their group who tried to sneak a cup of beer from a keg during a Hoot, drawing the attention of everyone there to the loud sucking sound it made because the keg was empty. He also told me about running "pell-mell" down Old Baldy at the meeting in Wimberley. He said he remembered the Cox family better than any other members they had met, and the two families got to know each other quite well over the next several years. The Dean children would visit the ranch Sid Cox had told them about in that first paper, and Keith still remembers the names of some of the goats they had.

Keith and Lou Ann told me they first met at the Hootenanny at the 2004 meeting in Allen. Lou Ann had been telling stories, and each had been playing around with some of the instruments. It got pretty late, and most people had turned in for the night. Keith asked if Lou Ann would like some wine, and—they both tell this part with humor and mutual understanding—when Lou Ann said "yes," Keith apparently pointed to the table and said, "It's right over there." After the meeting, they talked on the phone and began emailing each other. It turned out that they were both at a re-starting point in their lives, so Lou Ann agreed to go to Berkley to help Keith transport his belongings back to Texas.

Upon arriving in California, Lou Ann discovered that part of her job was to help Keith finish packing, something she thought had already been completed. They say that what really pulled them together was spending twenty-four hours a day together during that trip. What did they do for all that time? Lou Ann says they talked. They learned about one another. They shared their interests, their concerns, and their histories. They had some unexpected twists and turns on the trip to Nacogdoches, and they even kept a piece of the wood from the hotel overhang that they hit with a U-Haul truck. They rented a house pretty close to ours before moving out to the A-Frame, which the Deans had built themselves—as a family—during the summers from 1975 to 1977.

When I finally interviewed Tom and Janell Chesnut for this paper, their story about how they met matched the one Sarah had told me—mostly.[9] Tom had been to two or three meetings, but he didn't know anyone too well, which was okay with him, he says, because he went to hear the papers, not to socialize. Little did he know about how the Texas Folklore Society pulls people in. He says he was in "the tail end of a marriage that was going down fast" when he attended the 1996 meeting in Abilene. It snowed that year, as anyone who was there will recall, and Tom said he couldn't even go across the street to a shopping center. This is where Janell broke into the story, saying that *everyone* at the meeting that year got to know one another better.

Janell met Tom as they were both looking at tapes on the tables at the back of the room. They started discussing their interests, and Tom suggested a tape he thought Janell would like. However, when she went back for it, the last one had been sold. Tom mailed her his copy after the meeting, and he says he was a little surprised when he received a letter from her thanking him. Janell had been attending meetings for years with Sarah, a neighbor of hers in Gilmer, and she already understood the personal nature of the Society. However, even she admits that she did not expect to find romance at a conference. They laugh as they tell about the note they received from Ab after they paid their dues (for a family membership) for the first time after getting married in November of 2000: they say Ab wrote something like, "If you all are still together at the next Folklore meeting, I'll see you there."

I can give other examples of how people in this organization have become family, and not just ones who have become romantically involved. Kenneth Davis first got me started in this whole business. He was my professor at Texas Tech University long before I ever heard of the Texas Folklore Society. I was taking his course on the Western novel when my friend Buddy had an unfortunate experience with a research paper. Buddy needed to see "Dr. Davis" about his grade, but for some reason he was worried about going to his office. As a side note, it *was* a scary place, where rumor has it that some cleaning personnel may have gotten lost in the debris, and were never heard from again. I agreed to accompany my friend, and somehow during the conversation Buddy mentioned that I was a police officer. I distinctly remember Kenneth's response, although I still don't understand it. He replied, "Yes, and I am the emperor, Napolean Bonaparte." I thought he was pretty kooky, but he was also a fairly good professor, so I took him for another course, which happened to be about folklore.

After we had a discussion about graffiti and folk art, he encouraged me to write a paper and submit it for presentation at a conference, which I did; I eventually presented a version of that paper at the 79th annual meeting in Ft. Worth in 1995. Kenneth, who was still Dr. Davis to me back then, retired the same year I finished my undergraduate degree, and I ran into him in the hall at school one day as he was cleaning out his office (a process that would actually take months to complete.) He suggested that since he was no longer my professor, we should maybe have lunch one day. We had lunch, and sometime later I invited him to dinner at our home. We attended his church, then joined. Eventually, he became like a grandfather to our children. It was Kenneth who told me, "Going to the Folklore Society meetings is like going to a family reunion when all the cousins are on speaking terms," a quote he attributes to Syvia Grider.[10] Whoever said it is right. In fact, I don't recall ever having attended one of my own family reunions where people got along as well as they do at meetings of the Texas Folklore Society.

The TFS family continues to grow. I look forward to seeing *all* of the members each year, but we have, as is natural, formed strong bonds with a few people, including Tom and Mary Crum, Jim and Mary Harris, the Deans and the Coxes, the Hansons, and the Hailes, whose daughters grew up at these meetings. Some of these relationships have formed because of the children, but members all probably have their little groups, which is normal. I don't believe any of them, however, are exclusive to the group as a whole. And yes, we even occasionally see people crying as they leave these annual gatherings, sad that it will be another year before they can get together again.

The next generation of folklorists in Texas

A few years ago, my wife Tierney proudly served as Chair for the first Youth Session that was part of the regular program. In 2004, our daughter Miché became the youngest member to ever read a paper at a meeting. These are important milestones for our family. Not just the Untiedt family, but ours—the Texas Folklore Society family. Families grow and diversify naturally, and I know that the TFS family will continue to thrive. However, it doesn't hurt to work consciously at it. Ab has spoken of the natural cycle of life, as new blood must come in to carry on what was started by those before them. We are trying hard to make sure that the younger members who attend feel welcome and are an active part of these meetings. We're also working on other ways to involve them, including the camp we put on in cooperation with Treetops-in-the-Forest, just west of Nacogdoches. John Mellencamp, a favorite songwriter of mine, says, "There is nothing more sad or glorious than generations changing hands."[11] I believe that must be true. Our family will carry on. The kids are the future. Everyone I talked to about this paper agreed: they're anxious to see what they will contribute.

ENDNOTES

1. F. E. Abernethy. *The Texas Folklore Society: 1909–1943.* Denton: University of North Texas Press, 1992. 18.
2. Mody Boatright. "The Family Saga as a Form of Folklore." *The Family Saga: A Collection of Texas Family Legends.* F. E. Abernethy, Jerry Bryan Lincecum, and Frances B. Vick, eds. 7.
3. Ibid.
4. Ibid. 7–8.
5. Dow Cox. Phone interview, January 30, 2005.
6. Videotape of Cox/Dean wedding.
7. Ibid
8. Keith and Lou Ann Dean. Personal interview, February 11, 2005.
9. Tom and Janell Chenut. Phone interview, March 19, 2005.
10. Kenneth W. Davis: ". . . that's the way I heard the comment and it was attributed to Sylvia Grider, who is on the TAMU faculty. Who knows what the original statement was? Repeating 'quotings' of a statement will lead inevitably to modifications. But the version I gave above is the one I recall."
11. John Cougar Mellencamp. *Scarecrow* liner notes.

BOOKS, PAPERS, AND PRESENTATIONS:

TEXAS FOLKLORE SCHOLARSHIP

James Ward Lee

COLLECTING AND READING FOLKLORE

by James Ward Lee

At the forty-first meeting of the Texas Folklore Society in Nacogdoches in 1967, John Q. Anderson, a past-president of the organization, read a paper titled "Magical Transference of Disease in Texas Folk Medicine." What Anderson presented was a series of remedies he had collected. At the evening banquet, William A. Owens delivered a full-blown attack on Anderson's paper in his "Texas Folklore: A Challenge to the Creative Artist." The main focus of his excoriation of Anderson's work was that the paper was merely a compilation of remedies. Nothing more. No analysis. No attempt to make sense in some large context. No transference from collection to art. It was an uncomfortable thirty minutes, and all eyes kept turning to John Q., who was visibly shaken and angered. As vice-president and program chairman, I was embarrassed that I had put together a program that lent itself to such vituperation. My only escape was that the banquet speaker was chosen by the local arrangements committee or the secretary-editor or some entity that could pay travel expenses. Nevertheless, I was most uncomfortable.

There was no question that William A. Owens had credentials. He had just published *This Stubborn Soil,* one of the two or three finest memoirs ever written about Texas. He was a professor and dean at Columbia University, and he had achieved success as a folklorist with two books—*Swing and Turn: Texas Play-Party Games* (1936), and *Texas Folk Songs* (1950)—and as a novelist with *Walking on Borrowed Land* (1954), *Fever in the Earth* (1958), and *Look to the River* (1963). In addition to his publications, he tells us in the third volume of his autobiography, *Tell Me a Story, Sing Me a Song. . .* (UT Press, 1983), *how* he had served time as "a professional collector." He says he was a professional "if being paid makes one a professional." That was in 1941, when he went to work collecting folksongs for the University of Texas. He worked under Roy Bedichek in the Extension Service. "Bedichek brought me close to his closest friends: J. Frank Dobie and Walter Prescott Webb. The three were instrumental in creating my job and getting me appointed to it." From them he learned of the land and the people and the meaning of folk life. "I eventually came to know that the people has a great, perhaps greater, need to lose themselves in an old ballad . . . and that the songs they treasured were as much as anything else a key to understanding who they were and what they were. The realization was slow in coming but it came: if I wanted to know the people I had to work from inside out, beginning with songs and stories deeply embedded in their minds."[1]

At the time Owens worked with Dobie, Bedichek, and Webb, the Texas Folklore Society was in full flower, Dobie having served as secretary-editor from 1922 until 1943. And while some of the focus of the Texas Folklore Society involved assessing Texas culture by analyzing the songs, tales, and superstitions, much of the emphasis of the Society was on collecting and introducing this Texas lore to the rest of the world. During the early years of the TFS, there were a number of notable collectors, the most famous being John A. Lomax, collector of cowboy songs, who later, with his son Alan, was discoverer of Huddie Ledbetter, the great black blues and folksinger. Dobie helped to develop J. Mason Brewer's talents as a collector of black preacher tales from the Brazos. Before the Dobie era, the best known collector was Dorothy Scarborough, who used her knowledge of Texas folklore to write a series of novels, most about the cotton country along the Brazos. Of course, her most famous work was *The Wind,* set in and around Sweetwater in West Texas.

It has always seemed to me that J. Frank Dobie's main interest was, like Scarborough's and Owens's, using folklore as a vehicle for his own writing, and much of Dobie's writing was an attempt to capture the flavor of "western" life in Texas—tales of cattle drives and cow camps, of mustangs and longhorns. His works were, in the broadest sense, cultural, for Dobie and others in the Society were concerned with capturing "old Texas," of showing nineteenth-century Texas to the world. Francis Abernethy in his history of the Texas Folklore Society quotes one of Dobie's valedictory comments on his work as a Texas folklorist. "Folklore has inter-

John Q. Anderson, author of *Texas Folk Medicine*

ested me to the extent that life and life's romance, vitality, flavor, humanity, humor, gusto, drama, songs . . . and hundreds of other factors of the land I belong to are inherent in it. Folklore to me is an expression of folks, the essence of a cultural inheritance."[2]

Dobie was followed as secretary-editor by Mody Boatright, and later Boatright and Wilson Hudson. A few volumes during and after the Dobie era had additional editors—Donald Day and Harry Hunt Ransom are two of the best known—but most of the work before Francis Abernethy became Secretary-Editor was done by Boatright and Wilson M. Hudson, both professors of English at the University of Texas at Austin. Boatright was a significant collector of cowboy and oil field lore, but his *Folk Laughter on the American Frontier* is an analysis of the kind of humor that grew out of both the exuberance and despair of the early settlers. There was indeed analysis of folklore during the early and middle years of the Society, but much of the emphasis was on collecting.

I can't be certain, now that forty years have passed, what William Owens found so unpalatable about John Q. Anderson's collection of folk remedies and magical transferences since he had called himself a professional collector. But I suspect that some of what Owens attacked was Anderson's failure to go beyond the collection and see how the remedies told us about the people who were his informants and how all this fitted into the framework of folk life and folk superstitions. More than that, any collection of magical transferences should lead to a consideration of the enchanted world his informants lived in. Still, it seemed rude and unnecessary for Owens to come back from his success in New York to crush a minor folklorist from Texas A & M.

Owens was wrong in his comments. But he was also right. He was wrong in attacking the collector who did no more than assemble data; after all, somebody has to do it. But he was right in that the mere collection of folklore is not the ultimate end of the discipline. And yet no one can deny, I think, that some of the grandest names in folklore were those of collectors. It should be remembered that all Francis James Child did was to collect his *English and Scottish Popular Ballads.* He never explained his methods, but in his defense, it must be said that he died before he annotated the work. Still, we don't know what he would have said about all those now-famous Child Ballads. George Lyman Kittredge and Child's daughter, Helen, put the book together, and even they did not know his rationale for choosing the ballads he did or why he left out some that seem worthy of inclusion. Jacob and Wilhelm Grimm merely collected the folktales from the Black Forest, *Kinder-und Hausmarchen (Children's and Household Tales)*, and Charles Perrault put together *Contes de mir Mere l'Oie (Tales from My Mother Goose)*. It was left to later scholars to write commentary on the Brothers Grimm and Perrault. The collecting was important, as was John Q. Anderson's folk medicine. But I agree a little with Owens that the collector should apply some art to his collecting. It seems to me necessary, or at least desirable, for folklorists and popular culturists to pay attention to the subtexts of much that is amassed. Folklorists should "read" the material they collect. The idea of reading the folklore and popular

John Q. Anderson's 1970 publication for the Paisano Book Series

culture that folklorists collect is not an old idea. Some of the impetus came from the Annales School of history, which began in France in the 1920s. But I think it is also true that all historians, folklorists, and literary critics have always read between the lines when they consider folk artifacts, historical events, and literary productions.

Those of us who study literature have become heartily sick of the "theorists" who hijacked English departments in the seventies and eighties. Fortunately, the malady has passed off, even though the melody lingers on in some quarters. That surge in theory, in what most remember under the term "deconstruction," was, like the Annales historians, a French scheme. But no matter how much we poke fun at the deconstructionists, we all must admit that there is something to be said for "reading a text." They made serious points about reading texts, and they defined texts as all sorts of productions—from "La Belle Dame Sans Merci" to *The Mary Tyler Moore Show*. And they were wrong. And they were right. There is more meaning in all sorts of texts than traditional critics (and I count myself as one) admit. After all, a folktale is a text, a ballad is a text, a superstition is a text. And all of them can be read to our profit.

None of this is to suggest that the great collectors failed in what they were about. And I doubt that Owens, who collected songs and stories all through the thirties and into the early forties, would not deny that great work in folklore had been done by collectors. If we think of all the collections made in this country late in the nineteenth century and early twentieth century, we see a great many collections but not much analysis. I am thinking of such works as H. C. Belden's *Ballads and Songs Collected by the Missouri Historical Society*, *The Frank C. Brown Collection of North Carolina Folklore*, *Ozark Folksongs*, Vance Randolph's monumental collection, as well as the many volumes of folktales Randolph collected in the Missouri and Arkansas Ozarks. And certainly the world owes a debt to Louise Pound, Cecil Sharp, John Lomax, Frank Dobie, Dorothy Scarborough, and scores of others—Owens included—who worked in the field with pencils and paper and rudimentary recording devices operating off a car battery. In earlier centuries, even before the term "folklore" was used, collections like Walter Scott's *Minstrelsy of the Scottish Border* and Bishop Percy's *Reliques of Ancient English Poetry* established the primacy of collecting.

It was only in the 1920s, in France, that a group of cultural historians, the Annales School, began reading history from "the bottom up." Until the 1920s, the focus of historians had almost always been on "event history," the doings of captains of kings, the

William A. Owens

great social upheavals brought about by wars and shifts in philosophical thinking. It was more or less a new idea to study the history, as far as it could be reconstructed, of the lower orders, the middle classes, and those who were not involved in the power structure. One of the ways the members of the Annales School looked at what they called the *longue duree* (the long term) was to consider those structures that have existed for centuries, especially those found in the lives of common people. We might consider why some customs have existed from time immemorial: why we wear black at funerals, why we tell tales of animals that become humans, why cats are considered to be the companions of witches, and on and on with all the customs and superstitions and tales the folklorists have collected for years. In other words, the tales, songs, beliefs, and customs of the common people give us a valid picture of life down the ages. Not only in ancient times (folklore), but also in the present days (popular culture).

One of the early works of the Annales School was by one of its founders, Marc Bloch. His 1924 book *Les rois thaumaturges* (*The King's Touch*) was a discussion of the superstition that the king's touch could cure scrofula. It is easy to imagine how a discussion of such a belief had existed in the Middle Ages, when the king had powers given by God. Bloch's book treats folk beliefs, magical cures, and what Charles Taylor in his Templeton Award-winning book, *A Secular World* (Harvard UP, 2007) calls the enchanted world. Bloch, who was killed by the Nazis in 1944 for his work with the French Resistance, joined Lucien Fabvre in founding *journal Annales d'histoire économie et sociale,* a publication which helped spread the discipline they called *mentalitiés,* roughly translated as attitudes or cultural history.[3] It is this study of *mentalitiés* in our approach to folklore that I find important to an organization like the Texas Folklore Society and to Texas folklorists in general. What are we to learn about the cultural history of our world from the study of folklore? How can we, without becoming unspeakably pedantic, meld our collecting and our analysis?

A study such as Jan Harold Brunvand's *Folklore: A Study and Research Guide* or his *The Study of American Folklore* lists hundreds of books and articles discussing various collections, studies, and theories of folklore and popular culture. Brunvand, however, does not in those works give detailed analyses of the kind of information the Annales historians were concerned with. Brunvand suggests readings, so many in fact that only the dedicated folklore graduate student or his professor can absorb them all. Still, the books are valuable guides to the many theories that folklorists, anthropologists, psychologists, and literary critics have expounded in the past fifty or so years.

One book that will make clear what the *Annales* School was about and lead us to a discussion of *mentalitiés* is Robert Darnton's *The Great Cat Massacre and Other Episodes in French Cultural History* (Basic Books, 1984), especially the first chapter, "Peasants Tell Tales: the Meaning of Mother Goose." That chapter is a good starting place to begin a discussion of the reading of folklore texts, which, after all, is the focus of this essay. In his *The Great Cat Massacre,* Darnton *goes* into great detail to explain what lay behind the tales Perrault collected and other "episodes" in the cultural history of early modern France. What Darton does in that essay is to show how the tales collected by Perrault give us a picture of life in early modern France "from the bottom up." In those tales, one can see how poverty worked its way into the stories people told: How a farmer and his wife with a large family could not support all their offspring; therefore, the second and third sons were often sent out on the roads to beg or starve or find work, or perhaps to encounter an enchanted figure that could by spells and magic cause the wanderer to prosper.

Darnton's essay on the cat massacre of 1707 ("Workers Revolt: The Great Cat Massacre of the Rue Saint-Severin") is both his consideration of the sociology of the apprentices' revolt against their masters by slaughtering cats, as well as some enlightened commentary on animal torture. The apprentices to Paris printers were fed poor food, while the masters' cats ate far better fare and lived what the young men considered lives of luxury. So, after seeing masters who kept as many as twenty-five cats, who had their kitties' portraits painted, and fed them better fare than the apprentices ate, the apprentices revolted and went on a rampage of cat killing. In one night they killed pampered cats, alley cats, and all cats that came within their reach. They held cat trials, hanged cats, and "got their own back" on the masters and on the cats, cats who often yowled all night and kept the already sleep-deprived apprentices awake.

That is the story. What does it mean beyond the simple sociology of the hard lot of the apprentices? What does it say about cats, about animal torture, about the world of witchcraft? I commend your attention to Darnton's book, but let me offer a sample of what he says about kitty torture:

> The torture of animals, especially cats, was a popular amusement throughout early modern Europe. You have only to look at Hogarth's *Stages of Cruelty* to see its importance, and once you start looking you see people torturing animals everywhere. Cat killings provide a common theme in literature, from *Don Quixote* in early seventeenth century Spain to *Germinal* in late nineteenth-century France. Far from being a sadistic fantasy on the part of a few half-crazed authors, the literary versions of cruelty to animals expressed a deep current of popular culture, as Mikhail Bakhtin has shown in his study of Rabelais. All sorts of ethnographic reports confirm that view. On *dimanche des brandons* (burning the Valentines) in Semur, for example, children used to attach cats to poles and roast them over bonfires. In the *jeu du chat* at the Fete-Dieu in Aix-en Provence, they threw cats high in the air and smashed them on the ground.[4]

The game of *jeu du chat* is like tennis or squash with cats as the balls. I have no information that people today play "cat tennis," but the torture of cats did not die out in the Middle Ages or in early modern France. Somewhere, a few years ago, I saw a reference to a magazine called *Kitty Torture Quarterly*, though I suspect that the title was a joke since I have not been able to locate it anywhere. But a Google search of cat torture lists 352,000 hits. One of the articles listed comes from Salt Lake City's *Deseret News* and tells of nineteen cat mutilations in "the Avenues" section of Salt Lake City.[5] Utah later enacted laws against animal cruelty which the *Deseret News* called "one of the strongest in the nation."[6] A Google search turns up more than a million hits under the rubric "Kitty Torture"—one listing in 2008 mentions that more than one cat in North Dallas was "sliced open with a knife."

A consideration of stories and tales and superstitions about cats may offer a short course in "folklore reading." Why are cats so often the object of torture even today? What do cats mean in our culture? How long have the prejudices about cats been a part of western culture? Of course, not all cultures have seen evil in cats and subjected them to mutilation. The Egyptians elevated some cats to the godhead. The earliest Egyptian feline goddess was named Mafdet, and the most famous was Baslet, pictured in Egyptian mythology as having a female body with the head of a cat. There was even a festival devoted to the worship of Baslet, and statues of her/it can be seen in books of Egyptian art. Many cats were revered as household goddesses by the Egyptians. Mohammed had a famous cat named Meuzza, and the *Koran* mentions the cat as a symbol of purity. Even in Norse mythology the goddess Freyja had her own special cat. But—and this may be important—there are no cats mentioned in the Bible. It may be that the Egyptian adoration of cats rankled during the Hebrew children's long sojourn in Egypt. The luxurious treatment of cats by the Pharos, the mummification of cats, the graven images of cats, and the sanctification of felines may account for the revulsion felt by ancients Jews and early Christians. And, despite the love of cats by many today, there is in the Christian world some holdover of fear from ancient times.

Charles Taylor, in *A Secular Age,* says that between 1500 and 2000, the western world moved from being an enchanted world to being a disenchanted world. That is, people in the Middle Ages believed in angels and ghosts and witches and devils. People in the Medieval Period relied on magical cures, and believed in spells and things that went bump in the night.[7] Today, we are much less likely to think that magic is the best medicine, that ghosts walk the earth after darkness falls, rather that witches have no power over us, and that it is unlikely that one can make a pact with the devil to give powers beyond the human.

I wonder how much of what Taylor thinks is really a secular world is indeed that. I think if we take a careful look at cat lore—and translate that to many other kinds of folklore—we may see that the superstitions of the ancient world, of the *Mother Goose Tales*, of the Great Cat Massacre, are still with us. So, let's focus our attention on cats and see if that will open a door to "reading" folklore. First, why are cats hated by so many? Of course, not everybody does, but it is probably fair to say that the world can be divided into cat fanciers and those who detest cats. I am not sure how to account for the adoration of cats by moderns, just as I am at a loss to understand the old woman who dies in a house with thirty-six cats—in a house covered in feces, decaying feline corpses, and smells that would, to use the folk term, "gag a maggot." But we read about such people about three times a year and see at least two disturbing television reports of old crones who have fallen prey to cats and die among them. Some are men, but more often they are women. Men, as a group, are not as taken with cats as women, though I must admit to having been servant to more than one cat in my life. I can't prove that more men than women "take against" cats, but I believe it to be true.

Let's consider the case against cats. For one thing, cats aren't good for anything. They can't be trained, and they are remarkably aloof, even those that rub up against one's legs and clamber onto the lap. But they only do it when they want to. As to their worthlessness, they don't provide food, they don't function as beasts of burden, and they do no work. Dogs can be trained to herd cattle and sheep; they work as guard dogs; they can function as dope sniffers and cadaver hunters. Dogs can be trained to do tricks, to kill animals, to hunt foxes and raccoons and birds, to retrieve fallen ducks and partridges and grouse. And, as pack animals, they are affectionate and treat their masters as pack mates. Cats do none of these things. About the only excuse for cats as hunters is to kill mice and the occasional bird or snake. But none of that really explains why cats are so often seen as evil by many in our culture.

First, cats are nocturnal creatures, and that puts them in a folklore category with bats and witches and vampires and ghosts and

Members of the Old School TFS: William Owens, Paul Patterson, Wilson Hudson, and the author, James Ward Lee

goblins. They wander at nights and may join with spirits that exist "on the dark side." They can see in the dark, and that makes them suspicious because we cannot. Who knows what companions they find when they roam abroad. Certainly, we associate them with witches and call them witches' familiars. Black cats are especially suspect, and we picture them on Halloween (the eve of all ghosts, all saints, all "haints"). We are all familiar with the icons of Halloween besides the pumpkins—bats, witches on brooms, ghosts. Cats roam abroad with what Shakespeare calls "the sheeted dead." And then at dawn, cats slink home with the expression of sinister glee. They look like "the cat that ate the canary."

Second, many see cats as pure evil. As every folklorist knows, cats will suck the breath out of a sleeping baby and kill it. And in country circles, when people sat up with the dead, it was commonly known that cats would gather round the house where the corpse lay and set up a great yowling. Of course, as everyone knew, if no one sat up with the dead, a cat might slip in and eat the face of the decedent. Maybe these are rural legends, but if they are widely believed, then the cat has another bad mark against him. Among the most common superstition is that a black cat crossing in front of a person will bring serious bad luck, though it should be mentioned that Everett Gillis and Kenneth W. Davis found an informant who said a white cat crossing would bring good luck.[8] Despite the Gillis-Davis informant, most superstitions about cats of all colors mark them as evil.

Though we may live in a disenchanted world, it seems clear to me that a great many of the folk still show vestiges of the enchanted world. Many believe in evil cats, screech owls presaging death, and ghosts that "squeak and gibber in the Roman streets." Many believe in spells and charms. There is—or maybe was—a dime store on Beale Street in Memphis that had a whole section devoted to love potions and charms of all sorts. I once bought a vial of High John the Conqueror root there. That root will give one power, the way Love Potion Number Nine will find a lover more rapidly than eHarmony.com. Don't think for a minute that the folk have moved beyond the enchanted world. The sophisticates may have, and may live in what Taylor calls "the secular age," but New Orleans is full of voodoo shops, and people regularly go to witches to get spells cast upon someone. Or have spells removed. A policeman I knew from East Texas told of the number of people who came to the police station (the unenchanted world) to get spells cast off. The police would have them place a hand on the Xerox machine, select the button marked "copy," run the light across the hand, and remove the spell. That proved to be a certain amount of trouble, so some policeman persuaded the supplicants that a newer and better machine existed for spell removal. He simply aimed the radar gun at the enchanted person and eliminated the hex.

Back now to the disenchanted world, the world of the Texas Folklore Society and its role in a secular (?) age. The Society has changed from the days of its founding at the hands of George

Youth members take part in a presentation at a recent TFS meeting

Lyman Kittredge, Leonidas Payne, and John Lomax in 1909, through the Dobie-Boatright-Hudson era to the days of Francis Edward Abernethy and Ken Untiedt. And it is still changing. Where it is going is not altogether clear, but one direction is toward popular culture and away from the oral tradition of songs, tales, customs, etc. that marked the early years of the Society. There was a time when Brownie McNeil collected and sang the English and Scottish ballads, as well as Mexican folk music. At about that same time Américo Paredes introduced the Society to the corrida and sang the songs of the Texas-Mexican Borderlands and the songs from the Mexican interior. There were still papers on cattle drives, on bit and spur making, and on the language of the cow camps. But as the Society changed, the papers both read and published became more focused on present-day life, on pop culture. There were papers that would have seemed foreign to the ears of Lomax and Payne and Dobie—"Cobras at K-Mart," "Tire-Shrinker to Dragster," and "The Penny Dreadful in the Man's Magazine."

It is my observation in attending most of the meetings of the Texas Folklore Society between 1959 and the present, that members of the Texas Folklore Society still do the occasional paper on Old-time Texas. There are still the stories of the Old West, of cowboys and cowgirls, of nesters and barbed wire and cooking over open flames. There are recipes, remedies, and superstitions. But I have noticed some changes that bear remark. There are nowadays, a good many stories about events in the life of the speaker. These stories are largely nostalgic and are only tangentially connected to folklore. There are more and more popular culture papers, papers about cyberspace, television, and wonderful papers about urban legends, the picturesque language of modern social groups—teenagers, instant messengers, and bloggers. There are rules for games from drag racing to bridge. And then there are the purely—or impurely—humorous presentations which do not do much to further the business of folklore or popular culture.

I know a great deal about this kind of folklore presentation, for I think I am the worst offender. Except for an early paper on folk songs, and a banquet speech on the uses of folklore, I have done little but deliver fluff. I have no excuses except that I am a show-off, but it ought to be noted that I am not alone in that tendency in the Society. Nevertheless, I hope the Texas Folklore Society can rise above me and my ilk and produce not only collections but also analyses of the material collected. I doubt that we should imitate the Annales School slavishly, but I think we ought to encourage members to look more deeply at the tales, superstitions, customs, games, and language we collect. We can look at folklore "from the bottom up." We should imitate what William Owens says in *Tell Me a Story, Sing Me a Song* . . . and "know the people I had to work [with] from the inside out."

ENDNOTES

1. William A. Owens, *Tell Me a Story, Sing Me a Song. . . A Texas Chronicle.* Austin: University of Texas Press, 1983. 10–11.
2. Abernethy, Francis Edward. *The Texas Folklore Society: 1909–1943, Volume I.* Denton: University of North Texas Press, 1992. 279.
3. Marc Bloch. *Le Rois Thaumaturges (The King's Touch).* Strasbourg: Faculty of Arts Press, 1924.
4. Robert Darnton. *The Great Cat Massacre and Other Episodes in French Cultural History.* New York: Basic Books, 1984. 90–91.
5. "Killing Cats Isn't Art—It's Pure Evil," Salt Lake City: *The Deseret News*, July 6, 2003. AA01.
6. "Landmark Pet-Abuse Case Hailed." Salt Lake City: *The Deseret News*, May 7, 2007, B05.
7. Charles Taylor. *A Secular World.* Cambridge: Harvard University Press, 2007.
8. Kenneth W. Davis and Everett A. Gillis. *Black Cats, Hoot Owls, and Water Witches.* Denton: University of North Texas Press, 1989.

Len Ainsworth

BOOKS OF THE TFS

by Len Ainsworth

Books drew me to the Texas Folklore Society. I began to read TFS books in high school without paying attention to the publisher, being drawn to them by the editor and frequent contributor, J. Frank Dobie. A ranch-oriented small-town boy in the 1940s, books such as *Pitching Horses and Panthers* just suited me. The illustrations by Will James, another favorite, were icing on the cake. Reading *Mustangs and Cow Horses* was akin to a religious experience and the subject of much discussion with a best friend. We had grown up with horses, and recognized Dobie, Boatright, and Ransom as the gurus (although we wouldn't have understood the word) or founts of greater knowledge about a Texas still much alive in our thoughts. We even expanded our taste to beyond Dobie offerings, insofar as our school library provided them. Someone in the school must have developed a fair collection of the earlier TFS publications for them to be available at least a dozen years later. We read some of the Mexican tales (*Puro Mexicano*, 1935), even though they weren't always about horses. And, perhaps not to the credit of the TFS, I "learned" that Jim Bowie had his tongue cut out before being killed at the Alamo (for this article I hunted it up again, and that's the story told in the 1939 publication *In the Shadow of History*).

I suppose I knew there was a "society" or at least a group that put the books together, but as a young reader that made almost no impression. I was only mildly interested in most of the authors' names. It was the content that fascinated me. The books were "library books," in the school-community library, and it didn't occur to me that individuals owned them or collected them. They were sources of undoubted information, and even guides to action. My friend and I practiced some of the loops described in one of the

TFS Secretary-Editors Kenneth L. Untiedt and F. E. Abernethy

articles on roping (by Frank Goodwyn, in *Backwoods to Border*). We fancied ourselves becoming the kinds of cowboys that could throw the *laso voltiado* or the *manganas* with skill. We surreptitiously practiced on unsuspecting calves. We also delighted in the occasional Spanish phrasing that appeared in a number of articles.

The series has been a means of preserving and communicating about the borderlands and the Mexican heritage that is so much a part of Texas. From the first volume through the last, particularly *Both Sides of the Border* edited by Abernethy and Untiedt, these have been important elements. As *Hecho en Tejas* (1991) focused on folk arts and crafts from braided ropes and rawhide quirts to musical instruments and construction styles, so the 2002 volume *Charreada* portrayed the flavor of the Mexican rodeo. Legends, stories, and "fright" tales from the border, many emanating from Spain, have long been a rich part of the publication series. These resonated with me and other West Texas youth as being part of our living heritage.

A sampling of Publications of the Texas Folklore Society, as diverse as their editors and contributors

I discovered that those books edited by Hudson and Boatright and Day held the same fascination—they were about a Texas that I could appreciate, if not always understand. As I have collected many of the earlier publications over the past several years, I realized the scope of content in them is remarkable. The Dobie-Boatright-Ransom 1939 volume roamed from the Alamo to sheep ranching to the roadrunner in fact and lore. The 1924 *Legends of Texas* wandered from lost mines to names of flowers and streams, but also included the story of the White Steed of the Prairies, by Walter Prescott Webb. That's probably where I first learned of the Pacing White Stallion, but that horse was firmly fixed in my mind by the superb rendition by Tom Lea at a later time. Lea, Jose Cisneros, and many other recognizable artists' names are associated with various TFS offerings. Thinking of those earlier books makes me realize that my own children probably didn't read them with the same interest, as they didn't have the same rural/ranch associated background. But I'll now be sure many of those stories, along with some discussion of context, are available to my grandchildren.

Reflecting on the series brings to mind the emphases given to music, both for content and the historical value of preservation, such as of the "corridos," called "versos" by Dobie in the 1925 publication, and of other ethnic songs. First were the "Play Party Songs" of earlier generations in *Round the Levee*, (TFS Publication Number 1), edited by Stith Thompson. The attention to music continued through the in-depth treatment of African-American music development in *Juneteenth Texas*, edited by Abernethy, Mullen, and Govenar in 1996. And a fuller treatment of *Texas Folk Songs* was provided by William Owens, and in an extra publication edited by Francis Abernethy called *Singin' Texas.*

The various editors have been important to maintaining the richness and diversity of the books. But so have the multitude of authors, many of whom are not easily found in print elsewhere. While Dobie has been referred to as the "patron saint" of the society and Elmer Kelton holds a current position of high esteem, they aren't the only writers of note. There are simply too many to call to mind, but a number have won continuing attention in regard to collectible Texana. They range from J. Marvin Hunter, Walter Prescott Webb, and John A. Lomax of earlier days to J. Evetts Haley, Americo Paredes, and T. Lindsey Baker as examples of those whose works have appeared in many other formats. And there have been a number of folks that know a lot about books whose bylines appear in TFS. Al Lowman, Ron Tyler, Lou Halsell Rodenberger, and James Ward Lee immediately come to mind. They have written, developed, and critiqued notable volumes apart from the folklore genre.

In short, the publications of the Texas Folklore Society have been a pleasure to read, and continue to bring pleasure upon rereading—as they will to those who discover them anew. As F. E. Abernethy wrote about the publications in a poignant preface to the 1972 *Observations and Reflections*, "These make up our umbilicus, the visible chain of the Society's being that makes us all a part of it from its inception in 1909." That chain reaches from the first publication through the mysteries of death pondered in number LXV of the series, in 2008, with unexplored links yet to be added.

From the beginning to the present, and on into the future

Al Lowman

TEXAS BOOKLORE: IF IT AIN'T FOLKLORE, THEN WHAT THE HE(CK) IS IT?

by Al Lowman

Or maybe a more descriptive subtitle might have been "An Idiosyncratic Reminiscence of Book People I Have Known In and Out of the Texas Folklore Society." On Good Friday 1967, in Nacogdoches' Fredonia Hotel, I presented my first paper to the Society. Its title was "Charlie Coombes and his *Prairie Dog Lawyer.*" Coombes' book had been published in 1945 as the final volume in the Society's Range Life Series. Unfortunately, it betrayed the earmarks of having been written by a lawyer. Coombes, though reputedly a superb storyteller in the oral tradition, was no prose stylist. The stories Charlie had left out of his book had come to me indirectly from James A. Hankerson, Sr. by way of his son, James, Jr., who was—hands down—the very finest raconteur I have ever known. Hank, as he was generally known, was in those days my colleague at the old Texas Research League in Austin. Hankerson, Sr. had been a land lawyer at Wichita Falls, and when the oilfields in that vicinity had played out, he moved to Tyler. One of his tales had initially been told by Frank Fisher, whose storytelling skills were legendary. In his day, Fisher was well-known and widely loved in the legal profession. He was also an unsuccessful gubernatorial candidate in the Democratic primary of 1938, which was won by "Pappy" O'Daniel. At state bar gatherings, lawyers would flock to Fisher's suite after-hours to drink his whiskey and listen to his stories, one of which involved a friend from his Oklahoma boyhood, who had become the lieutenant-governor of the state.

Fisher had been employed by the father of an inmate who was up for parole after having been incarcerated on cattle rustling charges. Fisher went to the Capitol at Guthrie to plead his case before the Oklahoma Parole Board, presided over by none other than the aforesaid lieutenant-governor. This official, whose education was rudimentary to say the least, announced right off the bat that there would be no paroles that day for murderers, rapists, or horse and cattle thieves, at which point two-thirds of the audience filed out of the room. For the first time the lieutenant-governor noticed his boyhood chum.

"Why hello thar, Jedge Fishuh. Whut brings you to ouah fair city?"

Fisher mumbled a response.

"Speak up Jedge, ah caint heah yuh."

Fisher thought quickly before responding, "Well, your Excellency, it's embarrassing to come right out and say it, but the fact is that my client purloined a heifer."

"He done WHUT?!" thundered the lieutenant-governor. Then, after a moment's reflection, his Excellency continued, "Wall now, I reckon *all* us ole country boys done thet a time or two, but thet ain't no reason to keep a feller in jail the rest of his life."

Without so much as a glance at his fellow board members, the lieutenant-governor banged his gavel and boomed: "Parole granted."

[Hmmm! I think I like that story better now than I did forty-two years ago. As Frank Dobie might have said, "God pity the poor wight who can't improve on his own story." God knows Dobie probably *did* say that, or something similar.]

Now, I had forgotten this tale until 2004, when the Honorable James Ward Lee repeated it at the Friday luncheon of the Texas State Historical Association meeting in Austin. Jim contrived to make it sound as if a member of *my* family had purloined the heifer. There you have it: a case study in how folklore gets started and distorted.

But back momentarily to our Nacogdoches meeting in 1967. I brought along my friend, Hank, who spoke on the old-time East Texas oil-promoter, one of whom had been on trial in the federal court at Tyler. This old fellow was being tried for using the federal mails to swindle money from unsuspecting investors in his fraudulent stock. A mistrial had to be declared when it was discovered that

Paul Patterson, in the '60s

he had talked his way past the guard posted at the jury room door and was found inside trying to sell the same worthless stock to members of his *own* jury! Ah, well, a feller's gotta do what he's gotta do.

Before he died in 1991, Hank wrote a little book containing some of his dad's best stories. The title is *Old Maid's Folly, Black Venus and Other Texas Lawyer Tales.* Hank asked me who I would recommend to design and put it into print for him. I suggested Bill Holman. The little book is a real gem both in content and design. Limited to 250 copies, it will never be common.

I have one other recollection of that meeting: Paul Patterson was president. I never think of Paul without remembering one of his sayings, which I have certainly come to appreciate: "I'm to the age where yesterday is just as big a mystery to me as tomorrow." So much for that 1967 meeting. I had joined the Society two years earlier when Wilson Hudson was Secretary-Editor. A decade before that, I had been his student in a course on the Life and Literature of the Southwest, in which our principal text was *Texas Folk and Folklore* (Austin: Texas Folklore Society, 1954). I had never intended to take the course until I had word from the registrar's office that I was pyramiding too many courses in my major field.

Soon after joining the Society, I mentioned to Hudson that I might like to do a paper on the folklore of Texas book-collectors and collecting. He enthusiastically endorsed the idea. Finally, I have decided to write mostly about book people I have known in the context of the Folklore Society itself. I really shouldn't be discussing some of this, but frankly, I have outlived most of those who could have done it better. My nominee for the job would otherwise be Johnny Jenkins, an Austin-based bookseller who had an endless supply of stories about book people. He once began a tale by saying, "Okay, let's have a show of hands; who wants the facts and who wants a good story?" Johnny had character flaws that could not be overlooked. If he sized up a potential customer as having more money than sense, that's when his shark instinct kicked in.

Suddenly, he became the potter and you were the clay. He could mold you and make you, regardless of whether you were yielded and still; he could hold o'er your being absolute sway. And when the hapless victim left Jenkins' clutches, his wallet would be lightened, but he would be happily embarked on a bibliographic journey with Johnny as an ever-attentive guide to the more esoteric, albeit expensive, byways of bibliographical pleasures. He was a master of situational ethics who could always justify the means to any end he desired. Bill Holman calls him a scamp. But he was far more: he was a scoundrel. He was ultimately found dead of a gunshot wound in the Colorado River near Bastrop, a mystery not entirely resolved to this day. For all his faults, I prefer to remember Johnny's generosity to those he deemed serious about their scholarship or their book collecting. Not to imply that the two are mutually exclusive.

Johnny had the gift—as all good salesmen do—of pointing out some unique feature of his merchandise. Dewey Bradford had this gift. For years, he owned and operated the Bradford Paint Company at 401 Guadalupe Street in Austin. Now, this was no adjunct of a lumberyard where they sold house paint. It was an art gallery, where art supplies were also sold. Porfirio Salinas was an artist greatly loved by those who cherish paintings of Texas wildflowers, bluebonnets in particular. From the owners of Salinas' paintings would come such statements as, "This is the *only* time that Salinas ever depicted a fawn in one of his pictures; Dewey Bradford told me so." Or, "Look at the wild verbenas in this picture. Dewey Bradford told me that in all Salinas' other paintings the purple was significantly faded, but this one has held its color better than any of the others." And so on and on. Apparently, Bradford attended some TFS meetings in the early '40s; he was on the program in 1943.

Glancing over Ab's three-volume history of the Society, other familiar names rise to the surface, among them Dr. Cecil E. Evans, president of the local college, or Texas State University–San Marcos, as it is known today. Prexy Evans, as he was affectionately called by faculty and students alike, welcomed the TFS to the campus in late April 1917. The San Marcos meeting was held at the behest of Lillian T. Shaver of the college English faculty, who was serving as president of the Society, that year.

I remember Dr. Evans well; he was an old family friend and indeed was an exemplary figure. Later, I wondered if he were trying subconsciously to compensate for the actions of his younger brother, Hiram W. Evans, a Ku Klux Klan leader who, from 1922 to 1936, served as its Imperial Wizard. Prexy Evans' entry in the *New Handbook of Texas* makes no mention of this fact; indeed, the person who wrote the entry may not have been aware of it. Certainly the *Handbook* editors weren't. When I was nineteen and a college sophomore, Dr. Evans had been retired as president since

1942, after a thirty-year career in that job. He seemed a somewhat lonely figure on campus, living proof that there is no quicker, more certain path to oblivion than to be the ex-president of *anything*. Dr. Evans was given a carrel in the library where he devoted his retirement years to researching and writing his book, *The Story of Texas Schools* (Austin: The Steck Company, 1955).

In his day, a university president lacked the stature of those now serving. In fact, his wife, Allie Evans, found it her uncompensated responsibility to prepare meals for visiting regents. In those more primitive days, Mrs. Evans kept chickens cooped in the presidential backyard. Whenever she got word of an imminent regental visit, she hastened to prepare a chicken dinner. She would saunter to the rear of the manse, catch a chicken, wring its neck, dip the carcass in boiling water, pluck its feathers, carve it up, and fix a meal for the regent. My, how times have changed!

So one day, Dr. Evans had word of an impending visit by a regent. Mrs. Evans had her eye on a particular hen whose turn in the pot had come. Early that morning Mrs. Evans went looking for the hen in question. It was *gone*! Lyndon Johnson, who was Prexy Evans' secretary at the time, lived out back in the garage apartment. Dr. Evans commented drily, "You know, I'll be convinced 'til the day I die that Lyndon beat Allie to that old hen." This bit of suspected chicken thievery did not prevent Evans from giving a full-throated radio endorsement of LBJ in the 1948 Senate race.

I repeated this account years ago to David Conrad, one of three co-authors of *Lyndon Baines Johnson: The Formative Years* (San Marcos: Southwest Texas State College Press, 1965). Dave shot back, "Oh darn, Al, I wish you had told me about that earlier; we could have called our book 'The Chicken Thief in the White House.'"

Had I not already told my J. Frank Dobie story in the July 1988 issue of the *Southwestern Historical Quarterly*, I could devote much time to discussing his contribution to southwestern literature. I wrote in that article about my visit to the Dobie home on Park Place in the fall of 1963. I wrote of mustering the courage to "ring his doorbell." Elsewhere in that same issue, Johnny Jenkins wrote of having done the same thing. Within the week, Bill Wittliff was quoted in the *Austin American-Statesman* of having rung the doorbell at the Dobie home. Now, with three distinct and unequivocal recollections, you would think the matter would be settled with some degree of finality. But here comes a communication from Dudley Dobie, Jr., who had bought the Dobie home from Willie Belle Coker, "Pancho" Dobie's long-time secretary. Dudley, Jr. had re-modeled it and he and his wife Saza were the current occupants. Dudley Jr. said, "Al, I hate to tell you this, but there never *was* a door-bell in that house." What did I say earlier about how folklore gets started and distorted?

The current generation of students seems little interested in J. Frank's output but, in my opinion, he still has relevance for at least two reasons: 1) if you want to know how your grandparents and that generation thought and talked, read Dobie, and 2) if Dobie wrote a review, say in 1930, predicting that a particular book was destined to become a classic, then his prediction was likely to be on target. He was a remarkably fine judge of literature.

If you have any tenure at all in the Texas Folklore Society and are old enough to vote, you will surely remember Martha Emmons. She joined the Society in 1924, became president the first time in 1935–36, and again in 1969–70. In 1979, she became the first and only recipient of the Grasshopper's Library Award. Martha was always the Society's grande dame until her death in 1990. She took a particular shine to children, including my own son and daughter, after they had met her at earlier TFS meetings that we had taken them to.

For years Martha took a summertime break at the old Aquarena Springs Hotel and Resort in San Marcos. My wife and I used to haul our children there to the swimming pool. One day my daughter, then about five, rushed up to where my wife and I were seated and said, "Look, Daddy, there's Miss M&Ms." Sure enough there she was! Martha was vastly amused at, and took a certain pride in, being called "Miss M&Ms."

I never knew Gates Thomas of the English faculty at Southwest Texas State Teachers' College, but he lives on in local legend. He

The Grasshopper's Library Award, presented to Martha Emmons, and now part of the TFS archives

had been president of the Texas Folklore Society in 1926–27. Prior to that time, he was one of my mother's college English teachers. I *do* remember Thomas' widow, a gracious lady who delighted in decorating her Belvin Street home at Christmas-time for the pleasure of every child in the community. I was taken there as a ten-year-old when my fifth grade class embarked on a mid-morning excursion. Every inch of the living room floor was taken up with fanciful animals and humans cavorting in fairyland proximity with each other. Although only recently widowed, it would be difficult to say who enjoyed the visit more—she or her young visitors.

The Thomas house itself still stands at 809 Belvin. It was built in 1923 of river rocks hauled painstakingly to the building site by the professor himself, plus a handful of his students, one of whom owned a flatbed truck. Carl Sandburg was an overnight guest there on two occasions. Alas, there is no record of my own 1945 visit. Professor Thomas was a self-professed atheist, and local legend has it that he was buried facing west. If you happen to be familiar with Terry Jordan's *Texas Graveyards: A Cultural Legacy* (Austin: University of Texas Press, 1982), you will understand the significance of this gesture. Yet, his widow made a big to-do about Christmas. Go figure. Before he had any experience pushing up daisies, Gates Thomas raised prize-winning dahlias in his backyard.

Otherwise, my only connection to the Thomases is that I once owned his copy of Volume I of the TFS publications, which Mrs. Thomas had given to Ralph Houston who, in turn, had given it to me. That copy is now with my J. Frank Dobie holdings in the Southwest Writers Collection at Texas State University–San Marcos. Its cover is reproduced on page seventy of the first volume of Ab's history.

During Gates Thomas' tenure as TFS president, the Society had two notable additions to its roster. J. Evetts Haley appeared on a TFS program for the first time in 1927; he served as a councilor in 1930, and was on the program again in 1931. Haley's association with the Folklore Society began during a lull in the usually stormy relations between the conservative Mr. Haley and the liberal Professor Dobie. This lull produced a feature article by Dobie in *The Country Gentleman* about the two of them hunting Bighorn Sheep in the Sierra Madres of Mexico (J. Frank Dobie, "Hunting Bighorns Below the Border" in *The Country Gentleman*, April 1930, pp. 22–23, 147–48).

Years later, I heard a story about the fiery-tempered Haley from Mrs. Grey Golden, then the receptionist at the Texas State Library. She and her husband, J. B., had both attended West Texas State Teachers' College and knew Evetts Haley there. In fact, Evetts and J. B. were on the school's football team. J. B. and another team member were given an unusual assignment: they were to sit on either side of Haley and hold him on the bench to keep him from running onto the field and getting physically involved whenever a referee's call went against his team.

Let me fast-forward a few decades to illustrate my point. If there was a political gulf between Haley and Dobie you can only imagine what it would have been between Haley and Ralph Yarborough. On a Saturday morning in the spring of 1974, Carl Hertzog, El Paso's legendary book designer/printer, had agreed to a 9:00 a.m. conference at Guynes Printing Company with J. Evetts Haley concerning Haley's forthcoming family history book (*Rough Times-Tough Fiber: A Fragmentary Family Chronicle*, Canyon, Texas: Palo Duro Press, 1976). But at 8 o'clock the phone rang at Hertzog's residence. It was Ralph Yarborough in town to address a steelworker's convention; he had a satchel full of Hertzog books he wanted the designer to autograph. Due to scheduling problems, it had to be done right away. Hertzog told him of the 9:00 meeting with Haley. Undaunted, Yarborough replied, "I'll meet you there."

Hertzog's stomach knotted as he remembered how these two had nearly come to blows on a campaign platform at Hearne, Texas, during the 1956 Democratic gubernatorial primary. Later, when Hertzog told Haley to anticipate Yarborough's interruption, Haley puffed a bit, then paid Yarborough an unexpected compliment: "At least he's honest; you always know where he stands." When Yarborough appeared, the two greeted each other with wary cordiality, but when it came time to sign the books, it just happened that five of them had been written by Haley himself. Haley was in quite an expansive mood when Yarborough asked if he would mind adding his inscriptions to Hertzog's. Yarborough was amazed and gratified as Haley's inscriptions ran to full pages and more.

Never reluctant to embellish a perfectly good story, Hertzog would later claim that he feared so much as to go to the bathroom lest the two get in a political argument. Sure enough, when the book signings were finished, the conversation turned political and highly animated as both men began telling war stories and discovering that each had been sold out at one time or another by some of the very same people. Time flew as each would top the other's tales of betrayal and ethical hanky-panky! Here were disclosures of political history that had never been—and never will be—made public. After Yarborough left for his speechmaking assignment, Hertzog recalled Haley's earlier words: "At least he's honest; you always know where he stands." A love of books and Texas history overcame whatever political animosity may have existed between the two.

Parenthetically, my great friend, Bob McCubbin of Santa Fe, has collected books about the Southwest for at least sixty years. Bob sagely observes that marriage has been the ruination of more promising book collecting careers than any other force on the planet. Now twice-divorced, Bob's observation cannot be casually dismissed. My own story is somewhat different. When I met my wife in a book establishment over four decades ago, she was my most expensive acquisition to that point, but remains my most treasured first edition. (You simply have no idea the amount of grief I would have saved myself had I thought of that punch line at the outset of our marriage.)

The other addition to the Texas Folklore Society's roster during Gates Thomas' term as president was Mody Boatright, whose association endured until his death in 1970. He was president in 1942–43 and, immediately thereafter, succeeded Dobie as Secretary-Editor, which position he retained (albeit tenuously) until he was officially succeeded by Wilson Hudson in 1964.

I recall returning from a meeting of the Western History Association in the late 1960s and telling Boatright what a wonderful experience that had been. I told him, "I met people who wrote books, people who illustrated them, people who designed and printed them, people who bound them, and people who sold them." Boatright's laconic response was, "Yes, but did you meet *anybody* who reads them?" Good question. Which calls to mind an inscription that W. H. Hutchinson once put in my copy of one of his books: "For Al Lowman with the thought that a devoted reader is the noblest work of . . . himself." Hutch was on the English faculty at Chico State College in California.

Gates Thomas was succeeded as TFS president by Martin L. Crimmins, a retired army colonel from San Antonio. I never knew Colonel Crimmins either, but I heard much about him from Dudley Dobie, Sr., the San Marcos rare bookseller and first cousin to J. Frank. He was part of a coterie of San Antonio book people with whom Uncle Dud consorted. Others were realtor Paul Adams, lawyer C. Stanley Banks, Southern Pacific Railway attorney Chris Emmett (later Crimmins' biographer) Dr. William E. Howard, President George P. Isbell of the Southern Steel Company, and politician Maury Maverick.

Crimmins had been a Rough Rider and a veteran of the Philippine Insurrection. A year before his elevation to the TFS presidency he had been medically discharged at San Antonio. I have been told that he had been a veterinarian in the horse cavalry days and had been instrumental in developing an anti-venin for snakebites. More than any of these, he was a renaissance type, a scholar, and adventurer.

Another character from that era was Betty Smedley, whose husband, Graham B. Smedley, was a lawyer at Wichita Falls and later in Fort Worth. Eventually, he was appointed to the Texas Supreme Court. Betty was active in the Folklore Society, first appearing on the 1930 program and in the yearbook that followed. She was on the program again in 1931, and was elected a vice president in 1932, during Jovita Gonzales' second term as president, following which she seems to have dropped from the Society's roster.

But in 1969, she was an Austin realtor, who decided at age seventy-five to become an antiquarian bookseller. Her objective, she claimed, was to get into a more benign, dignified, honorable, less stressful and cut-throat occupation, plus have a little fun and earn a modest income. In no time at all she was setting new benchmarks for out-of-print book prices and finding fools to pay them.

Six months later, she wrote Carl Hertzog that she preferred doctors and lawyers for clientele "because they're the only ones who have money." Her customers were mostly among the once young lawyers that she and the judge had befriended on their way up.

With entree to Austin's finest old homes, Betty would occasionally spot a rarity with which the owner was reluctant to part. More than once she told me with intense Methodist fervor, "Son (any male at least twenty years her junior was Son), Ah'm prayin' evah night, just as hard as Ah know how, that that book is gonna come mah way. Ah just know in mah heart that the Good Lord intends for me to have it. Ah've got at least three customers who'd pay me a *fortune* for it!" I could never quite believe she was serious. Although we are told that God moves in mysterious ways His wonders to perform, I had perhaps mistakenly assumed that He might be preoccupied with weightier matters. Years later I saw letters in which she confirmed that she was indeed taking her trials and temptations to the Lord in prayer. Perhaps the closest she ever came to divine assistance was when she encountered her "little Baptist preachuh friend" from East Texas who, she bragged, was a superb book scout with an unbelievable success rate. He was consistently turning up stuff which was breathtakingly rare. One morning I picked up the *Austin American* to read that her "little Baptist preachuh friend" had been arrested for stealing excessively rare books, documents, maps, and other items not nailed down from courthouses and special collection libraries throughout the Southwest. Betty was certainly not implicated in any way, but she had forgotten the time-worn admonition, "If it sounds too good to be true, it probably is."

Bill Owens, from Pinhook, Texas appeared on the scene in 1936, when Dobie was casting about for a publishable manuscript. Had Dobie been the praying type, Owens might have been the answer to a prayer, because Owens put before Dobie the manuscript of *Swing and Turn: Texas Play Party Games*, which became the Society's publication for 1936 (Dallas: Tardy Publishing Company, 1936).

I cannot remember when or where I first met Bill Owens, but it would have been after publication of *This Stubborn Soil* (New York: Charles Scribners Sons, 1966). But I *do* remember our last encounter in October 1985. He and Lyman Grant had collaborated in editing the *Letters of Roy Bedichek* (Austin: University of Texas Press, 1985). They were given an autograph party at Rosengren's bookstore in San Antonio. On these occasions, Florence Rosengren invariably served sherry and cheese—nothing fancy, either Wisconsin or Monterey Jack. From time to time Bill Owens would put down his pen to savor a bite of cheese. Consequently, my copy of the Bedichek letters is not only inscribed by Owens, but his signature is further authenticated with cheesy fingerprints on the front endpaper and bastard title page.

Now comes Leland Sonnichsen. I already had my say about Doc Sonnichsen as a member of the folklore panel at the Texas State Historical Association conference at El Paso in 2000. This presentation was subsequently published in PTFS LXI, ("Doc Sonnichsen Holds His Own" in *Both Sides of the Border*, Denton: University of North Texas Press, 2004). Sonnichsen was an English professor (chairman of the department at the University in El Paso from 1933 to 1960) who wrote and published numerous works of what he called "grass-roots history." He quickly discovered that nothing so enrages history faculty as a colleague from another department successfully challenging them on their own turf. "Historians don't like outsiders crowing on their dung-hill," he once put it. While departmental chairman, he also taught a course on Life and Literature of the Southwest with such success that the summer of 1938 and again in 1939, he was invited to pinch hit for J. Frank Dobie himself on the Austin campus of the University of Texas.

Since the mid-1930s, Dobie and others had been trying to wangle a joint meeting of the Texas Folklore Society and its New Mexico counterpart, the New Mexico Hispanic Institute. The meeting was foreordained to happen in El Paso. A local arrangements coordinator was needed, someone who would assume the

C. L. Sonnichsen, 1982

presidency. That someone proved to be none other than Doc Sonnichsen. Commenting acerbically on his own rise to the TFS presidency, he said later, "As soon as a comparatively sane, able-bodied El Pasoan showed up, he was going to be president, whether he liked it or not." There are many wonderful stories to tell on and about Doc Sonnichsen, and many (not all) can be found in the aforementioned TFS yearbook.

Fred Gipson's one and only appearance on a TFS program came at the San Antonio meeting in 1949. I remember vividly my single encounter with Gipson. My wife and I were attending the Friday evening banquet of the Texas State Historical Association, which was held in the Crystal Ballroom of the Stephen F. Austin Hotel in his namesake city. I reckon this to have been in the early seventies. (My wife agrees; she has a wonderful memory. She remembers things I haven't even said yet.) The regularly scheduled speaker had failed to appear for whatever reason, and Wallace Stegner happened to be in town. Ron Tyler seems to think he may have been there to address the Texas Institute of Letters. At any rate, Stegner gave an uncharacteristically dull, listless performance, which called to mind Alben Barkley's story about his debut as a speaker at the outset of his political career. When it was over, he made the mistake of asking an elderly auditor for a frank assessment of his effort. Came the opinion that he, Barkley, had solicited: "Well, All-ben, in the first place, you read it; in the second place, you read it poorly; in the third place, it wadn't wuth readin'."

My wife wasn't about to give up on Stegner; she had paid for the evening meal and a speech to follow. But others in the audience were more easily daunted and were seen quietly leaving the gathering. My wife and I were seated at the back of the room at a table where a residue of the meal was still in evidence. We had turned our chairs away from the table in order to face the speaker's podium.

Then came the sound of a late-comer noisily pulling a metal chair from under the table and plopping themselves into its groaning frame. I waited an appropriate length of time, then turned to see who the late arrival might be. Facing me was a bleary-eyed Fred Gipson who was not less than three sheets to the wind. It seemed neither the time nor the place for introductions. In a moment Gipson pronounced his judgment on Stegner by falling asleep to the accompaniment of his own loud snoring.

It is perhaps noteworthy that the Texas Folklore Society has drawn not only participation but leadership from the length and breadth of the state. Several presidents of the organization have hailed from El Paso, beginning in 1938–39 with Leland Sonnichsen and continuing through Haldeen Braddy, John O. West, James Day, and currently Lucy Fischer West. It can be said without fear of successful contradiction that no TFS president was as intimately familiar with every nook and cranny of the Juarez *juzgado* as Haldeen Braddy, who spent many nights there as a guest of the city for the offense of S.W.I. (stumbling while intoxicated). Nonetheless, Braddy managed a steady hand at the Society's helm from 1951–53.

Braddy produced his last book, *Three Dimensional Poe*, in 1969. It was dedicated to Carl Hertzog who, at least, had the good judgment to get drunk on this side of the border. As he gave me a copy (El Paso: Texas Western Press, 1969) Carl remarked, "This is a book involving three drunks—one dead, one practicing, and one reformed," although there lingers some doubt about that last one.

Another personality from near west Texas was Boyce House, then living in Fort Worth, prior to which he had lived in several oil-towns, including Eastland and Ranger. Ab Abernethy relates in his third volume that House gave several papers before the Society, was one of its vice-presidents in 1941, and was responsible for circulating the tale of Old Rip, the horny toad that survived a thirty-year entombment in the cornerstone of the Eastland County Courthouse. He also covered the Santa Claus Bank robbery in nearby Cisco.

I remember that in my mid-teens Boyce House had a weekly radio program called "I Give You Texas" and later wrote a book by that title, maybe more than one. The radio program went off the air in 1950 when House campaigned a second time for lieutenant-governor and lost to then state senator Preston Smith from Lubbock. Apparently, there weren't enough folklorists in Texas to put him over the top. House's entry in the *New Handbook of Texas* seems somewhat ambivalent. On one hand, he is charged with relying on second-hand sources; on the other, he is given implicit praise for interviewing eyewitnesses to the history he is writing about.

Between 1973 and 1999, annual publications of the Texas Folklore Society have been enhanced with contributions from the eminent, energetic, and versatile historian T. Lindsay Baker, presently director of the W. K. Gordon Museum at Thurber, Texas. He is originally from Rio Vista (to hear him tell it the natives pronounced it Rye-O-Vista—to rhyme with mistah or sistah. I will defer to his expertise). Lindsay, on the strength of his many contributions to Texas and western American history, will surely rate his own entry in a future edition of the *Handbook of Texas*. He doubtless would already have done so had he not met one critical qualification. He ain't dead yet! Some years ago, I paid good money to acquire a copy of his *Field Guide to American Windmills* (Norman: University of Oklahoma Press, 1985). Perhaps foolishly, I asked for his inscription in the book. After almost no thought at all, he carefully wrote: "For Al Lowman, who can blow enough hot air to sail every windmill on the South Plains." I cherish this tacky inscription above nearly any other in my collection.

Moving right along, the Texas Folklore Society met in Galveston in 1987. I remember Galveston as it was nearly thirty years ago, about the time my wife and I made a tour-guided trip to Italy. At dusk, as the bus crossed the causeway into Venice, the colored lights of the city were reflected in the calm, black waters of the lagoon. Our guide, a young Roman seated at the front of the bus, was searching for every adjective in his English vocabulary to describe an intensely romantic scene that, by its very nature, was indescribable. My wife and I were near the back of the bus in close proximity to a sixtyish blonde seated at the very back between her two equally blonde and thirtyish daughters. Finally, mama had had enough of the tour guide's effort and said, in a throaty baritone that carried two-thirds of the way to the front of the bus: "WELL! . . . he just hasn't seen Galveston yet!"

As a Texas newspaperman said on hearing General Sherman's comment that if he owned both, he would rent out Texas and live in hell, "Damn any man who won't stick up for his own country."

Well, I've seen Galveston, and I hope to see it again—if not in this life, then surely in the next one. Above all, I hope to meet characters who've made this life such an entertaining and exhilarating one. When author, editor, and bookman Clifton Fadiman died at ninety-five a few years ago, he was remembered as having once said, "I haven't had an interesting life; I've just known a lot of interesting people." You are well on your way to living that kind of life if you are fortunate enough to be a member of the Texas Folklore Society.

Frances Brannen Vick

HOW I CAME TO BE A PUBLISHER OF TEXAS FOLKLORE SOCIETY PUBLICATIONS

by Frances Brannen Vick

E-Heart Press, named after our father's old family cattle brand, was founded by my brother, J. P. Brannen, and myself when our father died and we ended up with a little cash from the sale of his cattle. We had also rediscovered his memoirs from World War I, written many years before, and decided they should be published. That was the original thought about starting E-Heart Press. It seemed the logical and right thing to do—publish our father's memoirs with the proceeds from the sale of those cattle he loved and petted, and even named on occasion. It had been very painful for me to sell Sophia Loren, whom he had raised by hand since her mother had died at her birth. Sophia was more like a pet dog than a cow. She knew who her parent was and followed him lovingly whenever he was around. But back to E-Heart.

I was teaching English at Baylor University at the time and got involved with students working for the Baylor student newspaper. They came to me with a scheme to buy some old typesetting equipment, which I foolishly thought we could use to typeset the World War I memoirs. I am foggy about where that typesetting equipment came from—Baylor or an ad the kids saw somewhere and knew where a sucker was that would help finance their grand schemes. The plans for publishing the memoirs got put on hold when Bill Wittliff quit publishing the Publications of the Texas Folklore Society and Ab Abernethy could not find another publisher to take his place. Thus, in my ignorance of publishing (and almost everything else I sometimes think), Roger Lindstrom and I decided we could take on the job and got in touch with Ab with our plan. Ab and I met at the Red Lantern Cafe in Buffalo during one of those Texas northers that blow through sometimes, freezing Texans' bones, and we struck a deal.

Built in Texas, PTFS XLII, 1979

As far as I am concerned, I started publishing very close to the top with the Texas Folklore Society publication *Built in Texas*, edited by F. E. Abernethy, published in 1979. Ab became my mentor in publishing, as J. Frank Dobie had been to Bill Wittliff. However, unlike Wittliff, I was learning from the bottom up since I knew absolutely nothing about publishing. I had been teaching English all those years before, so it was a fast learning curve. Of course, I *would* start out with a coffee table book, full of Ab's photographs and Reese Kennedy's sketches. Just to make it more difficult to design, print, and bind, it was in an 8 ½ × 11 format, bound on the short side. Furthermore, we would run Ab's photographs in duo-tones, not quite as expensive as 4-color, but almost. No point in starting out with something simple.

Built in Texas was designed and typeset by Roger, who was also one of those students who had talked me into buying that typesetting equipment. If my memory serves me right, that was the only book typeset on that equipment. We found a printer, Motheral in Fort Worth, to print the book, and I took out a loan at the bank to pay for all of this foolishness. Daddy's cow money wasn't enough. Today, I occasionally see the banker who made the loan and he still teases me about it. At the time, he acted as if he didn't want me to take out the loan because it was not a good deal for me but I talked him into it. He laughs at that since he was ecstatic to get the loan. He finally had something to show the feds when they showed up for examinations. He could show that he was fulfilling his obligation to help out minorities with his loan to a woman. We've come a long way, Baby—at least I think we have.

Bill Shearer was part of the marketing arm of Texas A&M University Press, and when he went to the different stores selling books for that press he would mention a new press that was publishing the Texas Folklore Society books, so some marketing was going on in spite of my still-naïve knowledge of publishing. It is a real miracle that these books came out and the public bought them, when you think about it. It was a case of my dumb luck in falling into some of these things, like my friendship with Bill.

Ab would find Extra Books (ExB) for some of the years in between his own editing of the Society's books. In 1980, he found *Mexican Folktales from the Borderland* by Riley Aiken (ExB-17). So those would be off years from TFS Publications for me, and a welcome relief. Ab gripes about the books always being late to the membership, but when you consider all that goes into getting a book into production, I think we were doing pretty good, particularly since one of us had no notion of what the heck she was doing most of the time.

The next book Ab came up with was *Legendary Ladies of Texas*, published in cooperation with the Texas Foundation for Women's Resources in 1981. Motheral also printed that book for us, but we had wised up on this typesetting business by that time and went with one of the best—G & S Typesetting in Austin. Eje Wray was the designer on that book, which had an excellent design, but sometimes it was difficult getting the finished product on the press. I was reduced on many occasions with most of the first books to cajoling, threatening, and finally being reduced to all but weeping to get the books on press. In spite of all that, however, both *Built in Texas* and *Legendary Ladies of Texas* were very good sellers and are still in print today in paperback reprints.

Thinking we were on a real roll, Ab came up with *T for Texas: A State Full of Folklore.* So far, I had been doing fairly well for someone who was still in a state of ignorance about a lot of the workings of the publishing industry. However, things kinda fell apart on us with this one. Eje Wray was the designer on this one as well, and clearly we were not communicating. I still do not like the typeface, the textbook look, really the whole design. And again, I finally had to threaten to go to Austin to get the book before we finally got something to go on press. Ab still will not discuss this book and there is no reason to go into any details here and get him stirred up again. Suffice it to say, this was not our finest hour. This was PTFS XLIV, published in 1982.

Ab had been working on a book on Texas folk music, and my brother and I wanted to publish it. So, the next E-Heart Press book was *Singin' Texas*, and the Society picked it up as ExB-18 for 1983. That book became a real adventure to produce. Dan Beaty arranged the music and fortunately knew of a typesetter in Korea who could typeset the music. So, off that went to Korea and came back to the designers, Whitehead & Whitehead in Austin, who put the whole thing together. Ab's photographs were included as well. Joe Pat decided that since he couldn't read music there ought to be a tape to go with the book so people (mainly him) could hear the songs. Ab traveled to Dallas to the studio my son Ross III had set up in a closet in his condo, and Ab would pick and sing and Ross would record. That all worked out pretty well, actually. We had the tapes reproduced here in Dallas and sent them to the printer who shrink-wrapped them with the book. You can see what can happen if folks sit around and start thinking up things to do. As it turned out, that was a really fine book, which is also still in print, sans the tape, of course, since that format is as obsolete today as are most other ways of production we were using then.

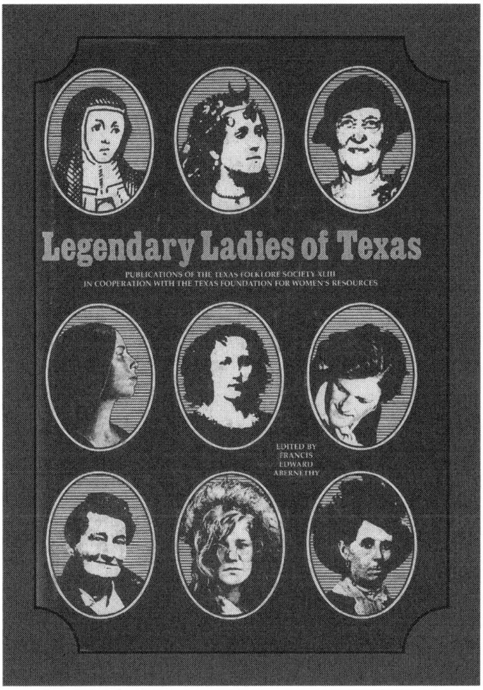

Legendary Ladies of Texas, PTFS LXIII, 1981

It seemed to me that it was time for the Publications to go back to a university press, and since they had been at Southern Methodist University Press before and it was right down the street from me in Dallas, that was the logical place. Trudy McMurrin was the director of SMU Press and was agreeable to taking on the TFS books, so she produced *Folk Art in Texas*, published in 1984, and *Sonovagun Stew*, published in 1985. You need to read *The Texas Folklore Society: 1971–2000, Volume III* if you want to know about the adventures of producing those two books.

Trudy left for the West, Nevada I think, and Keith Gregory came in as director of SMU Press. Suzanne Comer moved to SMU Press as editor with Keith Gregory, so that press was blowin' and goin'. Suzanne agreed to take on the Publications of the Texas Folklore Society. Under her direction SMU Press produced *Hoein'*

Singin' Texas, TFS Extra Book #18, 1983

the Short Rows, published in 1987, and *Texas Toys and Games*, published in 1989. Then tragedy struck. We lost Suzanne to esophageal cancer in 1990. She was a terrific editor and a good friend, and a loss to Texas publishing.

Meanwhile, in 1987 Jim Lee, Chairman of the English Department at the University of North Texas, and A. C. Greene hit on the bright idea of starting a press there and called me to see if I wanted to come run it. Did I ever! I hopped up there and we kicked around ideas of what we would do until finally, President Al Hurley gave me enough money to publish a pictorial history of UNT for the school's 100th anniversary. So, the University of North Texas Press was born when that book came out in 1989. Then a miracle happened, as far as I was concerned. Keith Gregory called me and asked if I wanted the Publications of the Texas Folklore Society back. Absolutely! I quote here from

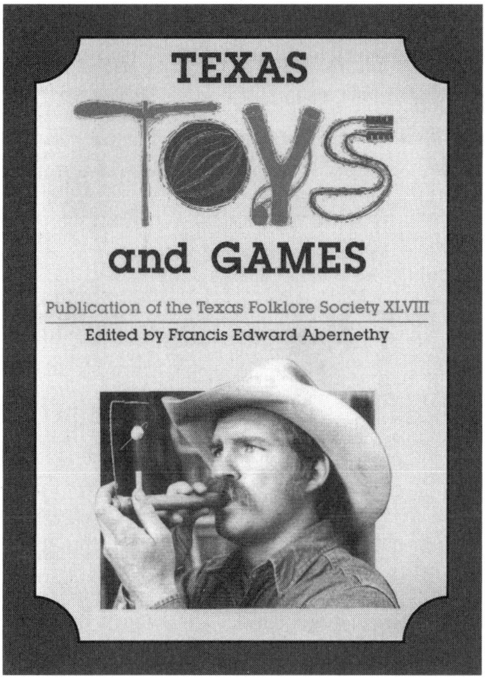

Texas Toys and Games, PTFS XLVIII, 1989—one of the most popular TFS books

what I wrote to Ab about this when he was putting together Volume III of the history:

> Suzanne was the one who was interested in Texas folklore and without her at the press there was no one to take the books through publication. I, of course, jumped at the offer and called the Society about it. Then came the most wonderful and generous gesture of all. Keith transferred ALL of the Texas Folklore Society publications to the University of North Texas Press! That included all of the facsimile books from 1916 to the books SMU Press had produced under Allen Maxwell, et al, to the brand new books that Trudy and Suzanne had produced. So this new UNT Press now had a

> built-in backlist of books to build a publication list on, with the promise of a TFS publication each year thereafter. It was a tremendous gift to us and one that our Vice President of Fiscal Affairs [Phil Diebel] spent time trying to figure out. He was sure that we would get some whopping bill for all the books that would put UNT Press in the red forever. That generous gift is what started me on my quest of getting all of the TFS publications under one umbrella. We finally accomplished that when [Bill Wittliff's] Encino Press transferred the books they had to UNT Press. . . . I had already transferred all rights from my own E-Heart Press to UNT Press with the reprinting of *Legendary Ladies* and *Singin' Texas.*

Now all Publications of the Texas Folklore Society were available at one spot—the University of North Texas Press. I considered that a major accomplishment.

So, Ab and I were back in business again. *The Bounty of Texas* was the first book out after the reunion of the two of us. It was published in 1990, designed by Whitehead & Whitehead. Then Ab had another brainstorm. He would have other Society members edit some of the books. I think this was because Ab was deep into writing the history of the Society. In any case, the first one we did, with Ab still as series editor, was *Hecho en Tejas: Texas-Mexican Folk Arts and Crafts*, edited by Joe Graham, published in 1991 and again designed by Whitehead & Whitehead. That was a homerun for us. That book is still in print in paperback, and I think it is one of the jewels of the Texas Folklore Society. It was a great loss when we later lost Joe Graham. He was wonderful to work with.

It was a good thing that Ab had Joe to rely on for *Hecho en Tejas*, for he was hard at work on what would be a three-volume history of the Texas Folklore Society. He was the only one who could do it, the only one who knew where all the bones were buried, so to speak. *The Texas Folklore Society: 1909–1943, Volume I* was published in 1992. I found a designer in Austin, Caissa Dowes, who worked with tremendous Texas artist, Charles Shaw, to produce the art work for the cover and the illustrations we would use for all three volumes. He was the most astounding artist who understood all things Texan. When I would ask him for cover art he would not do anything until I could send him a manuscript of the book. Then he could somehow capture the soul of the book in the art he produced. Charles Shaw was another enormous loss to the state. We all miss him and his art.

The Society publication in 1993 was *Corners of Texas.* This book was designed by Nancy Land and put together by a group in Crockett, Texas, Publications Development Company. Ab had found this group while driving down the highway, for all I know. You will have to ask him. This was followed by *The Texas Folklore Society: 1943–1971, Volume II* in 1994. In 1995 we had ExB-21, *Through Time and the Valley* by John Erickson.

I was extremely proud of the publication in 1996—*Juneteenth Texas: Essays in African-American Folklore*, which introduced me to the spectacular art of John Biggers, whose work we used on the cover. The Biggers piece we used was *Shotguns, Fourth Ward.* The book was designed by a young woman I found in Denton, named Amy Layton. She did an outstanding job on the book. This book was edited by Ab, Patrick B. Mullen, and Alan B. Govenar. Whatever trouble there was in putting this book together was before I got involved in the publishing end of it, for I was very pleased with the finished product and still am.

The 1997 publication was *Between the Cracks of History: Essays on Teaching and Illustrating Folklore*, followed by ExB-22 in 1998, *The Best of Texas Folk and Folklore 1916–1954*, edited by Mody C. Boatright, Wilson M. Hudson, and Allen Maxwell. I dearly hate to see a book go out of print, and for a Texas Folklore Society Publication to be out of print was a scandal as far as I was concerned. So, we put this one back in print. Ab said we would get static, which we did. I asked him if he ever got tired of being right. I still think it was the thing to do. All of this was before books on demand had ever been thought of, so there is no longer any reason for any book to be out of print, but there was at the time.

The next book was again turned over to an editor from the Society, Jim Harris. He edited *Features and Fillers: Texas Journalists on Texas Folklore* for the 1999 PTFS. Angela Schmitt, living in Denton and working at UNT, had come into my world, so she was the typesetter and designer. Angela was busy having babies and tried to quit on me several times, but she couldn't turn me down when I offered to come over and rock babies while she designed and typeset books. She was wonderful to work with.

In 2000, Volume III of Ab's history came out and I had finally found a young man to take over the University of North Texas Press. It was time for me to go. I retired from the Press in 2000, and turned it over to Ron Chrisman, who I could not be prouder of if he were my own son.

The Publications of the Texas Folklore Society were the hook on which I hung my entire publishing career, both E-Heart Press and the University of North Texas Press. There is no way to discount their importance to me and to the presses I was involved with. I not only published the Publications, but they brought to me many writers who were members of the Society, such as Jim Lee with his *Classics of Texas Fiction* and later *Texas, My Texas.* Other folklorists I published were Joe Graham with his work on the ranches and people and folklore of South Texas. Alan Govenar and Jay Brakefield brought their work on Deep Ellum in Dallas. Roy Bedichek's letters to his family kept me laughing when I wasn't musing about his observations. Kenneth Davis just kept me laughing, with his *Black Cats, Hoot Owls and Water Witches.* The title alone gives pause, you have to admit.

Archie McDonald called me one day with what I was sure would be a treatise on Texas history. What he brought me instead was *Helpful Cooking Hints for Househusbands of Uppity Women,* a cookbook that took him all the way to *The Today Show* in New York City because of *his* title. His uppity woman was the mayor of Nacogdoches at the time. The mayor of Huntsville was another uppity woman, Jane Monday, who would lure me into writing in

Juneteenth Texas: Essays in African-American Folklore, PTFS LIV, 1996

later years. You have to watch out for East Texas uppity women. They can be very cunning.

I never published Elmer Kelton's novels; Judy Alter got to do that out of TCU Press, but I published him in Texas Folklore Society books, and I published Judy Alter's critical biography of him.

John Erickson delighted us with the antics of his cowdog, Hank, who is in charge of security on the ranch in Ochiltree County in the Panhandle, which I unfortunately did not publish. However, he also wrote of his own adventures as a cowboy and his observations of the people of the Panhandle, and I was lucky enough to publish those.

Joyce Roach, that "high-toned woman" from the Cross Timbers, sometimes gets the rest of us tickled with her escapades at revivals and other places, but she also informs us of high-toned women in general and of *The Cowgirls* and of *This Place of Memory: A Texas Perspective,* with cover art by Charles Shaw. She on occasion fights it out with Robert Flynn about who has the best hometown—Chillicothe or Jacksboro. Flynn, with his Baptist boots firmly planted in the West, keeps us entertained but he also makes us think about the travails as well as the joys of the old folks who went before. There was B. W. Aston's *Along the Texas Forts Trail*, Lawrence Clayton's, *Benjamin Capps and the South Plains*, and Kent Biffle's *A Month of Sundays.* These were all Texas Folklore Society members who I published other than in a PTFS.

It also gave me great pleasure to see the names in our stable who I didn't publish but who came before me and were there in the old TFS Publications: J. Frank Dobie, Wilson Hudson, Mody Boatright, Harry Ransom, Stith Thompson, Allen Maxwell. Not a bad bunch to have on your list. Not a bad bunch at all. I used those writings of the old ones when I began authoring my own books. I extensively used the work of Américo Paredes, Jovita Gonzalez, and some of the other writings in the Society publications in *Petra's Legacy: The South Texas Ranching Empire of Petra Vela and Mifflin Kenedy.* Jane Monday and I wanted to recreate, as much as we could, the world in which Petra moved. The folklore I found in the old books was invaluable in helping us do that. I found material in *Backwoods to Border*, edited by Mody Boatright and Donald Day; *Madstones and Twisters* and *Singers and Storytellers*, edited by Wilson M. Hudson and Allen Maxwell; *Southwestern Lore, Happy Hunting Ground, Texas and Southwestern Lore,* and *Man, Bird and Beast*, all edited by J. Frank Dobie; and *Coyote Wisdom*, edited by J. Frank Dobie, Mody Boatright and Harry H. Ransom. These Texas Folklore Society works were extremely helpful in capturing Petra's world.

Later, in *Literary Dallas*, I used the work of J. Mason Brewer, Lou Rodenberger, Bob Compton, John Neal Phillips with Andre

L. Gorzell, Pat LittleDog, Stanley Marcus, Lon Tinkle, Frank X. Tolbert, Ruthe Winegarten, and many others that I had been introduced to from their work in Publications of the Texas Folklore Society and in their work influenced by PTFS, as well as from talks with them at Society meetings. The Publications of the Texas Folklore Society are extremely valuable in the collecting and disseminating of Texas folklore, and indeed in the saving of the old folklore that is fast being lost in a Texas world increasingly peopled by folk from other parts of the country and the world. For example, I find myself to have become quite "quaint" to these folk in my use of expressions—expressions that were as much a part of my speech and my parents' and grandparents' speech as the air we breathed. I use them unconsciously and only realize I have done so when the listeners pause and smile after I have used an expression. So, that is the importance of the Publications of the Texas Folklore Society for me—in the collecting and the publishing of folklore.

By the way, my father's memoirs did get published, but it was not by me. It was by the press at one of his alma maters, Texas A&M University Press. They titled it *Over There: A Marine in the Great War.* No lesser authority than Frank Vandiver, who had written the biography of John J. Pershing and was at the time the president of Texas A&M University, recommended that it be published. C. A. Brannen would be greatly pleased and astounded that such a thing had taken place. Had I figured that out in the beginning there would have been no E-Heart Press, which eventually led me to the University of North Texas Press. Had that happened, though, I would certainly have missed out on a lot of fun and lasting friendships. That should tie up all this publishing business in a not-so-neat little package. Anything else you want to know, read the three volumes of *The Texas Folklore Society* by Francis Edward Abernethy. He tells it all and does it very well.

L. Patrick Hughes

AN ENDURING RELATIONSHIP: THE TEXAS FOLKLORE SOCIETY AND FOLK MUSIC

by L. Patrick Hughes

A commitment to the preservation, analysis, and enjoyment of folk music underlay the 1909 creation of the Texas Folklore Society. As it was in the beginning, so it remains. Over its century-long existence, the Society has been a nurturing home for collectors and interpreters such as John A. Lomax, William A. Owens, Américo Paredes, and others. Its publications are replete with both scholarly and popular examinations of cowboy songs, train songs, field hollers, border corridos, the blues, and Old World ballads that made their way to Texas. Annual meetings have consistently featured presentations on various aspects of folk music by both academicians and lay aficionados. Groups as varied as the Southwest Texas Sacred Harp Convention, the Jubilee Choir, Four Boys from the Brakes, and the East Texas String Ensemble have performed the songs of our collective past at TFS convocations all across the Lone Star State. Nor would any annual meeting be complete without the hootenanny that has been a TFS tradition for the last half-century. It has been and remains a symbiotic relationship that through all the years has enriched both the Society and folk music.

The Society owes its existence in no small measure to John A. Lomax's fascination with the drover songs of the open range. He grew up as a child in Bosque County among men who'd been up the cattle trails to Kansas, and began collecting their songs long before receiving his baccalaureate degree from the University of Texas at Austin. Graduate studies at Harvard University under professors George Lyman Kittredge and Barrett Wendell led to academic legitimation and encouragement of his collecting efforts. The results were impressive. Lomax, pursuing every possible lead, rescued and preserved melodies and lyrics for "The Old Chisholm Trail," "Git Along, Little Dogies," and "Buffalo Skinners" among others. Returning to Texas in 1909, graduate degree in hand and

Cowboy Songs and Other Frontier Ballads in the works, the forty-two-year-old musicologist, working with University of Texas linguist Leonidas W. Payne, launched the Texas Folklore Society. Payne agreed to serve as president and Lomax as secretary. In part, Lomax was repaying Professor Kittredge for his kindnesses by following through on his mentor's suggestion that he start such an organization upon his return home. Creation of the Society, perhaps more importantly, served his own professional interests as he readily admitted in a May 25, 1910, letter to Wendell: "I hope the Folk-lore Society is going to help me in my ballad collecting; in fact, that is my only interest in it."[1]

While hyperbole, Lomax's statement foreshadows the centrality folk music would play in Society affairs during its critical first years. Seeking to broaden its base, the Society issued a circular in 1910 announcing its existence, stating its goals, and soliciting new members. Crafted by Payne, it nonetheless bore Lomax's imprint. Various folklore topics worthy of study included legends, dialects, superstitions, omens, cures, games, and dance. The category of "Songs and Ballads," however, was first on the list:

> We want the "Play Party" songs of both negro and white . . . the songs the negroes improvise and sing, the native Spanish ballads, and the many songs that have grown up in the state or have been brought to it from the other states celebrating local conditions and events—such as battles with Indians or Mexicans, the career of the desperado, the deeds of the ranger, and the life of the rancher, the freighter, the bummer or the cowboy.[2]

The number of presentations on such types of music must have been pleasing to Lomax once the Society began its annual meetings in 1911. In its first six gatherings, one out of every three papers involved folk music. Programs featured papers on "The Ballad of the Boll Weevil," "A Batch of Mexican Border Ballads," "Negro Ballads and Reels," "Some Hobo Ballads," and "Folklore in

Appalachian Mountain Music" among others. Nor was the topic slighted once the Society went to print. First came the 1912 publication in pamphlet form of Will H. Thomas' presentation from earlier that same year entitled "Some Current Folk-Songs of the Negro and Their Economic Interpretation." The Society's first book followed four years later. A miscellany titled *Publications of the Folk-Lore Society of Texas, Number 1*, known after its 1935 reissue as *Round the Levee*, contained three music-oriented articles, including R. E. Dudley and Leonidas W. Payne's "Texas Play-Party Songs and Games" and Ben D. Wood's "A Mexican Border Ballad."

Burdened down with a hectic but profitable speaking schedule and job responsibilities as secretary of the University of Texas' Alumni Association, Lomax surrendered his TFS duties in 1915. His impact had been profound, organizing the Society and setting it upon its path. His greatest contributions, nonetheless, were yet to come.

Traveling on behalf of the Library of Congress' Archives of American Folklore at the depths of the Great Depression, Lomax, new wife Ruby, and sons John, Jr. and Alan captured the musical pulse of a nation. Their instrument was a three-hundred-pound acetate disc recorder the folklorist somehow sandwiched into the trunk of his Ford sedan. Between 1933 and 1939, the Lomaxes visited prisons, churches, music festivals, plantations, work sites, and private residences from one end of the country to the other and back again. Along the way, commoners from all walks of life performed their songs for Lomax, each one recorded by his strange machine. Ten thousand ballads and blues, corridos and fiddle tunes, spirituals and field hollers that might otherwise have been lost to posterity found their way to the Library of Congress repository as a result. Books containing the Lomax discoveries appeared one after the other: *American Ballads and Folk Songs* (1934), *Negro Songs as Sung by Lead Belly* (1936), *Our Singing Country* (1941), *Folk Song: U.S.A.* (1947), and *Adventures of a Ballad Hunter* (1947). Given a life of such accomplishment, it came as no surprise in 1941 when the Texas Folklore Society awarded John Lomax its highest honor, designation as "Fellow."

William A. Owens was no less pivotal a figure in the collection and study of folk music in the Southwest. Clawing his way out of the abject rural poverty of Pin Hook in Lamar County, Owens earned a high school diploma from East Texas State Normal College and taught in small country schools before landing at Southern Methodist University in 1930. There he fell under the tutelage of Professor Henry Nash Smith, member and future president of the Texas Folklore Society. As Kittredge and Wendell had encouraged Lomax at Harvard, Smith convinced Owens of the academic legitimacy of studying the rural folkways of his own heritage. The young man from Pin Hook excelled under Smith's direction, completing his undergraduate studies and receiving his Master's degree in 1933. His thesis examined the folk tradition known as "play parties," social functions for the young featuring singing and dancing but devoid of the fiddle music and intimate physical contact fundamentalists considered evil. Frank Dobie, Lomax's successor at the TFS helm, jumped at the chance to publish Owens' manuscript. *Swing and Turn: Texas Play Party Games*, the Society's 1936 publication, established Owens as a comer in folklore circles.

The years between 1937 and 1941 found Bill Owens teaching English at Texas A & M in College Station while conducting the field recordings across his native state that became the basis for a doctoral dissertation at the University of Iowa. Utilizing a secondhand Vibromaster machine, he recorded sermons and spirituals in black Brazos bottom churches, Big Thicket ballads in the Pineywoods, Cajun songs along the Texas-Louisiana border, and Tejano music deep in the Nueces Strip chaparral. Owens also did collection work for the University of Texas' Extension Division under Roy Bedichek between January and August 1941. Writing years later, Owens recalled: "He [Bedichek] thought I could do for other kinds of songs what Lomax had done for the cowboy." Bedichek "... gave me the freedom to roam where I would and record what I would. Whatever was not recorded, he was certain and I believed him, would soon be forgotten and lost. He laid the task on me."[3] The music that would otherwise have vanished was thus preserved.

William A. Owens' Texas Folk Songs, PTFS XXIII, 1959

Dissertation accepted and doctorate in hand, Owens subsequently taught at Columbia University in far away New York City for a quarter of a century following his military service in World War II. TFS members at annual meetings through the years delighted in his presentations, including "Recording Folk Songs and Fiddle Music," "Negro and Cajun Songs," and "English Ballads in the Big Thicket." Today, nearly two decades after his passing, many of his field recordings from the 1930s are available in collections maintained at both the University of Texas and Texas A & M University. Additionally, any study of folk music in Texas invariably leads to Owens' *Texas Folksongs*, published by the Society in 1950, and *Tell Me A Story, Sing Me A Song* (University of Texas Press, 1983). His was a life fully lived.

No examination of the TFS-folk music relationship would be complete without recognition of the path breaking work of Américo Paredes. Society members had been preserving and analyzing the ballads and corridos of the Rio Grande border since the organization's inception. Paredes, however, would attain international renown and recognition during his long tenure at the University of Texas as the foremost scholar of such music.

The Brownsville native first set foot on the Austin campus as a thirty-five-year-old junior in 1950 following newspaper and radio jobs as well as wartime service in the Pacific theater. Paredes quickly earned his bachelor's degree and immediately began graduate studies in folklore, researching the songs of the border. Professor Mody Boatright, TFS secretary from 1943 to 1963, recognized Paredes' talents, introducing him to the Society and endorsing his applications for research assistance. "I know of nobody better equipped by experience and training to do this work than Paredes," wrote Boatright. "He grew up in the region and knows the people and their culture. At the University of Texas he has demonstrated a critical insight and an aptitude for scholarship as gratifying as it is rare."[4] The TFS secretary's faith was more than rewarded. "Don Américo," as he would affectionately come to be known, gave presentations at Society meetings, authored articles appearing in TFS publications, and topped off his graduate work in 1956 with a dissertation titled "El Corrido de Gregorio Cortez."

Published by the University of Texas Press in 1958 as *With His Pistol in His Hand: A Border Ballad and its Hero*, folklorists immediately recognized it as landmark research and analysis. The story of Cortez's fatal 1901 shooting of Karnes county Sheriff W. T. Morris, celebrated flight for freedom, and subsequent capture and imprisonment was well known. Paredes recounted and analyzed the corrido that had sprung up along the border even as Cortez fled southward at the turn of the century. More importantly, he placed the event and the ballad in context, challenging the racist simplicity of the traditional Anglo version of events and examining

Américo Paredes performing one of his corridos

the corrido as an expression of justified Tejano resistance to subordination in a land that had once been theirs.

Even as he established himself as a professor of both English and anthropology at his alma mater after graduation, Paredes continued to be one of the Society's most active members. Serving as president in 1962, he appeared regularly as a presenter and his articles on folk music continued to grace its annual miscellanies. He played pivotal roles on campus as well, training a new generation of folklorists and successfully lobbying for creation of both the Center for Intercultural Studies of Folklore and Ethnomusicology and the Center for Mexican-American Studies. His influence continues to this day, though he himself is gone. *A Texas-Mexican Cancionero: Folksongs of the Lower Border*, published in 1976 and reissued in 1995, remains the definitive compilation of the music he so loved.

The numbers wax and wane through the course of a century, but the Society has never been without its students of song. Dorothy Scarborough wrote of the blues in *On the Trail of Negro Folk-Songs*, and might well have made it her life work had not the success of her novel *The Wind* led her in a more literary direction. Hermes Nye, TFS president and originator of the Society's hootenannies, hosted a Dallas radio folk music program and performed regularly at Metroplex venues during the popular revival of such music at mid-century. He shared billing with Pete Seeger, Huddie "Leadbelly" Ledbetter, and Woody Guthrie on *The Life Treasury of American Folk Music* in 1961, and Nye's six Folkways albums reflect the depth of his familiarity with the genre's classic material. College professor and TFS fellow John Q. Anderson researched British murder ballads and their Texas variants, and entertained fellow paisanos with his rendition of "The Waco Girl." F. E. "Ab" Abernethy, long-time TFS secretary-editor and dog-house bassist with the East Texas String Ensemble, carried the tradition on through century's end. His *Singin' Texas* (1983) is required reading for lovers and performers of folk music, and his turn at each year's hootenanny is a treat not to be missed. As the Society celebrates its centennial and begins its second hundred years, students and performers of the people's music continue to find the TFS a nurturing home.

Another reflection of the Society's interest in and contributions to folk music is the comprehensiveness of its members' scholarship in the field. Ethnomusicologist Gary Hartman argues cogently that Texas music owes its richness to location and cultural diversity. According to Hartman, "The number, variety, and placement of the state's ethnic communities are unique in all of America, and they have allowed for a prolific cross-pollination of musical cultures that has given Texas music its special character."[5] Situated at the confluence of the Deep South, Great Plains, Southwest, and Republic of Mexico, Texas' varied landscapes and climates lured people of numerous races and cultures: Anglos and blacks from the Deep South, Hispanics from Mexico, and various European immigrant groups among others. Each brought its own distinctive musical traditions, but each also borrowed from the others with the passage of time. The end product was a mélange of sounds as diverse as the people who made them to express joy and sorrow, triumph and tragedy.

An examination of TFS records reveals almost 250 meeting papers and published articles on musical topics since the Society's founding in 1909. With amazing equality of numbers, they reflect the musical heritage of the major ethnic groups who came to Texas. Society members have recounted and analyzed the European ballads that made their way to the New World and spread down the Appalachians to the ever-advancing frontier. Presentations and articles on the music of black Texans abound: Negro spirituals, plantation and works songs, and the country blues of the Colorado and Trinity River valleys. Frank Dobie, Brownie McNeill, Américo Paredes, and Longino Guerrero among many others have chronicled the Tejano and Mexican ballads and corridos of the Rio Grande border. Studies of the sacred harp or shaped note singing of both Anglos and blacks, camp meeting spirituals, the music of the "holy-rollers," and singing conventions have all dealt with how Texans of various ethnicities express their personal faith through song.

TFS members have explored as well the folk roots of commer cial music and the many Texans who have made major contributions to that field of entertainment. Annual programs have included presentations such as "Bob Wills and Folk Music," "From Folk Music to Hillbilly to Country," and "Robert Earl Keen: Texas Folk Traditions in Popular Music." Published articles have examined the evolution of black folk music into ragtime, jazz, bebop, the urban blues, and zydeco, as well as recounted the contributions of Mance Lipscomb, T-Bone Walker, and Lightnin' Hopkins. Jose Reyna's "The Development of Chicano Music in Texas" and Wayne Albro's "Conjunto and the Mexican-American Community" provide additional evidence of the Society's appreciation of the multiracial nature of popular music emanating from the Lone Star State and its historic roots.

Students and scholarship notwithstanding, the informal hootenanny marking the beginning of each year's annual meeting is perhaps the purest and certainly most joyous expression of TFS members' love of folk music. Inaugurated in 1956 at the suggestion of Hermes Nye, we gather on Thursday evenings before the formal meeting commences to renew old friendships and share our fascination with folklore in its various forms. Storytellers tell their tales, singers sing their songs, and everyone present knows there is no place they'd rather be. There is a special feeling and folk music always plays an integral part. Perhaps no one captures the feeling more eloquently than "Ab" Abernethy in recollecting a special moment at his first Texas Folklore Society meeting in 1960:

> . . . Hermes, Américo Paredes, John Q. Anderson, and I and three or four others congregated in a dim corner of the banquet room. Everybody else had gone. Hermes had a guitar, and we circled up our chairs and began to sing singly and as a group or in duet, depending on who knew the songs and then pass the guitar around. A soldier wandered in and joined the singing circle, and a dozen other folks sat in the darkness around us. We loved it. Nobody hogged the guitar. Everybody enjoyed everybody else. I sang "Precious Jewel" and "Little Green Valley" and "Sally Goodin," none of which they had heard. It was a close encounter, and I felt a sense of belonging with them and the Society that I have never gotten over.[6]

The "sense of belonging" to which Abernethy refers is one shared by all who attend Society gatherings. And music—the songs through which untold generations of plain folk have expressed every aspect of their lives—has been and remains no less integral a part of the TFS experience.

Endnotes

1. Abernethy, Francis Edward. *The Texas Folklore Society: 1909–1943.* Denton: University of North Texas Press, 1992. 8; Porterfield, Nolan. *Last Cavalier: The Life and Times of John A. Lomax.* Urbana: University of Illinois Press. 1996. 142.
2. Abernethy. *The Texas Folklore Society: 1909–1943.* 28–30.
3. Owens, William A. *Tell Me a Story, Sing Me a Song: A Texas Chronicle.* Austin: University of Texas Press, 1983. 10–11.
4. Abernethy, Francis Edward. *The Texas Folklore Society: 1943–1971.* Denton: University of North Texas Press, 1994. 87.
5. Hartman, Gary. *The History of Texas Music.* College Station: Texas A&M University Press, 2008. 7.
6. Abernethy. *The Texas Folklore Society: 1943–1971.* 115–56.

Recommended Readings

Abernethy, Francis Edward. *The Texas Folklore Society: 1909–1943.* Denton: University of North Texas Press, 1992.

Abernethy, Francis Edward. *The Texas Folklore Society: 1943–1971.* Denton: University of North Texas Press, 1994.

Abernethy, Francis Edward. *The Texas Folklore Society: 1971–2000.* Denton: University of North Texas Press, 2000.

Abernethy, Francis Edward. *Singin' Texas.* Dallas: E-Heart Press, 1983.

Barkley, Roy, et al., eds. *The Handbook of Texas Music.* Austin: Texas State Historical Association, 2003.

Hartman, Gary. *The History of Texas Music.* College Station: Texas A & M University Press, 2008.

Owens, William A. *Tell Me a Story, Sing Me a Song: A Texas Chronicle.* Austin: University of Texas Press, 1983.

Paredes, Américo. *With His Pistol in His Hand: A Border Ballad and Its Hero.* Austin: University of Texas Press, 1958.

Paredes, Américo. *A Texas-Mexican Cancionero: Folksongs of the Lower Ballad.* Urbana: University of Illinois Press, 1976.

Porterfield, Nolan. *Last Cavalier: The Life and Times of John A. Lomax.* Urbana: University of Illinois Press, 1996.

Willoughby, Larry. *Texas Rhythm, Texas Rhyme: A Pictorial History of Texas Music.* Austin: Texas Monthly Press, 1984.

Bruce A. Glasrud

AFRICAN AMERICANS AND TEXAS FOLKLORE

by Bruce A. Glasrud

One Sunday in early fall, 1932, in a well known and often referenced tale, a young, emerging black Texas folklorist called the office of Texas Folklore Society secretary-editor and University of Texas English professor, J. Frank Dobie. The black folklorist received an encouraging and welcoming invitation to visit, and shortly entered and deposited a shoebox full of African-American folk stories on Dobie's desk. As Dobie subsequently remarked, thus he discovered the writer who became the nationally acclaimed folklorist, John Mason Brewer. Dobie recognized Brewer's talent, and edited and published his folktales. Brewer's aptly named tales, "Juneteenth," reflecting liberty and freedom, were found in the 1932 publication of the Texas Folklore Society, *Tone the Bell Easy.* The following year the TFS publication *Spur-of-the-Cock* included a collection of Brewer's stories entitled "Old-Time Negro Proverbs," together with his insightful interpretations of the proverbs' meanings.[1]

There are a number of intriguing aspects to this story. First, that Brewer located Dobie and sought his assistance. Second, that the white Texan, Dobie, accepted Brewer's material, and realized its value for what it was—classic stories of Texas slave days compiled by a black Texan. Third, that the Texas Folklore Society already had established a record of publishing black folklore. Fourth, that the previous African-American folklore published by the society had been collected by white folklorists. And, finally, that for most of its history (except for the excellent Texas Folklore Society publication, *Juneteenth Texas: Essays in African-American Folklore*, as well as the 1974 publication, *The Folklore of Texan Cultures*), J. Mason Brewer remained the only African-American folklorist to present and to publish folklore in the proceedings of the

Texas Folklore Society.[2] What do all these situations have to tell us? Do these items have any significance? The answers, I think, are important. The interplay of these factors provides a measure of Brewer's importance to Texas folklore and the contributions of the Texas Folklore Society to black studies in the state.

Born in Goliad, Texas, in 1896, Brewer's own family background was rich in stories and lore, especially of the west. Part of a "literary-minded family," as James W. Byrd noted, Brewer was encouraged to study history, to read, and to write. He graduated from high school in Austin, Texas, received a B.A. degree from Wiley College in Marshall, Texas, and during World War I served in France with the American Expeditionary Forces. After the war, he taught school in Fort Worth and worked for an oil company, part of the time in Colorado, where he published stories and poetry, including a small book, *Glimpses of Life* in 1923. By 1926, he assumed a teaching position at Samuel Huston College in Austin, when he probably first met Dobie. Throughout his career at Samuel Huston, Brewer continued his research and publications in folklore, history, and poetry, sometimes in concert with his students. Brewer eventually studied folklore with W. Stith Thompson at Indiana University, where he earned a master's degree. Brewer returned in 1943 to Austin and the renamed Huston-Tillotson College until 1959, when he moved to Livingston College in North Carolina. He returned to Texas in 1969, to become distinguished visiting professor at East Texas State University. Still active, he died in January of 1975.[3]

J. Mason Brewer was a remarkable scholar, teacher, and author. However, as Texas folklorists know, he excelled at collecting, interpreting, and publishing African-American folklore.[4] He received rave national reviews for his collection *American Negro Folklore*, the study that helped establish him among the best of folklorists; in fact, Brewer and black Florida folklorist, Zora Neale Hurston, were the two greatest black folklorists of the twentieth century and among the greatest of any grouping. While in North Carolina he published two award winning collections, *Humorous Folktales of*

J. Mason Brewer speaking at a TFS meeting

the South Carolina Negro and *Worser Days and Better Times: The Folklore of the North Carolina Negro*, which enhanced and advanced his reputation.[5]

It was his Texas work, however, that provided us with exciting and informed publications, especially his three classic studies—*Aunt Dicy Tales: Snuff-Dipping Tales of the Texas Negro*, *Dog Ghosts and Other Texas Negro Folk Tales*, and *The Word on the Brazos: Negro Preacher Tales from the Brazos Bottoms of Texas.* Brewer also published two additional selections with the Texas Folklore Society, "John Tales" in *Mexican Border Ballads and Other Lore*, and "More of the Word on the Brazos" in *Observations & Reflections on Texas Folklore.*[6] The following example from "John Tales" illustrates Brewer's ability to collect, relate, and publish African-American folklore:

> Cotton picking season was the time of year that the hands on the Southern plantation had most money, but this was only true when they had a good crop year. Whenever these good crop years came, John and several of the hands on the other plantations always gambled. They usually went down to Colonel Clemon's cotton gin every Sunday afternoon and shot dice until the sun went down and it got too dark to see. There were always a large number of bales of cotton there on Sunday, so the crapshooters hid behind the bales of cotton where they could not be seen. None of the white folks knew that gambling was going on at the gin until Steven, one of the hands from another plantation, lost a lot of money on Sunday and accused some of the others of cheating in the game. It happened that Steven went to town the next Saturday. While there, he visited the sheriff's office and told him about John and the other hands gambling every Sunday afternoon, down at the Colonel's gin. So the sheriff took two deputies with him out to the Colonel's plantation the next Sunday and arrested the gamblers. When the day for the trial came, the Judge questioned each one of the hands separately as to his guilt or innocence. John was the last one called to the stand. The others had been tried, found guilty, and fined ten dollars for gambling. Everybody in the court-room was wondering whether or not John, who could usually get himself out of trouble, was going to be able to fool the Judge this time and keep from paying a fine. When

> John's turn came, the Judge called him to the stand. Everybody was so quiet you could hear a pin drop in the courtroom. "John," said the Judge, "didn't I tell you the last time you were here that I would fine you if I ever caught you winning money in games of chance?" "Yas suh, Judge," replied John, "but Ah wasn't winnin', Ah was losin'." And this is how John got out of paying a fine for shooting dice.[7]

John epitomized Brewer's ability to collect folklore and to tell a story.

Prior to Brewer's TFS folklore publications in 1932 and 1933, the African-American folklore mantle in the Texas Folklore Society was borne by white folklorists. The first publication of the TFS, for example, was Will H. Thomas' 1912 booklet, *Some Current Folk-Songs of the Negro.* Thomas' collection, reprinted in *Rainbow in the Morning* (1926), is comprised of a dozen or so songs, along with his brief economic interpretation that forms part of the introduction. At the time, Thomas was president of the TFS.[8] Will Thomas was not alone in collecting African-American folk songs; so too did his brother Gates Thomas, whose "South Texas Negro Work-Songs: Collected and Uncollected," also was published in *Rainbow in the Morning.* In that same volume, Natalie Taylor Carlisle contributed "Old Time Darky Plantation Melodies." Carlisle paternalistically asserted that she had "known well the old fashioned negro," whom she described as "the old time faithful, trusting, and to-be-trusted darky."[9]

Collecting black Texas folk songs was popular in the 1920s, as attested by the work of two other authors—Dorothy Scarborough and Mary Virginia Bales. Bales completed a master's thesis at Texas Christian University on the topic of black folk songs and published "Some Negro Folk-Songs of Texas" in *Follow de Drinkin' Gou'd.* Famed Texas writer Dorothy Scarborough published "The 'Blues' as Folk-Songs" in *Coffee in the Gourd* (1923). Scarborough, like Brewer, searched beyond Texas for information, and in 1925 she published her well-known *On the Trail of Negro Folk-Songs* that included Texas songs as well as African-American folk songs from across the nation. Collecting and publishing these folk songs was an exceptionally valuable effort then and now; however, in an important early reminder (1926), Texas Tech professor R. C. Harrison's "The Negro as Interpreter of His Own Folk-Songs" (*Rainbow in the Morning*) pointed out the increased desirability of African American interpretation and study of their folk songs. As Harrison phrased it, "we are forced to recognize the advancement of the Negro as an interpreter of his own folk-lore."[10]

Folk songs were not the only source for white folklorists who collected and published African-American works during the twenties, thirties, and forties; they also collected and published black Texas folklore and folk tales. Two of the best known early white Texas folklorists were A. W. Eddins and Martha Emmons. Eddins contributed black folk tales from the Brazos Bottom, beginning with the TFS's first volume in 1916; his knowledge of Afro-Texan lore of the Brazos Bottoms surfaced in selections for *Round the Levee*, *Coffee in the Gourd*, and *Southwestern Lore*. Martha Emmons, referred to by Dobie "as the foremost master of Negro dialect that Texas has produced," provided black folklore selections for at least four TFS publications, and ultimately published *Deep Like the Rivers: Stories of My Negro Friends.*[11] Other white folklorists who published selections in TFS publications prior to the end of World War II included such prominent individuals as Walter Prescott Webb, J. Frank Dobie, H. B. Parks, Bertha McKee Dobie, Ruby Terrill Lomax, and John Lomax.[12] The entire list is overwhelming.

As Francis E. Abernethy noted in his essay "African-American Folklore in Texas and in the Texas Folklore Society" in the excellent TFS publication *Juneteenth Texas*, "the first nineteen volumes, to 1944, contained thirty articles" on black Texas folklore. In this author's own count, a total of thirty-nine selections were published before the end of World War II. In either case, this output was exceptional; it meant an average of at least two selections per volume on the topic of black Texas folklore in the first nineteen publications of the TFS. However, with the exception of J. Mason

Brewer, this folklore came to us from white folklorists; some, as F. E. Abernethy reminded us, filled with "condescension and paternalism and stereotyping."[13]

Despite the dated viewpoints, these contributions were valuable. Before 1945, the contributions of the Texas Folklore Society to Afro-Texas folklore consisted principally of original folklore and folk tales collected, interpreted, and published by whites, with the sole exception of Brewer. This research is especially important to scholars and lay persons today. Without the scholarship of these early folklorists, we would not have these tales and stories to help us understand the black community of earlier years, nor the perspective on black-white relations.

In the years after World War II, the Texas Folklore Society published twenty-eight selections of black folklore in its volumes. There exist a few exceptions to this assertion. In 1954, the society published *Texas Folk and Folklore*, a reprint of some of the best folklore from previous years that included eight pieces of folklore about black Texans, one a reprint of Brewer's "Juneteenth." That number is not included in the original twenty-eight. That volume, *Texas Folk and Folklore*, was reprinted in 1998 as *The Best of Texas Folk and Folklore, 1916–1954*, and it is not included in the calculations, either.[14] There is one other major exception: the number twenty-eight does not include the twenty essays on African-American folklore located in the distinguished volume edited by Francis E. Abernethy, Patrick B. Mullen, and Alan B. Govenar and published in 1996, *Juneteenth Texas*.[15] If we *do* total the original (not reprinted) publications, the number of selections published by the Texas Folklore Society on black Texas folklore—thirty-nine to 1945, twenty-eight after that date—we arrive at a grand total of sixty-seven. This is an imposing total by any standard. The Texas Folklore Society has much of which to be proud. With the current volume of TFS publications, number 66, the society has published an average of one selection on black folklore in every volume. If the twenty from *Juneteenth Texas* is included the output (87), the total becomes even more impressive.

A survey of the African-American folklore publications and authors since World War II shows that, once more, most of the authors, folklorists, were white. The topics the folklorists of the latter twentieth and early twenty-first century found interesting included music, seers, "The Yellow Rose of Texas," and evaluations of black folklore and its study. One of the most prominent, and best, of these authors was James W. Byrd. Byrd, a friend and colleague of J. Mason Brewer, published a first-rate investigation of Brewer's "Aunt Dicy" that was published in *Legendary Ladies of Texas*. Brewer's Aunt Dicy was a heroic, strong, and admirable woman. One of the stories that Byrd appreciated concerned Aunt Dicy's trip to Houston, when not everything worked quite as well as it might have:

> Aunt Dicy boarded the train, and shortly after it left the station she took out a can of "Levi Garrett" snuff and took a dip. They had spittoons on the train coaches at that time, since so many people chewed tobacco and dipped snuff. But Aunt Dicy had never seen a spittoon before. She didn't know what it was. Consequently when she got ready to spit her snuff-juice out, she spat on the other side of the spittoon to keep from spitting in it. Every time Aunt Dicy would spit snuff-juice on the floor the Negro porter would pick the spittoon up and put it in the spot where Aunt Dicy had spit last. This kept up for a long time until finally Aunt Dicy called the porter over to where she was seated and said, "Look a here Bub; let me tell you something—you better take that thing and put it out of the way, 'cause if you keep on putting it over here close to me, I'm going to spit in it afterwhile."[16]

Byrd also published a biography of Brewer, "Dr. J. Mason Brewer," in *Features and Fillers* (1999) that originally served as Brewer's eulogy. Byrd's third article, "Folk Anecdote Survives in

Black Fiction," found in *The Folklore of Texan Cultures*, discussed the origin and use of the negative connotation, "gone Democrat."[17] Other folklorists pursued additional studies with their Texas Folklore Society publications.

The role and influence of music in the African American community was one example that was reflected in the folklorist's choices. Two sections in William A. Owens' TFS publication *Texas Folk Songs*, "Afro-American Spirituals" and "Afro-American Secular Songs," are notable contributions. Owens concentrated on both secular and spiritual African-American music. Alfreda Iglehart described and explained the motion and meaning of "Waco Jive" in *The Folklore of Texan Cultures*. The background and influence of zydeco in black Texas music was explained in Joseph F. Lomax's "Zydeco—Must Live On!" from the TFS book *What's Going On? (In Modern Texas Folklore)*. In *Corners of Texas*, Alan Govenar depicted the special style that sprang from "The Blues and Jives of Dr. Hepcat."[18]

Two authors, William A. Owens and Henry Wolff, Jr., described the life and role of seers in the black and white community. African-American seers, perhaps best depicted as fortunetellers, clairvoyants or finders, generally were women. Owens, then a professor of English at Columbia University, followed the stories of Texas oil pioneers, and wrote about the "Seer of Corsicana," Annie Buchanan, in an article for *and horns on the toads*. Prolific newspaper writer and storyteller Henry Wolff, Jr. produced more than 6,000 columns for the *Victoria Advocate*. While researching for his columns, he discovered black Victoria seer "Madame Blackley: Seer of South Texas," and turned his discovery into an article for the TFS publication, *Folklore: In All of Us, In All We Do*. Both Buchanan and Blackley used their gifts for the benefit of their community; both advised individuals on where/how to locate items, and both told for black or white clients.[19]

The emergence and spirit of Texas' African American communities and the individuals who resided in them also received attention from folklorists. Thad Sitton depicted the beginnings and roles of near-black communities in his first-rate study, "Texas

Freedman's Settlements in the New South," published in *Both Sides of the Border: A Scattering of Texas Folklore.* Michael Mott described "Johnny W. Banks, Black, Man, Texan, Artist," in *Folk Art in Texas.* In *and horns on the toads*, Girlene Marie Williams collected and told "Negro Stories from the Colorado Valley." In that same volume, Fred O. Weldon, Jr. discussed "Negro Folktale Heroes." Perhaps Weldon's article led Roger Abrahams to consider "The Changing Concept of the Negro Hero" in *The Golden Log.*[20]

One topic that received considerable attention by folklorists in the latter twentieth century was connected to the song, "The Yellow Rose of Texas." For many years legends circulated that the song was written by a free black Texas man seeking his estranged lover, Emily West/Morgan who, again according to lore, aided the Texas revolutionary cause by (either willingly or unwillingly) being in Santa Anna's bed at the time of the battle of San Jacinto. Five folklorists have written about this story in the pages of TFS publications. The first, then Director of the Institute of Texan Cultures, R. Henderson Shuffler, in "San Jacinto, As She Was: Or, What Really Happened on the Plain of St. Hyacinth on a Hot April Afternoon in 1836," published his version of the story in *Observations & Reflections on Texas Folklore.* Shuffler argued that Emily, beautiful and sexual, willingly engaged Santa Anna in his quarters. In fact, Shuffler used the story as a way of exploiting the alleged sexuality and promiscuity of black women.[21] As Trudier Harris noted, "West is a joke upon whom he [Shuffler] can hang all the sexual baggage he carries about black female bodies."[22]

Martha Anne Turner's "Emily Morgan: Yellow Rose of Texas," found in *Legendary Ladies of Texas*, is bright, beautiful, a Texas patriot, and willing to do what she can for the cause of Texas independence. The first academician to argue that Emily Morgan was the "yellow rose of Texas," Turner published a book on the topic, *The Yellow Rose of Texas: Her Saga and Her Song.* One other book-length work is fiction, Anita Bunkley's *Emily, The Yellow Rose: A Texas Legend.*[23] The third TFS author to investigate the "Yellow Rose" story is Trudier Harris, professor of literature at Emory

University. A black woman, Harris accepted the basic tenets of the story, but tried to fit Emily West into her actual role as a black woman in those circumstances. The title of her article, "'The Yellow Rose of Texas': A Different Cultural View," gives us an awareness of her approach. Accepting that she likely was "the yellow rose of Texas," Harris' West was not a sexual, promiscuous person; she was not a black mammy; she was a black woman who was taken illicitly for sex and companionship. She was raped.[24]

Two presenters at the Texas State Historical Association's 1997 meeting, James Lutzweiler and F. E. Abernethy, took on the stories about Emily D. West/Morgan and her relationship to the song, "The Yellow Rose of Texas." They looked at the available, though limited, evidence, and provided us with a furtherance of the discussion. The papers were published in *2001: A Texas Folklore Odyssey*, a volume of the TFS, as James Lutzweiler's "Emily D. West and the Yellow Prose of Texas: A Primer on Some Primary Documents and Their Doctoring," and F. E. Abernethy's "The Elusive Emily D. West, Folksong's Fabled 'Yellow Rose of Texas.'" Lutzweiler determined that the woman in Santa Anna's tent was Emily D. West, that she was a free woman of color, and that she was not the "yellow rose of Texas." An officer of the Texas army, none other than Sam Houston, reported the incident to an acquaintance, William Bollaert. Abernethy continued the overall assault, and asserted that "I certainly have never found anything to tie the song to the Texas Revolution, San Jacinto, or Emily West-Morgan."[25] This author suspects that both Lutzweiler and Abernethy presumed to stop the discussion of Emily as the yellow rose, but doubts it will happen. However, do remember that Emily D. West, not Emily Morgan, is the name of the black woman who remained in Santa Anna's tent. However, she is not the basis for the song "The Yellow Rose of Texas." Since Sam Houston reportedly told us so, she did occupy the tent with Santa Anna when the battle of San Jacinto began. Or did she?

Although the aforementioned Trudier Harris was an African-American writer and teacher/folklorist, few of the other articles mentioned above from the 1950s and on were written by blacks. As mentioned, J. Mason Brewer published two selections, his "John Tales," and "More of the Word on the Brazos." Two original essays published by black authors, a reprint from Brewer entitled "Tales from Juneteenth," and white author James Byrd's "Folk Anecdote Survives in Black Fiction" were included in a section entitled "The Negroes" in *The Folklore of Texan Cultures* (1974). The two original articles were Alfreda Iglehart's "Waco Jive" and Lorece P. Williams' "Country Black." Iglehart's article was mentioned earlier. Williams discussed rural events and lifestyles among rural blacks in Texas; she discovered that ceremonies and traditions were important.[26] For collecting and interpreting the folklore of black Texans, skin color makes a difference, as we also noticed in the essay by Trudier Harris. For additional insight, read Patrick B. Mullen's thoughtful essay "The Rabbit, The Lion, and The Man: Race Relations in Folklore Fieldwork" in TFS publication *Corners of Texas*. As Mullen pointed out, "we have not always recognized the fact that when a white folklorist interviews black informants it is within a political context."[27]

From the perspective of African-American folklore in Texas, and the Texas Folklore Society, the marvelous publication *Juneteenth Texas* deserves special comment. Published in 1996, the collection includes twenty essays, eleven by whites and nine by blacks, with a Preface from Patrick B. Mullen and Alan Govenar, and an opening article by Francis E. Abernethy. The topics are wide-ranging, and cover sacred harp singing, African-American foodways, blacksmithing, singing cowboys, Juneteenth, West African fiddles, zydeco, and the "Texas Trailblazer Project." Individuals are considered as well, and include Henry Truvillion, Mance Lipscomb, John Biggers, Lightnin' Hopkins, and "Bongo Joe." Trudier Harris' article on "The Yellow Rose of Texas" is incorporated. Dave Oliphant considers "From Bebop to Hard Bop and Beyond: The Texas Jazz Connection." Author of *Waiting in Line at the Drugstore*, James Thomas Jackson, who studied at Budd Schulberg's Watts' writer's workshop after Watts exploded, explored "Once

Upon a Time in Houston's Fourth Ward."[28] Perhaps the most entertaining, most spirited, and most insightful selection is Clyde Daniel's "Where the Cedars Grove." Using poetry, Daniel's discussed his community, and provided insight into the folklore of that community. As he wrote in "Our Town":

> The world didn't revolve
> Around Cedar Grove,
> But our lives did.
> For this was our nest,
> Our niche in the universe,
> Yet, less than a neutron—
> In an atom—in a molecule
> Of dust—in eternity.[29]

For anyone interested in black Texas folklore, *Juneteenth Texas* is one volume to peruse carefully.

The black folklore published by the TFS, whether in *Juneteenth Texas* or in the sixty-seven other selections published in the sixty-six volumes of the Texas Folklore Society, is significant. Over the past century, those responsible for collecting the folklore and disseminating their findings have made a substantial contribution to locating the history and culture of black Texans. Their varied interpretations, from a white or black perspective, from an orthodox or unorthodox approach, or from a liberal or conservative viewpoint, yet enable us to discuss some of the issues that arise from the study of black Texas folklore as depicted by articles in the volumes of the TFS. During the one hundred years of its existence, the Texas Folklore Society has played a vital role in collecting, disseminating, and critiquing African-American folktales and lore from Texas. Over the past century, on average the TFS has published more than one African-American folktale, folksong, or essay per volume. That is a grand performance.

ENDNOTES

1. J. Mason Brewer. "Juneteenth." *Tone the Bell Easy* (PTFS 10). J. Frank Dobie, ed. Dallas, TX: Southern Methodist University Press, 1932. 9–53; J. Mason Brewer, "Old-Time Negro Proverbs," in *Spur-of-the-Cock* (PTFS 11). J. Frank Dobie, ed. Austin: Texas Folklore Society, 1933. 101–105. For the fall 1932 meeting, see J. Frank Dobie, "A Word on *The Word*," in *The Word on the Brazos: Negro Preacher Tales from the Brazos Bottoms of Texas*, by J. Mason Brewer. Austin: University of Texas Press, 1953. vii–xii. It should be noted that an additional part of the story is overlooked in Dobie's rendition, as happens with folktales. As James W. Byrd pointed out, Dobie met Brewer in 1926; he encouraged Brewer to devote his efforts to collecting African American folklore rather than writing poetry. See James W. Byrd, "John Mason Brewer," *The Handbook of Texas Online* http://www.tshaonline.org/handbook/online).
2. Francis E. Abernethy. "African-American Folklore in Texas and in the Texas Folklore Society." *Juneteenth Texas: Essays in African-American Folklore* (PTFS 54) Francis E. Abernethy, Patrick B. Mullen, and Alan B. Govenar, eds. Denton: University of North Texas Press, 1996. 1–13; Francis Edward Abernethy and Dan Beaty, eds., *The Folklore of Texan Cultures* (PTFS 38). Austin: Encino Press, 1974.
3. Although there yet is no definitive biography of Brewer, one can start with James W. Byrd, *J. Mason Brewer: Negro Folklorist.* Austin: Steck-Vaughn, 1967. See also Kenneth W. Turner, "Negro Collectors of Negro Folklore: A Study of J. Mason Brewer and Zora Neale Hurston" (Master's thesis, East Texas State University, 1964); Bruce A. Glasrud, "John Mason Brewer," *BlackPast Online Encyclopedia* (http://www.blackpast.org); Bruce A. Glasrud, "From Griggs to Brewer: A Review of Black Texas Artists, 1899–1940. *Journal of Big Bend Studies* 15 (2003): 195–212; Lorenzo Thomas, "The African-American Folktale and J. Mason Brewer." *Juneteenth Texas: Essays in African-American Folklore* (PTFS 54). Francis E. Abernethy, Patrick B. Mullen, and Alan B. Govenar, eds. Denton: University of North Texas Press, 1996. 223–23; Darwin T. Turner, "J. Mason Brewer: Vignettes," *CLA Journal* 18 (June 1975). 570–577; James W. Byrd, "Dr. J. Mason Brewer." *Features and Fillers: Texas Journalists on Texas Folklore* (PTFS 56). Jim Harris, ed. Denton: University of North Texas Press, 1999. 168–171; J. Mason Brewer, *Glimpses of Life* (nc: privately printed, 1923).
4. Brewer also collected and published numerous works about other aspects of black Texas contributions; these included poetry, history, and education. See, for example *Heralding Dawn: An Anthology of Verse*, J. Mason Brewer, ed. Dallas: June Thomason, 1936; J. Mason

Brewer. *An Historical Outline of the Negro in Travis County.* Austin, Tex.: Samuel Huston College, 1940; J. Mason Brewer, *Negrito: Negro Dialect Poems of the Southwest.* San Antonio: Naylor Printing, 1933; J. Mason Brewer, *Negro Legislators of Texas and Their Descendants: A History of the Negro in Texas Politics from Reconstruction to Disfranchisement.* J. Mason Brewer, ed. Dallas: Mathis Publishing, 1933; *A History of the Dallas High School for Negroes.* Dallas: privately printed, 1938; J. Mason Brewer, *The Life of John Wesley Anderson . . . in verse . . .* Dallas: C. C. Cockrell, 1938.

5. *American Negro Folklore.* J. Mason Brewer, ed. Chicago: Quadrangle Books, 1968; J. Mason Brewer, *Humorous Folktales of the South Carolina Negro.* Orangeburg, S.C.: South Carolina Negro Folklore Guild, 1945; J. Mason Brewer, *Worser Days and Better Times: The Folklore of the North Carolina Negro.* Chicago: Quadrangle Books, 1965.
6. J. Mason Brewer. *Aunt Dicy Tales: Snuff-Dipping Tales of the Texas Negro.* Austin: privately printed, 1956; J. Mason Brewer. *Dog Ghosts and Other Texas Negro Folk Tales.* Austin: University of Texas Press, 1958; J. Mason Brewer. *The Word on the Brazos: Negro Preacher Tales from the Brazos Bottoms of Texas.* Austin: University of Texas Press, 1953; J. Mason Brewer. "John Tales." *Mexican Border Ballads and Other Lore* (PTFS 21). Mody C. Boatright, ed. Austin: Texas Folklore Society, 1946. 81–104; J. Mason Brewer. "More of the Word on the Brazos." *Observations & Reflections on Texas Folklore* (PTFS 37). Francis Edward Abernethy, ed. Dallas: Southern Methodist University Press, 1972. 91–99. For more on Brewer as depicted in TFS publications, see Thomas, "The African-American Folktale and J. Mason Brewer;" Byrd, "Dr. J. Mason Brewer."
7. Brewer., "John Tales." 98–99.
8. Will H. Thomas. *Some Current Folk-Songs of the Negro.* Austin: Texas Folklore Society, 1912; Will H. Thomas. "Some Current Folk-Songs of the Negro and Their Economic Interpretation." *Rainbow in the Morning* (PTFS 5). J. Frank Dobie, ed. Hatboro, Penn. Folklore Associates, Inc. 1926. (facsimile edition, 1965): 191–203.
9. Gates Thomas. "South Texas Negro Work-Songs: Collected and Uncollected." *Rainbow in the Morning.* 154–180; Natalie Taylor Carlisle. "Old Time Darky Plantation Melodies." in *Rainbow in the Morning.* 137–143.
10. Mary Virginia Bales. "Negro Folk-Songs in Texas: Their Definition and Origin" (Master's thesis, Texas Christian University, 1927); Mary Virginia Bales, "Some Negro Folk-Songs of Texas." *Follow de Drinkin' Gou'd* (PTFS 7). J. Frank Dobie, ed. Austin: Texas Folklore Society, 1928. 85–112; Dorothy Scarborough. "The 'Blues' as Folk-Songs." *Coffee in the Gourd* (PTFS 2). J. Frank Dobie, ed. Austin: Texas Folklore Society, 1923. 52–66; Dorothy Scarborough. *On the*

Trail of Negro Folk-Songs. Cambridge: Harvard University Press, 1925; R. C. Harrison. "The Negro as Interpreter of His Own Folk-Songs." *Rainbow in the Morning.* 144–153.

11. J. Frank Dobie. *Straight Texas.* J. Frank Dobie and Mody C. Boatright, eds. Austin: Texas Folklore Society, 1937. A. W. Eddins. "'How Sandy Got His Meat'—A Negro Tale from the Brazos Bottoms." *Round the Levee* (PTFS 1). Stith Thompson, ed. Austin: Texas Folklore Society, 1916,1935. 47–49; A. W. Eddins. "Brazos Bottom Philosophy." *Coffee in the Gourd* (PTFS 2). J. Frank Dobie, ed. Austin: Texas Folklore Society, 1923. 50–51; A. W. Eddins. "Brazos Bottom Philosophy" *Southwestern Lore* (PTFS 9), J. Frank Dobie, ed. Austin: Texas Folklore Society, 1931. 153–164; Martha Emmons. "Confidences from Old Nacogdoches." *Follow de Drinkin' Gou'd*, (PTFS 7). 119–134; Martha Emmons. "Dyin' Easy." *Tone the Bell Easy.* 55–61; Martha Emmons. "Cats and the Occult." *Spur-of-the-Cock* (PTFS 11). J. Frank Dobie, ed. Austin: Texas Folklore Society, 1933. 94–100; Martha Emmons. "Walk Around My Bedside." *Straight Texas* (PTFS 13). J. Frank Dobie and Mody C. Boatright, eds. Austin: Texas Folklore Society, 1937. 130–136; Martha Emmons. *Deep Like the Rivers: Stories of My Negro Friends.* Austin: Encino Press, 1969.
12. W. P. Webb. "Negro Songs and Stories." *Coffee in the Gourd* (PTFS 2). 45–49; J. Frank Dobie. "The Nigger Gold Mine of the Big Bend." *Legends of Texas* (PTFS 3). J. Frank Dobie, ed. Austin: Texas Folklore Society, 1924. 72–75; H. B. Parks. "Follow the Drinking Gourd." *Follow de Drinkin' Gou'd* (PTFS 7), 81–84; Bertha McKee Dobie. "The Ghosts of Lake Jackson." *Follow de Drinkin' Gou'd* (PTFS 7). 135–136; Ruby Terrill Lomax. "Negro Nicknames. *Backwoods to Border* (PTFS 18). Mody C. Boatright and Donald Day, eds. Austin: Texas Folklore Society, 1943. 163–171; Ruby Terrill Lomax. "Negro Baptizings." *From Hell to Breakfast* (PTFS 19). Mody C. Boatright and Donald Day, eds. Austin: Texas Folklore Society, 1944. 1–8; John A. Lomax. "Adventures of a Ballad Hunter." *From Hell to Breakfast.* 9–20.
13. Abernethy. "African-American Folklore in Texas and in the Texas Folklore Society." *Juneteenth Texas.* 1–13.
14. Mody C. Boatright, William M. Hudson, and Allen Maxwell, eds. *Texas Folk and Folklore* (PTFS 26). Dallas: Southern Methodist University Press, 1954; Mody C. Boatright, William M. Hudson, and Allen Maxwell, eds. *The Best of Texas Folk and Folklore, 1916–1954* (PTFS 57) Denton: University of North Texas Press, 1998. The eight reprinted selections follow (in a few cases the titles vary slightly from the original TFS publication): A. W. Eddins, "From the Brazos Bottom;" J. Mason Brewer, "Juneteenth;"

Bertha McKee Dobie, "The Ghosts of Lake Jackson;" H. B. Parks, "Follow the Drinking Gourd;" Gates Thomas, "Six Negro Songs from the Colorado Valley;" Mary Virginia Bales, "Some Texas Spirituals;" John H. Lomax, "Sin-Killer's Sermon;" J. Mason Brewer, "Old-Time Negro Proverbs."

15. Francis E. Abernethy, Patrick B. Mullen, and Alan B. Govenar, eds., *Juneteenth Texas: Essays in African-American Folklore* (PTFS 54) Denton: University of North Texas Press, 1996.
16. James W. Byrd. "Aunt Dicy: Legendary Black Lady." *Legendary Ladies of Texas* (PTFS 43). Francis Edward Abernethy, ed. Dallas: E-Heart Press, 1981. 123–131; Brewer, *Aunt Dicy Tales.* 60.
17. James W. Byrd. "Dr. J. Mason Brewer." *Features and Fillers: Texas Journalists on Texas Folklore* (PTFS 56). Jim Harris, ed. Denton: University of North Texas Press, 1999. 168–171; James W. Byrd. "Folk Anecdote Survives in Black Fiction." *The Folklore of Texan Cultures* (PTFS 38). Francis Edward Abernethy and Dan Beaty, eds. Austin: Encino Press, 1974. 139–140.
18. "Afro-American Spirituals." *Texas Folk Songs* (PTFS 23). William A. Owens, ed. Austin: Texas Folklore Society, 1950. 170–174; "Afro-American Secular Songs." *Texas Folk Songs* (PTFS 23). William A. Owens, ed. Austin: Texas Folklore Society, 1950. 175–181; Alfreda Iglehart. "Waco Jive." *The Folklore of Texan Cultures.* 129–139; Joseph F. Lomax, "Zydeco—Must Live On!" *What's Going On (In Modern Texas Folklore* (PTFS 40). Francis Edward Abernethy, ed. Austin: Encino Press, 1976. 205–223; Alan B. Govenar. "The Blues and Jives of Dr. Hepcat." *Corners of Texas* (PTFS 52). Francis Edward Abernethy, ed. Denton: University of North Texas Press, 1993. 239–245.
19. William A. Owens. "Seer of Corsicana." *and horns on the toads* (PTFS 29). Mody C. Boatright, William M. Hudson, and Allen Maxwell, eds. Dallas: Southern Methodist University Press, 1959. 14–31; Henry Wolff, Jr. "Madame Blackley: Seer of South Texas." *Folklore: In All of Us, In All We Do* (PTFS 63). Kenneth L. Untiedt, ed. Denton: University of North Texas Press, 2006. 95–105.
20. Thad Sitton. "Texas Freedman's Settlements in the New South." *Both Sides of the Border: A Scattering of Texas Folklore* (PTFS 61). Francis E. Abernethy and Kenneth L. Untiedt, eds. Denton: University of North Texas Press, 2004. 216–231; Michael Mott. "Johnny W. Banks, Black, Man, Texan, Artist." *Folk Art in Texas* (PTFS 45). Francis Edward Abernethy, ed. Denton: University of North Texas Press, 1984. 178–183; Girlene Marie Williams. "Negro Stories from the Colorado Valley." *and horns on the toads.* Mody C. Boatright, William M. Hudson, and Allen Maxwell, eds. Dallas: Southern

Methodist University Press, 1959. 161–169; Fred O. Williams, Jr. "Negro Folktale Heroes." *and horns on the toads.* 170–189; Roger Abrahams. "The Changing Concept of the Negro Hero." *The Golden Log* (TFS 31). Mody C. Boatright, Wilson M. Hudson, and Allen Maxwell, eds. Dallas: Southern Methodist University Press, 1961. 119–134.

21. R. Henderson Shuffler. "San Jacinto, As She Was: Or, What Really Happened on the Plain of St. Hyacinth on a Hot April Afternoon in 1836." *Observations & Reflections on Texas Folklore* (PTFS 37). Francis Edward Abernethy, ed. Dallas: Southern Methodist University Press, 1972. 121–130.
22. Trudier Harris. "'The Yellow Rose of Texas': A Different Cultural View." *Juneteenth Texas: Essays in African-American Folklore* (PTFS 54). 315–332.
23. Martha Anne Turner. "Emily Morgan: Yellow Rose of Texas." *Legendary Ladies of Texas* (PTFS 43). 21–30; Martha Anne Turner. *The Yellow Rose of Texas: Her Saga and Her Song.* Austin: Eakin Press, 1976, 1986; Anita Bunkley. *Emily, The Yellow Rose: A Texas Legend.* Houston: Rinard Publishing, 1989.
24. Harris. "The Yellow Rose of Texas." 315–332.
25. James Lutzweiler. "Emily D. West and the Yellow Prose of Texas: A Primer on Some Primary Documents and Their Doctoring." *2001: A Texas Folklore Odyssey* (PTFS 58). Francis E. Abernethy, ed. Denton: University of North Texas Press, 2001. 294–316; F. E. Abernethy. "The Elusive Emily D. West, Folksong's Fabled 'Yellow Rose of Texas.'" *2001: A Texas Folklore Odyssey* (PTFS 58). 323.
26. J. Mason Brewer. "John Tales." *Mexican Border Ballads and Other Lore* (PTFS 21). Mody C. Boatright, ed. Austin: Texas Folklore Society, 1946. 81–104; J. Mason Brewer. "More of the *Word on the Brazos.*" *Observations & Reflections on Texas Folklore* (PTFS 37). Francis Edward Abernethy, ed. Dallas: Southern Methodist University Press, 1972. 91–99; J. Mason Brewer. "Tales from Juneteenth." *The Folklore of Texan Cultures* (PTFS 38). 115–118; James W. Byrd. "Folk Anecdote Survives in Black Fiction." *The Folklore of Texan Cultures* (PTFS 38). Francis Edward Abernethy and Dan Beaty, eds. Austin: Encino Press, 1974. 139–140; Alfreda Iglehart. "Waco Jive." *The Folklore of Texan Cultures* (PTFS 38). 129–139; Lorece P. Williams. "Country Black." *The Folklore of Texan Cultures* (PTFS 38). 118–129.
27. Harris. "The Yellow Rose of Texas." 315–332; Patrick B. Mullen. "The Rabbit, The Lion, and The Man: Race Relations in Folklore Fieldwork." *Corners of Texas* (PTFS 52). 175–195. On the topic of

race relations and fieldwork, see also Roger Abrahams, "The Changing Concept of the Negro Hero." *The Golden Log* (PTFS 31). Mody C. Boatright, Wilson M. Hudson, and Allen Maxwell, eds. Dallas: Southern Methodist University Press, 1961. 119–134; James M. Lacy. "Folklore of the South and Racial Discrimination." *A Good Tale and a Bonnie Tune* (PTFS 32). Mody C. Boatright, Wilson M. Hudson, and Allen Maxwell, eds. Dallas: Southern Methodist University Press, 1962. 101–111.

28. Abernethy, Mullen, and Govenar, eds. *Juneteenth Texas.* The authors or titles mentioned in the paragraph follow: Patrick B. Mullen and Alan Govenar, "Preface," vii–xi; Harris, "The Yellow Rose of Texas," 315–332; Dave Oliphant, "From Be-bop to Hardbop and Beyond: The Texas Jazz Connection," 153–164; James Thomas Jackson, "Once Upon a Time in Houston's Fourth Ward," 41–47.
29. Clyde E. Daniels, "Where the Cedars Grove," 49–66.

An original sketch by the author, Charles Chupp

GEOCOCCYX

by Charles Chupp

Through minimum effort on my part I became a provider for a horde of hummingbirds in the season just past. Details of how and why Poverty Sink became a smorgasbord for these tiny avian creatures—and how Chihuahuas worked their magic on me—is of scant interest to you most likely, so the trigger for having me cook off batches of red dyed sugar water will remain shrouded in mystery.

Anyways, there's another thing I have fretted over for years, and the chaparral cock is an amazing quirk that I've not been able to cipher out. It's been an investigation that has been a thorn in my side for lo these many years.

Back in 1983, the *Texas Art Circles* magazine printed an article of mine that you may have missed, so here's a rerun. Should you have any information that might comfort me—I'd welcome your testimony. My old buddy, Buford, gave his deposition to me long ago, but Buford has no reason to tell me the truth.

As I applied the finishing touches to a pen and ink commission of a Geococcyx, it occurred to me that I'd never seen, in all my put-togethers, anything short of an adult of that specie.

"Zounds!" I expostulated to no one in particular.

Inquiring around, I was surprised to discover that nary a one of my friends or acquaintances could testify to ever having beheld a little 'un.

"Now, ain't that remarkable?" I asked my wife. "Young geococcyx are as rare as lawyers in Heaven!"

"Don't bug me!" she instructed. "You've apparently mistaken me for someone who cares."

They are all the same size and color. Their behavioral pattern does not vary a whit from one to the other. Their number is legion, and their presence is epidemic.

"I'll do a family portrait of that lily' ol' terrestrial!" I vowed with solemnity. "I'll show the mama and the papa and their offspring in all their radiant beauty. I will then go to print, thereby garnering a substantial chunk of the art market, merit the plaudits of my fellow artists, and make a nice piece of change to boot!"

My struggle for edification on the subject eventually led my flagging footsteps to the home of my good friend Buford.

Buford was in his front yard. He was busying himself by drilling holes in a railroad cross tie with his brace and bit (one of his hobbies).

He stopped, lit the wrong end of a Winston, and after a few draws, told me an astounding story.

"I've seen many a young Geococcyx in my time," he started, "but not many folks know where and when to find 'em. They hatch from eggs, of course."

"I had that figgered out," I responded as I moved back a little. The smoldering filter was emitting fumes that were hard on my sinuses.

"Welsir," Buford continued, "they all see daylight on the west slope of a tall dune out near Monahans, Texas.

"The mama lays them eggs in the spring when the sand reaches the exact temperature of 85 degrees.

"Naturally, them eggs start rolling down that dune as soon as they're layed, but they roll slow and gentle, thereby maintaining an incubating temperature for that little ol' geo-coccyx.

"It takes that egg 23 days to hatch out, but it's a 30 day roll down that dune.

"When that little bugger hatches out, he's awful dizzy and about the size of a Bic lighter. Since he's still on a slope of hot sand, he hits the ground arunning, and he runs at such a tremendous speed that he's invisible to the human eye until he reaches his full growth.

"Once they get away from that hot sand and their feet toughen up a little, they're full growed, and they begin to slow down and even stop once in a while. And that's when you're able to see 'em.

"They keep doing wind sprints their whole life, though, because like the salmon, they know they're gonna hafta run back out to Monahans in the sweet by and by to perpetuate their own kind."

Buford inhaled the last draw of his filter, dropped the cigarette to the ground, and promptly dropped beside it.

His eyes rolled in concentric circles for an instant, but his breathing returned to normal after a few moments. I thanked him and left.

Buford had no reason to lie to me, but as far as I was able to determine, he had no reason to drill holes in a cross tie.

So, loyal readers, if you really exist, and you have a photograph, or drawing, or even a word description that you will share with me on the young of the omnipresent Geococcyx Californianus, I shorely would be much obliged to hear from you.

Pecos Bill, as depicted in the original 1923 Century Magazine

PECOS BILL AND HIS PEDIGREE

by Charles Clay Doyle

Upon this anniversary of the Texas Folklore Society, like other long-time members, I have been moved to wander back down the lane of memories and tellings, especially ones that relate to my alma mater, The University of Texas. I have newly examined the early volumes of the Publications of the Texas Folklore Society, the earliest of which (edited by Stith Thompson), from 1916, gives the programs for the first five official annual meetings (1911–1915) and a membership list from 1916. The names are impressive and, to me, personally noteworthy. How strange that just two or three "degrees of separation" can link a century ago with the here-and-now!

My father, who died in 1965, had been a student of J. Frank Dobie's; I cherish a yellowed carbon copy of a letter of recommendation that Dobie wrote for him in 1939. In 1947, when I was a small child, Roy Bedichek—Dobie's friend and, evidently, my father's—was a houseguest at my family's home in Weimar, Texas (some ninety-five miles east of Austin; population 1,800); as a gift, he left an inscribed copy of his brand new book, *Adventures with a Texas Naturalist*, which the Society distributed to members as an "extra book" in lieu of a 1947 volume of PTFS.

I myself spent most of the 1960s at The University of Texas (B.A. 1964, Ph.D. 1969). As an undergraduate, I majored in mathematics; the mathematics department was housed in Benedict Hall—and H. Y. Benedict's name appears on the 1916 roster of the Society (as does the name Sidney E. Mezes; Mezes Hall stands adjacent to Benedict Hall). In graduate school my principal folklore mentor was Américo Paredes, and I worked for a year or two as paper-grader and research assistant for the elderly-seeming Wilson M. Hudson (he was about fifty-seven, several years younger than I myself am now. Hudson's hometown was Flatonia, a mere fifteen miles west of Weimar, and even smaller). My literary mentor,

Thomas P. Harrison, venerable and leonine Shakespearean, Spenserian, and Miltonist, did not belong to the Texas Folklore Society, but he once regaled me with an anecdote from his early years of professorhood: He had accompanied John Lomax and the visiting luminary from Harvard, George Lyman Kittredge (who—according to legend, at least—suggested to Lomax and Leonidas Payne the creation of the Society), to a Sunday service at an AME church in Austin. There Kittredge, an aged white man with a nimbus of white hair and a flowing white beard, was perhaps mistaken for Moses, or for God Himself; the congregants beseeched him to come forward and preach the sermon—which he did.[1]

I suppose it's normal, now, as I hurtle toward my own dotage, that I should reminisce a lot about my collegiate and post-graduate times at the University and my childhood years in Weimar. In fact, I think much about childhood in general. So, I took an acute interest recently when one of my little grandsons, who has no connection with Texas (other than genes), mentioned that troublesome Texas icon Pecos Bill. Had he learned about him on television? In a book? From elementary school teachers? Perhaps even from oral tradition on the playground? (My own first acquaintance with Pecos Bill certainly did not derive from oral tradition; I remember, quite particularly, meeting him in the pages of *Boys' Life* magazine.) How durable the character has proved in the imaginative life of American children! Here, then, I undertake, as a patriarchal duty, the following effort to clarify some points about the status and history of Pecos Bill—for the sake of new generations' understanding of old things.

Having meandered down Memory Trail, I now trudge back toward the present—but in the august footsteps, first, of Mody C. Boatright, one of the true giants of the Texas Folklore Society, friend and colleague of J. Frank Dobie, Roy Bedichek, and Wilson Hudson; and, next, of Dobie himself; and, then, of James M. Day, eminent historian of matters Texian and president of the Texas Folklore Society in 1978–1979. Day's article "Pecos Bill: His Genesis and Creators," in PTFS #44 for 1982, remains (remarkably) the most recent extended scholarly study of the subject, which members of the Society had pondered frequently during the preceding decades.[2]

Folklorists have generally come to accept the probability that the larger-than-life exploits of that riproaring cowboy, however prominently they may be featured in children's magazines, children's books, school curricula, journalism, and popular culture at large, have had virtually no existence in the oral traditions of rural Southwesterners—that Edward O'Reilly, cosmopolitan man of letters, invented the character in 1923 for an article in the *Century Magazine.*[3]

Jan Brunvand, in *American Folklore: An Encyclopedia* (1996), has epitomized the consensus of modern folklorists: "the character is clearly fakelore, not genuine folklore."[4] Brunvand continues, "In 1923 Edward O'Reilly published the first known Pecos Bill stories, probably inspired by the logger character Paul Bunyan. . . ." Other reference works easily accessible to a curious public have followed the scholarly line. The latest edition of *Encyclopaedia Britannica* (2002) reports, "Created by journalists, primarily Edward O'Reilly in *Century* magazine, the Pecos Bill character was based on little authentic oral tradition and no historical prototype." Richard Slatta's *The Mythical West: An Encyclopedia of Legend, Lore, and Popular Culture* (2001) states, "Edward O'Reilly, writing in *Century* magazine in 1923, created the figure, and subsequent writers added new tall twists and tales. Unlike some legendary heroes, we find no preexisting historical model or oral tradition about such a figure."[5] The *Penguin Dictionary of American Folklore* (2000) says, "Pecos Bill is a fictitious cowboy hero with superhuman abilities. While Bill resembles the kind of folk hero often created in the oral tradition, he is actually the creation of a journalist, Edward O'Reilly. . . ."[6]

Other reference works, though, are ambivalent on the point, or simply confused. An entry in the latest *World Book Encyclopedia* (1998) begins by calling the character "a cowboy hero in American folklore" but ends, "The legend of Pecos Bill developed from a magazine article written in 1923 by Edward O'Reilly." Of course, it is possible for a character "developed from a magazine article" to enter oral tradition, but likely not the oral tradition of actual cowboys. Avoiding the term "folklore," the latest *Encyclopedia Americana* (2001) calls the character "a cowboy-culture hero of the American Southwest" while noting, "The legend originated in a story by Edward O'Reilly for the *Century Magazine* in 1923." An article in the *Encyclopedia of Folk Heroes* (2001) recklessly begins, "According to nineteenth-century legend, Pecos Bill was weaned on moonshine and dies from drinking nitroglycerin," and concludes with this understatement: "Pecos Bill has been the subject of debate among folklorists, some of whom claim a literary rather than folkloric origin for the character."[7] The *Cassell Dictionary of Folklore* tries to have it both ways, calling Pecos Bill a "folk hero of the American Wild West, famed for his many remarkable feats. Actually a creation of the journalist Edward O'Reilly in the late 19th century [*sic*!], he soon passed into folklore. . . ."[8]

Still other reference works have not gotten the word at all. An unsigned entry in the encyclopedia *Cowboys and the Wild West* (1994) asserts, on the basis of no evidence, "The first Pecos Bill stories were told in the 1870s. . . . The stories were originally oral tales, passed from cowboy to cowboy"; the article does credit O'Reilly with the first *written* version of the tales.[9] The prestigious *Handbook of Texas* begins its entry, "Pecos Bill, a mythical cowboy, grew out of the imagination of southwestern range hands who told tall tales to pass the time and to out-do each other in boasting. His originator is unknown"; the article ends, "Pecos Bill exists in cowboy folklore as a hyperbole of the endurance, enterprise and other qualities required of cowboys"—with no mention of O'Reilly's well-known 1923 publication (a later collection by O'Reilly is listed in a very short appended bibliography).[10]

Among scholars, James Day stands virtually alone in his objection to Richard Dorson's characterization of Pecos Bill's exploits as fakelore and the protagonist himself as a fake hero. In 1941, Dorson enrolled Pecos Bill among the "knavish breed of blustering superheroes" inhabiting a "swashbuckling pantheon" of "comic demigods" presided over by Paul Bunyan.[11] Dorson returned to the subject in 1950, with his famously dyspeptic "Folklore and Fake Lore." That article begins, "In a democratic society the values of folklore rank especially high." However, in mid-century America, folklore had "been falsified, abused and exploited and the public deluded." Dorson anxiously saw an America recently emerged from the Great Depression and the war against Nazism, then in the throes of the Cold War, manufacturing and exploiting "folklore" in insidious ways: "These comic demigods are not products of a native mythology but rather of a chauvinist and fascist conception of folklore. They must be 100 per cent native American supermen, all-conquering, all-powerful, braggart and whimsically destructive. By such distorted folk symbols the Nazis supported their thesis of a Nordic super-race. . . ."[12] In an era of different anxieties, Day's 1982 article endeavored to establish Pecos Bill's "pedigree" not as a demigod at all but simply as a recurring character in the tall-tale telling of real cowboys.

Day drew an important distinction: A demigod, even a comic one, represents a significantly different character type from a tall-tale protagonist. Furthermore, Day clarified the separateness of two other issues: the narratives themselves—that is, what we might call the "tale types" (though most of Pecos Bill's exploits consist of single comic motifs, stylistically embellished to a greater or lesser degree)—and the presence in those narratives of a character specifically named Pecos Bill. Here is how Day approached the "pedigree" question: "To get at Pecos Bill's roots, young though he was, one has to look into his region, the Pecos River country of Texas and New Mexico. And he has to look into the early recorders of the legend: Alonzo Van Oden, Tex O'Reilly, and Mody Boatright."[13]

Boatright took an early interest in Pecos Bill narratives, giving a paper on the subject, "The Genius of Pecos Bill," at the Texas Folklore Society's 1928 meeting; with the same title, a version was published in 1929.[14] In Day's understanding, Boatright validated the folk provenance of the tales. Boatright had grown up in the West Texas ranching culture, and he gathered several Pecos Bill narratives into his slender volume *Tall Tales from Texas* (1934)—though less than a third of the material in that collection concerns Pecos Bill's adventures, which Boatright clustered in the last three chapters: "The Genesis of Pecos Bill," "The Adventures of Pecos Bill," and "The Exodus of Pecos Bill."[15] Day insisted that Boatright's tall tales came from oral sources, maintaining that "Boatright did not rely principally on the O'Reilly account" published in 1923, though Day also remarked, more hesitantly, that Boatright "had either read O'Reilly's account or . . . they used the same oral tradition sources."[16] The definiteness of the first assertion and the tentativeness of the second are both puzzling. Boatright himself acknowledged, in the introduction to his *Tall Tales from Texas*, "my chief indebtedness is to Mr. Edward O'Reilly's 'Saga of Pecos Bill,' published in the *Century Magazine* for October, 1923." Earlier in the same introduction, Boatright (who was now quoting from his 1929 article) minimized the role of Pecos Bill in the narratives told by cowboys: "Nor did cowboy fiction ever become unified around a single character. When a hero was needed, his name might be invented on the spot; the feats of daring might be ascribed to some local character; or the narrator himself might appropriate the honors. Certain names, however, were in rather general use, California Joe and Texas Jack being among the most common."[17]

No mention of Pecos Bill. When he did turn to Pecos Bill, Boatright noted, "This latter hero is apparently a late development, for few of the old-time cowmen have heard of him." Even within the narrative "frame" of the chapter titled "The Genesis of Pecos Bill," when the character Joe remarks, "Why, if Pecos Bill had a-done a thing like that, he would of been so ashamed of his self, he would of jest naturally laid down and died," the cowboy Lanky must inquire, "Who is this Pecos Bill I've heard you mention?"[18] Boatright may have regarded Pecos Bill as an emerging figure who might eventually seep into the lore of cowmen, but he hardly testified to the prevalence of the character in oral tradition. In 1949, he was more explicit: Pecos Bill, "put in print by Edward O'Reilly in 1923, though not generally accepted by actual cowboys, has become to outsiders the hero of the cattle country."[19]

The scarcity of Pecos Bill in cowboy lore has been further attested. Frank Shay, a very early compiler of Pecos Bill tales, hypothesized in 1930, "The viridity of the Bunyan legends has so choked out the other heroes that to-day not one in a hundred old-time cowboys ever heard of Pecos Bill; yet the lowliest buckaroo in the cow country knows of Paul. . . ."[20] Certainly the hypothesis is incorrect, although the circumstance that it sought to explain—the dearth of Pecos Bill lore—was real enough.

N. Howard "Jack" Thorp (1867–1940), a lifelong cowboy who in *Pardner of the Wind* (1941) chronicled life on the range and the tales told there, declared, "Cowboys never developed a mythical range rider on the order of Paul Bunyan of the lumber camp, but some of their tales were as tall as the mountains in whose shadows they worked cattle."[21]

The historian, social commentator, and fiction writer Brent Ashabranner stated in 1952:

> I have during the past five years examined scores of memoirs written or related to writers by old-time cowboys and cattlemen—the number who have recorded their range experiences is rather amazing—and I have found in them no mention of or allusion to a character called Pecos Bill. This is the case despite the fact that seldom did these men write the stories of their lives on the range without devoting considerable space to the hilarious tall tales told around the campfires.[22]

Marshall Fishwick, one of the deans of "popular culture" as a discipline, revealed in 1959:

> In 1951 Dr. [Ernest] Baughman made a survey of the "Pecos Bill Country" in the Estancia Valley, to determine whether any oral stories about Pecos were in circulation. The results were entirely negative. None of the ranchers, including those who

> had lived there for half a century, had heard of Pecos Bill. Another indication of the lack of a folk tradition is that the Writer's Project, while doing a detailed study of Texas during the Depression for the WPA, did not confront a single Pecos story.[23]

In 1998, writing in *The Dallas Morning News*, Bryan Woolley reported:

> Those who popularized the tales claimed Bill was an authentic folk hero invented by cowboys swapping yarns around their campfires. But Paul Patterson, an eighty-nine-year-old cowboy, teacher and poet who has lived along the [Pecos] river most of his life, doesn't think so.
>
> "Cowboys never thought much of Pecos Bill, because he could do anything without putting a strain on himself," he says. "That doesn't ring true with people of this country. You can't do anything here without straining yourself. Pecos Bill was a fabrication. Some writer made him up."[24]

Even Edward O'Reilly himself—who, according to Day, "first took Pecos Bill out of the oral tradition and put him in print"—finally had to unmask. J. Frank Dobie said of the character in 1955, "his name was unknown until Tex O'Reilly, a newspaperman, put him into the *Century* magazine (October, 1923), claiming him as a folk character. Later, when somebody else wrote a book about him, O'Reilly sued for money on the grounds of plagiarism, claiming that he had invented Pecos Bill. He had."[25]

Day emphasized O'Reilly's affinity for tall tales, noting that he belonged to the "famed Liar's Club" of his friend Lowell Thomas, who wrote the as-told-to memoir *Born to Raise Hell: The Life Story of Tex O'Reilly, Soldier of Fortune* (1936). In Day's opinion, that account (unlike O'Reilly's 1918 memoir *Roving and Fighting*) traffics heavily in hyperbole, if not outright prevarication. Perhaps it is significant that when the tall memoir was published serially in 1933, the first installment appeared on April 1![26]

Day's comments suggest to me to a sort of hypothesis: In his famous 1923 article in the *Century Magazine*, O'Reilly not only narrated (very briefly) a long series of tall tales, bestowing the name Pecos Bill on their protagonists, but he also framed those narratives with a tall tale of his own, about how he discovered or encountered the legends and the character. (In contrast, no irony frames James C. Bowman's 296-page collection from 1937, *Pecos Bill: The Greatest Cowboy of All Time*; its introduction bluntly and wrongly begins, "This is a volume of genuine American folklore.")[27]

O'Reilly's publication starts with a mention of Paul Bunyon [*sic*]; Pecos Bill, "born about the time Sam Houston discovered Texas," is introduced as Paul's blood brother: "they were both fathered by a liar." Is not that a sneaky admission? After all, Pecos Bill was in the very process of being fathered by a liar, O'Reilly himself, who would (naturally enough) claim the prerogative of naming his son. The progenitor proceeds, then, in the deadpan manner of a deft tall-tale teller, to relate both some "facts" about the character—whose "mighty deeds have been sung for generations by the men of the range"—and information about how the writer himself "during my boyhood days in west Texas" first heard Bill's "history told around the chuck-wagon by gravely mendacious cow-boys." If a gullible "stranger in cattle-land," hearing the tales, "shows an incautious curiosity," the raconteur will hold out some verbal bait, whereupon "the visitor walks into the trap"; then "he is sure to receive an assortment of misinformation that every cow-hand delights in unloading on the unwary." The tales themselves "will doubtless be familiar to cow-men, but deserve to be passed on to the larger audience,"[28] an audience which now, in fact, does comprise visiting tenderfoots and greenhorns—the unwary readers of the *Century Magazine*, Easterners and urbanites, including journalists and scholars and makers of books for children—who believe what O'Reilly tells them about the "folk" provenance of Pecos Bill!

Toward the end of his career, Richard Dorson, the great debunker of fakelore, remarked in passing, "Pecos Bill in 1923 came thundering out of a satirical piece in Century Magazine. . . ."[29] The characterization of O'Reilly's "Saga of Pecos Bill" as "a satirical piece" bears pondering. What exactly is being satirized? Among possible answers that one might pursue: He was satirizing (1) "Western" novels and short stories (as Jonathan Swift satirized the genre of travel narratives in that tallest of travel tales, *Gulliver's Travels*); (2) America's inordinate fascination with the "Wild West" of its past; (3) the gullibility of readers, who are eager to credit even a grotesquely distorted version of life in the West. O'Reilly's saga of Pecos Bill ends like this: "They say that he met a man from Boston one day, wearing a mail-order cow-boy outfit, and askin' fool questions about the West; and poor old Bill laid down and laughed himself to death."

Granted that some of the narratives of Pecos Bill may have had sources (some definitely had analogs) in oral tradition when O'Reilly wrote them and christened their protagonists with a single name, but what can be said about the name itself, its pedigree? Day quoted at some length from the diary of Alonzo Van Oden, a Texas Ranger, apparently from the early 1890s (the entries are undated). Oden encountered one Pecos Joe, "who started a lecture on stars and the heavens, and finally got around to religion."[30] Day called Joe "an ethereal character"—hardly resembling the boisterous Bill, except for the epithet "Pecos."

The epithet was not uncommon. A decade earlier, Robert Olinger, a federal marshal assigned to guard the outlaw William Bonney, incarcerated in the Lincoln County jail in New Mexico, was murdered by Bonney—a.k.a. "Billy the Kid." The marshal, apparently an unsavory gunman himself, sometimes went by the nickname Pecos Bob.[31] A short story from 1899, by the popular writer (of the time) Morgan Robertson, tells of three cowboys, "dark-faced, long-haired fellows with big hats," who have been kidnapped while drunk and impressed as crew members aboard a clipper ship commanded by a sadistic brute of a captain. When the cowboys awaken to their situation, they successfully mutiny.[32]

Crack marksmen all, they bore the names Laramie, 'Pache, and (the leader, a Texan) Pecos Tom. In 1920 the cowboy poet Jack Thorp (aforementioned author of *Pardner of the Wind*) published a poem "Pecos Tom" in the prestigious *Poetry* magazine.[33] Consisting of 24 lines, the poem opens like this:

> Where the old Fort Sumner Barracks look down on the
>   Pecos wide,
> In a dug-out near the crossin' we was a-sittin' side by side.
> Old Pecos Tom, the cow-man, en your humble servant
>   me,
> Was a-swappin' cow-camp stories in the fall of Eighty-
>   three.

Espying a lavishly expensive pistol on Tom, the persona inquires about it. Most of the poem is Pecos Tom's narration of his purchase of the item from "the Jew clerk" in a Chicago jewelry store. On the basis of Tom's apparel, worn and dusty from the northward cattle drive, the clerk doubts his ability to afford the gun, priced at $15,000. Indignant, Tom "grabbed him by the ear,/En he peeled off fifteen thousand to the Hebrew standing there,/Sayin', 'Don't judge western cow-men by the outfits that they wear!'"[34] That is the conclusion.

In 1913, a character named Pecos Pete appeared in an early one-reel silent film, *Pecos Pete in Search of a Wife*, a comedy about a New Mexico cowboy's multiple courtships before he finally gets snagged by a proper widow and reluctantly settles down on her sheep ranch. Curiously, Carl Sandburg in his long poem *The People, Yes* (1936) erroneously referred to our Pecos Bill as "Pecos Pete." Section 45 of the poem begins, "They have yarns"; then, notwithstanding Sandburg's keen ear and studious interest in the popular creations that "they" ("the People") cherish, he epitomized one of those yarns as "Pecos Pete straddling a cyclone in Texas and riding it to the west coast where 'it rained out under him.'"[35] In 1999, the literary historian and critic Emory Elliott wrote of Mark Twain, "He also knew well the popular writing of the American South and

West which had already introduced rustic characters and vernacular speech into American literature through the legends and stories of Daniel Boone, Davy Crockett, and Pecos Pete, among others."[36] The parallelism there is curious: Two historical figures—Boone, who died in 1820, and Crockett, who died in 1836—and then Pecos "Pete." Mark Twain himself died in 1910, thirteen years before Pecos Bill was "introduced"!

Ranger Oden, whom Day's article featured, actually met a Pecos Bill, so called—a purported murderer, William D. Barbee: "'Funny about this Pecos Bill,' the young lawman mused, 'so different from Pecos Joe—yet they are about the same age. . . . At that time he was well liked, and considered even tempered, honest, and fine. We arrested him for killing Albert Von Kleeser at Ozona, and we had word today that he is also accused of murdering a man by the name of Staggs.'"[37]

There were other Pecos Bills prior to Edward O'Reilly's 1923 article. In 1893, Alvin Sydenham published a narrative titled "The Lost Pine Mine" (perhaps fictional in part or in whole) of a young physician, the narrator, newly come to Arizona from the East, who is called to testify in a trial of two "White" men who turned themselves in to the sheriff for shooting a Mexican in the back. One of the defendants is named Pecos Bill. Despite the expert testimony of the greenhorn doctor, the jury renders a verdict of "not guilty":

> Pecos Bill celebrated his release from custody by leading the crowd, judge, bar, and jury, over to the licensed liquor-house presided over by one Honest Organ, a retired Methodist minister, noted as being the greatest single-handed liar in the Territory,—and there we irrigated. After many assurances that my mistakes had been misinterpreted, and that there was no ill will, I was permitted to mount and set out for camp.[38]

Tall-tale features abound in the narrative.

A 1903 story by Rothwell Brown, titled "Maria of the Maverick," begins, "Pecos Bill lay on the floor cursing a broken arm. Downstairs in the dance hall musicians were twanging their fiddles."[39] Bill is wanted for murder; the narrator does not deny his guilt. Maria, dark and lovely, works as a typesetter for a San Antonio newspaper (the *Maverick*), whereby she gains advance information concerning the intentions of the posse. She tricks them into seeking Bill at a nearby ranch. As the posse gallops down the wrong road, Maria and Pecos Bill mount up and head for Mexico—Maria brandishing the crippled Bill's gun in his defense.

Pecos Bill as "badman" is not an aspect of our character that has figured prominently in the books for children. However, O'Reilly unflinchingly included it:

> It wasn't long until he was famous as a bad man. He invented the six-shooter and train-robbin' and most of the crimes popular in the days of the West. . . .
>
> There is no way of tellin' just how many men Bill did kill. Deep down he had a tender heart, however, and never killed women or children, or tourists out of season. He never scalped his victims; he was too civilized for that. He used to skin them gently and tan their hides.
>
> . . . One day he met an old trapper and told him what he was lookin' for. "I want the hardest cow outfit in the world," he says. "Not one of these ordinary cow-stealin', Mexican-shootin' bunches of amateurs, but a real hard herd of hand-picked hellions that make murder a fine art and take some proper pride in their slaughter."[40]

In fact, the epithet "Pecos" itself might have suggested murderousness or other sorts of criminality. Some evidence exists from the decade in which O'Reilly published "The Saga of Pecos Bill" (1923)—if not earlier—that *pecos* could even be used as a verb. Dobie reported in 1929:

> If in the old days a man said of another, "He is a cowboy of the Pecos," that might mean many things. It might mean that this cowboy was unusually efficient in handling cattle or in riding horses. It might mean that he was a rustler. It might mean that he ran the risk of being "pecosed" either for his integrity or the lack of it; on the other hand, it might mean that he had helped to "pecos" some other rider of the range. To "pecos" a man one shot him and rolled his body into the river.[41]

"A real hard herd of hand-picked hellions"

Pecos Bill looking for a tough bunch

Other writings about the Old West, including glossaries of "western" or "cowboy" speech, record that sense of *pecos*; however, the authors may have derived their information from Dobie's notation (or from each other). Ramon Adams, in *Cowboy Lingo* (1936), noted that "to 'pecos' one meant to kill him and roll his body into the river."[42] Jack Thorp, in *Pardner of the Wind* (1941), elaborated slightly: "The very name of the river came to stand for murder, for when the freebooters of the valley killed a man, they were said to have 'Pecos'd' him, meaning, tied stones to his dead body and rolled it into the river."[43] And not necessarily even the Pecos river: in Dobie's *Coronado's Children* (1931), "they 'pecosed' him in the Rio Bravo." Somewhat at variance with that usage—and altering the specified manner of death—Dobie's appended glossary defines the verb *pecos*: "to throw into the Pecos River; hence, to kill by drowning."[44] A little later, the term "pecos swap" is also reported (as both a noun and a verb), meaning "a trade made without consent or knowledge of the other interested party, to steal."[45] In short, the Pecos River and its environs became a sort of metonymy for the "Wild West" itself—for its wildness—and some of the associations would have carried over to the use of "Pecos" as a personal epithet or nickname.

The most famous Pecos Bill of all—not counting our rider of cyclones and mountain lions—deserves special notice: William R. Shafter, soldier, medal-of-honor winner for his service in the Union army during the Civil War.[46] After the war he commanded forces in various parts of the West. The *Washington Post* on October 10, 1902, explained "How Shafter Won Nickname" (as the headline reads):

> "I'll tell you how I came to receive that designation," said Gen. Shafter to a group of friends last night, after having been addressed as "Pecos Bill." "It was out in that arid part of the Southwest country where water is a real luxury. We had been traveling for several days without water, and finally a captain of one of our companies, with tears in his eyes, said:
>
> "'Colonel, we are lost,' and begged that we turn back. 'We'll go straight ahead,' I replied. 'The

> Pecos River lies over there somewhere, and I intend going on until we meet it, if we have to circumnavigate the globe to do it.'
>
> "We reached the river that night. The water was muddy, but it was water. We simply had to go ahead; if we had turned back, we'd have starved to death."[47]

In that famous Llano Estacado campaign of 1875, most of Shafter's troops were Black cavalrymen—the (now) acclaimed "Buffalo soldiers"—along with "Seminole-Negro Indian" scouts; Shafter developed a great respect for the skill, stamina, and bravery of those often-marginalized military men. In 1898, when the United States declared war on Spain and prepared to invade Cuba, President McKinley appointed Shafter (now a major general) as commander of the armed forces, prominent among them being troops of Black cavalry and infantry. It was Shafter who accepted the Spanish surrender at Santiago de Cuba on July 17, 1898. Here is how a popular monthly magazine in that same month characterized him:

> He has an amiable, well-rounded front and weighs over three hundred pounds. He has risen from the ranks and one cannot help thinking he must have strained the ladder at every step. His hair and mustache are gray, his face is forceful and determined. . . . Long ago he was a popular hero in Texas, where to this day the people refer to him as Pecos Bill—and in that country they never lengthen their love of a man until they have shortened his name. He is a friend of the common soldier. In speech he is direct and forcible. With him, a spade is a spade and a fool is a fool. Size, good humor, a thorough knowledge of his business and a ready tongue are the chief elements of his magnetism.[48]

There was even a ballad called "Ol' Pecos Bill"; in 1898, it appeared anonymously in a floridly titled anthology *War-Time Echoes: Patriotic Poems, Heroic and Pathetic, Humorous and Dialectic, of the Spanish-American War*, where it is said to be reprinted from the *Denver Post*. The forty-line poem begins:

> Don't hardly reckon there ever was a tougher ol' soldier
> pill,
> In any way that you'd size him up, than that same ol'
> Pecos Bill,
> Fur to handle the reds when they showed their teeth, an'
> the whites that laughed at the law.
> A great big man with a great big heart, an' the proper
> sand in his craw.[49]

Although the designation "Indian fighter" would be accurate enough, the poem incorrectly attributes to Shafter the role of lawman purging the region of desperados: "When ol' Bill come to the Texas land the Pecos war' overrun/With the toughest outfit o' desperate men that ever handled a gun." Much of the poem is devoted to Shafter's disdain for "church going" and pious hypocrisy: "he never worried the Lord, I know, by recitin' a chestnut prayer/That died afore it war' half way up on the trail through the Texas air."[50] Here is the ending of the ballad:

> I allus said if a war 'd come an' they'd give the ol' man a
> chance,
> He'd lead the foes o' the Glory flag the liveliest sort of a
> dance,
> An' when I war' readin' the other day of his work on the
> Cuby shore,
> I ripped a streak in the Texas air with a firmament-shakin'
> roar!
> I danced the Apache victory dance, an' whooped like a
> painted brave,

At the way his Texican cowboy lads fixed Spaniards in
shape fur the grave.
An' I filled my system cl'ar to the neck with the snappiest
sort o' swill,
In visible honor o' Uncle Sam an' his pardner, ol' Pecos
Bill.[51]

Now, Edward O'Reilly, in his told-to-Lowell-Thomas memoir *Born to Raise Hell* as well as in his earlier memoir *Roving and Fighting*, said he had served in the Spanish-American War, specifically, in the invasion of Cuba with Company B of the Fourth Infantry, having volunteered at age seventeen—that he participated in the famous charge on El Caney and himself took a young Spanish soldier prisoner. Even if he exaggerated his own involvement—even if he was simply lying (he claimed that he had lied about his age in order to enlist)—still, he showed a fairly detailed knowledge of the war on the Cuban front. Certainly he knew who the commander was, and he could hardly *not* have known the commander was called Pecos Bill.[52]

There's more: In 1921—two years before the *Century Magazine* article gave birth to the "legends" of Pecos Bill—O'Reilly had been involved in the making of two silent western movies. He wrote the story for *On the High Card*, and he played the part of a lawman, Hank Saunders; the antagonist is known as Pecos Bill. O'Reilly also wrote the story for *West of the Rio Grande*, in which he played the role of a villain named Sinto—who goes by the alias Pecos Bill. In a celluloid sense, then, Tex O'Reilly *was* Pecos Bill!

Neither O'Reilly himself, therefore, nor the American public in 1923 was unfamiliar with the name Pecos Bill. It was available for O'Reilly to attach to his own begotten tall-tale protagonist. Obviously, the choice of the nearly-alliterating name proved highly satisfactory for the purpose, complementing the unmistakable appeal of the narratives themselves for generations of readers. If Pecos Bill as named protagonist has played little role in the folklore of cowboys, he remains a vivid presence in American culture at large.

The author, Charles Doyle, and his grandson Clay

Since the commencement of this genealogical investigation, I have ascertained that my grandson, Clay Doyle—age seven, of Marietta, Georgia, who is named for me and (more specifically) for my father—had his aforementioned encounter with Pecos Bill at a puppet theater production to which his mother's mother had taken him in Atlanta. So the tall tales survive, performed in diverse genres and media, far beyond the parched plains and dusty trails of the Southwest; such is the nature of "tradition." And Texas itself has moved into the modern, post-industrial world—perhaps ahead of the rest of the nation in acknowledging, in cherishing its multiplicity of traditions and rich variety of ethnic and occupational groups. Such is the case with the Texas Folklore Society, at least, as it has responded to the changing realities of the state; witness, for example, the plurality celebrated and examined in the 1974 volume of PTFS (number 38), *The Folklore of Texan Cultures.*[53] From the times of John Lomax, J. Frank Dobie, Roy Bedichek, Mody Boatright, and Wilson Hudson, the society lives on.

Endnotes

1. John Lomax gave an account of that "adventure" (with slightly different details, naturally) in his autobiography, *Adventures of a Ballad Hunter*. New York: Macmillan, 1947. 236–38. The incident is not included in the collection of "Kittredge" anecdotes presented by Duncan Emrich in *Folklore on the American Land*. Boston: Little, Brown, 1972. 322–26.
2. James M. Day. "Pecos Bill: His Genesis and Creators. *T for Texas: A State Full of Folklore* (PTFS 44). Frances Edward Abernethy, ed. Dallas: E-Heart Press, 1982. 135–47.
3. Edward O'Reilly. "The Saga of Pecos Bill." *Century Magazine* 106: (1923). 827–33.
4. Jan Harold Brunvand. "Pecos Bill." *American Folklore: An Encyclopedia*. Brunvand, ed. New York: Garland, 1996. 546–47.
5. Richard W. Slatta. *The Mythical West: An Encyclopedia of Legend, Lore, and Popular Culture*. Santa Barbara, CA: ABC-CLIO, 2001. 262. The article is unsigned.
6. Alan Axelrod and Harry Oster. *Penguin Dictionary of American Folklore*. New York: Penguin, 2000. 371. The article is unsigned.
7. Graham Seal. *Encyclopedia of Folk Heroes*. Santa Barbara, CA: ABC-CLIO, 2001. 201. The article is unsigned.
8. David Pickering. *Cassell Dictionary of Folklore*. London: Cassell, 1999. 227.
9. Don Cusic. *Cowboys and the Wild West: An A–Z Guide*. New York: Facts on File, 1994. 221. The article is unsigned.
10. *Handbook of Texas Online*. s.v. "Pecos Bill." http://www.tsha.utexas.edu/handbook/online/articles/PP/lxpl.html (accessed August 15, 2008). The article is unsigned. I do not believe any such book as the one cited there exists—"Edward Synnott O'Reilly, *Pecos Bill*. New York: Ridgway, 1935." The intended reference may be to a series of Pecos Bill tales that O'Reilly presented in *Adventure* magazine (published by Ridgway) during January and February of 1935: vol. 90, no. 5, 54–59; vol. 90, no. 6, 35–39; vol. 91, no. 1, 68–72; vol. 91, no. 2, 84–93.
11. Richard Dorson. "America's Comic Demigods." *American Scholar* 10 (1941): 389–401.
12. Dorson. "Folklore and Fake Lore." *American Mercury* 70 (1950): 335–43.
13. Day. 138.
14. Mody C. Boatright. "The Genius of Pecos Bill." *Southwest Review* 14: (1929): 419–28.
15. Boatright. *Tall Tales from Texas*. Dallas: Southwest Press, 1934. 68–99.
16. Day. 142–43.
17. Boatright. *Tall Tales*. xxiv and xxii.
18. Ibid. 70.

19. Boatright. "The Art of Tall Lying." *Southwest Review* 36 (1949): 362–63.
20. Frank Shay. *Here's Audacity: American Legendary Heroes.* New York: Macaulay, 1930. 11.
21. N. Howard Thorp (in collaboration with Neil M. Clark). *Pardner of the Wind.* 1941. Lincoln: University of Nebraska Press, 1977. 196.
22. Brent Ashabranner. "Pecos Bill—An Appraisal." *Western Folklore* 11 (1952): 21.
23. Marshall W. Fishwick. "Sons of Paul: Folklore or Fakelore?" *Western Folklore* 18 (1959): 279.
24. Bryan Woolley. "A Legend Runs Through It." (*The Dallas Morning News* June 28, 1998) *Features and Fillers: Texas Journalists on Texas Folklore* (PTFS 56). Jim Harris, ed. Denton: University of North Texas Press, 1999. 21.
25. J. Frank Dobie. *Tales of Old-Time Texas.* Boston: Little Brown, 1955. x. I simply cannot discover details of the law case that Dobie referred to. However, one bit of information may be relevant. Chroniclers of Pecos Bill's career in print have failed to note that in the late 1930s the versatile O'Reilly wrote a short-lived comic strip, illustrated by Jack Alonzo Warren. I will quote from an (unsigned) article "Jack A. Warren" in the online *Lambiek Comiclopedia*, said to be based on facts supplied by Warren's grandson: "Eventually, Jack and his old friend Tex O'Reiley [*sic*] created the 'Pecos Bill' strip for *The Sun.* The strip rose quickly to pre-World War II fame and earned Jack a career as a western-genre illustrator and cartoonist, cooperating on the strip with O'Reiley. When O'Reiley died in 1938 [*sic*], Warren created 'Pecos Pete' which ran for two years. This was during a squabble of the rights to 'Pecos Bill.' It was the same character only he had received a lump on the noggin', and forgot who he was (amnesia)." http://lambiek.net/artists/w/warren_jack.htm (accessed August 15, 2008). O'Reilly actually died in 1946. I am unable to corroborate the detail about the "squabble" over the name Pecos Bill. Could it have led to the law suit that Dobie mentioned?
26. Tex O'Reilly (as told to Lowell Thomas). "Born to Raise Hell." 11 weekly installments in *Liberty Magazine*, April-June 1933. Published in book form: *Born to Raise Hell: The Life Story of Tex O'Reilly, Soldier of Fortune.* Garden City, NY: Doubleday, Doran, 1936.
27. James Cloyd Bowman. *Pecos Bill: The Greatest Cowboy of All Time.* Chicago: Albert Whitman, 1937. The introduction is not paginated.
28. O'Reilly. "The Saga of Pecos Bill." 827.
29. Dorson. "Folklore vs. Fakelore—Again and Again." *Folklore Forum* 7 (1974). 60.
30. Ann Jensen, ed. *Texas Ranger's Diary & Scrapbook.* Dallas: Kaleidograph Press, 1936. 26–27.

31. Mitchel P. Roth. *Historical Dictionary of Law Enforcement.* Westport CT: Greenwood, 2001. 248.
32. Morgan Robertson. "When Greek Meets Greek." *"Where Angels Fear to Tread" and Other Tales of the Sea.* New Work: McKinlay, Stone & Mackenzie, 1899. 213–23.
33. Thorp. "Pecos Tom." *Poetry: A Magazine of Verse* 16 (1920): 240–42.
34. Ibid.
35. Carl Sandburg. *The People, Yes.* New York: Harcourt, Brace, 1936. 88. For the record, here is a "source" note on Sandburg's quotation, "it rained out under him." At the time Sandburg wrote his poem, four collections of Pecos Bill stories contained the cyclone-riding episode (it does not appear in Boatright's 1929 article—in which Bill rides a streak of lightning, though). The wording is quite different in Owen J. Remington's "The Legends of Pecos Bill." *Plain Talk* 4 (1929): 281: "That tornado was getting some tuckered by that time, so it pulled a mean trick. It just turned itself into rain and went right out from under Bill." The other three accounts include the same memorable phrasing—which Sandburg misquoted or slightly altered for effect, omitting *from.* O'Reilly's 1923 article says of the cyclone, "When it saw it couldn't throw him it rained out from under him. . . . Bill came down over in California" (831). Frank Shay's *Here's Audacity* (1930) says, "He rode it through three states but over Californy it got him. [¶] When it saw it couldn't throw him, it rained out from under him" (152). In Boatright's *Tall Tales* (1934), "Seeing it couldn't throw him, it jist naturally rained out from under him" (86). There, however, the alighting occurs in the Texas Panhandle, not California. So, we may conclude that Sandburg had been reading about Pecos Bill in either O'Reilly's original version or in Shay's adaptation.
36. Emory Elliott. Introduction to *The Adventures of Huckleberry Finn,* by Mark Twain. Oxford UK: Oxford University Press, 1999. xiv.
37. Jensen, ed. *Texas Ranger's Diary.* 36.
38. Lt. Alvin H. Sydenham. "The Lost Pine Mine." *United Service: A Quarterly Review of Military and Naval Affairs* 10, no.1 (July 1893): 53–59.
39. Rothwell Brown. "Maria of the Maverick." *Washington Post* (January 4, 1903): 35.
40. O'Reilly. "The Saga of Pecos Bill." 829.
41. Dobie. *Vaquero of the Brush Country.* Dallas: Southwest Press, 1929. 277.
42. Ramon F. Adams. *Cowboy Lingo.* 1936. Boston: Houghton Mifflin, 2000. 167.
43. Thorp. *Pardner of the Wind.* 170.
44. Dobie. *Coronado's Children: Tales of Lost Mines and Buried Treasures of the Southwest.* Dallas: Southwest Press, 1930. 163 and 365.
45. Ramon F. Adams. *Western Words: A Dictionary of the Range, Cow Camp, and Trail.* Norman OK: University of Oklahoma Press, 1945. 113.

46. In fact, a modern scholarly book by Paul H. Carlson bears the title *"Pecos Bill": A Military Biography of William R. Shafter*. College Station TX: Texas A&M University Press, 1989. Carlson has included extensive information about Shafter's life and military activities—but he does not cite the documents from which I shall be quoting here (except the article authored by Shafter).
47. "How Shafter Won Nickname: Refused to Turn Back When [*sic*] He Reached Pecos River." *Washington Post* (October 10, 1902): 13. When he finally *reached* the river, there would no longer have existed the temptation to turn back!
48. Irving Bacheller. "With the Waiting Army." *The Cosmopolitan* 25 (July 1898): 320. Shafter gave his own account of the Cuba campaign, "Capture of Santiago," which appeared (where else?) in the *Century Magazine* 57 (1899): 612–25. There he relates the following little story, which I include here simply because it's interesting and I haven't seen it given anywhere else; it shows Shafter's affection for and admiration of his Black soldiers: "The untiring qualities of Lawton's men were illustrated by an incident told by a correspondent, who, as they were coming in, observed a corporal of the Twenty-fifth Colored Regiment carrying one of the pets of the company, a little dog, in his arms. He said, 'Corporal, did n't you march all night before last?' 'Yes, sah.' 'Didn't you fight all day yesterday at El Caney?' ''Deed, I did.' 'Didn't you march all last night?' 'Yes, sah.' 'Then why are you carrying that dog?' 'Why, boss, the dog's tired'" (623). In the *Atlanta Constitution* (October 29, 1898): 4, amid a series of one-sentence, unconnected editorial comments (some of them clearly intended to be witty quips), this statement appears: "When Miles and Shafter shook hands there was the bridging of another bloody chasm, into which Pecos Bill was in danger of falling" (General Nelson Miles was an old friend and colleague of Shafter's, but the two were occasionally at odds during the war; I do not understand the "point" of the quip—other than a possible reference to Shafter's corpulence.)
49. James Henry Brownlee, ed. *War-Time Echoes: Patriotic Poems, Heroic and Pathetic, Humorous and Dialectic, of the Spanish-American War*. Akron OH: Werner, 1898. 104–6.
50. Ibid.
51. Ibid.
52. "At daybreak the next morning we marched to the village of Siboney. . . . General Shafter, commanding the expedition, made his headquarters in the village"; Major S. O'Reilly. *Roving and Fighting: Adventures under Four Flags*. London: T. Werner Laurie, 1918. 22. The memoirs do not specifically refer to General Shafter by his famous nickname.
53. *The Folklore of Texan Cultures* (PTFS 38). Frances Edward Abernethy, ed. Austin: Encino Press, 1974.

The Dannel Funeral Home, Sherman, Texas, circa 1950s

FUNERALS AND FOLKLORE: A SNAPSHOT FROM 1909

by Jerry B. Lincecum

Funeral customs and burial rites have been important issues in the lives of the folk at least as far back as the Neanderthals, and thus are frequent topics in history, anthropology, and folklore. A cursory review of the titles of papers presented at annual meetings of the Texas Folklore Society over the past hundred years shows that on occasion aspects of these topics were addressed in relation to folksongs about death ("Tone the Bell Easy," by Martha Emmons in 1932), burial traditions ("Grave Decoration" by Dorothy Jean Michael in 1943), and West Texas funeral homes "Funeral Homes in Small West Texas Towns in the Early Part of the Century" by Mildred Sentell in 1999). In addition, the annual volume for 2008, on the theme of "death lore," has an insightful essay on the funeral business by A. C. Sanders.

Over the past one hundred years, the rise of modern funeral homes and the larger role played by funeral directors have led to dramatic changes in the way most Texans relate to funerals and burials. Since this topic is too broad for a brief essay, I will focus on the funerals directed by one funeral home in Sherman, Texas, in 1909, the year the Texas Folklore Society began. In this way I can remind present-day readers of what the funeral business was like one hundred years ago, when the Texas Folklore Society had its beginning.

In 1908, The Sherman Undertaking Company had a new owner. John Carlton Dannel and his wife of one year, Flossie Wade Dannel, stepped off the train in Denison, Texas, eager to establish themselves and their business in Sherman. They had come from Illinois on the advice of the Shields family, long-time friends who operated the Short and Shields Undertaking Company in Denison, Texas.

The appeal of Sherman to a young couple looking to start a new business in 1908 is not surprising. When Grayson County was created by the Texas legislature in 1846, Sherman was named the county seat, and by 1900 it had grown into one of the premier towns of North Texas, with a population of over 10,000. It had been marketed as "Queen of the Prairies" and the "Athens of Texas," with the latter slogan boasting the presence of several distinguished educational institutions, including Austin College, Kidd-Key Conservatory, and Carr-Burdette College. As compared to other towns in North Texas, Sherman offered a promise of some cultural attractions, along with growth in population.

John C. Dannel came into the funeral business in typical fashion. His father, Charles Oliver Dannel, was a farmer who also owned and operated a furniture store and undertaking parlor in Greenfield, Illinois. The son, who was born near Kemper, Illinois, decided to follow in his father's footsteps by pursuing a career in the funeral business. In 1906, John graduated from the Barnes School of Anatomy, Sanitary Science and Embalming in Chicago, and the following year he married Flossie Wade. One hundred years after John and Flossie arrived in Sherman and started their undertaking business, Dannel Funeral Home remains one of Sherman's four oldest continuously operating businesses, and is one of only two still owned and operated by the original families.

When he directed his first funeral in Sherman on August 6, 1908, Mr. Dannel made the first entries in a large ledger, containing 300 pages, each with the heading "Record and Bill of Items for the Funeral of" printed at the top, followed by a blank line for the person's name to be written on. Almost half of the page was to be completed with detailed demographic information. On the lower half of the page was space to indicate the "bill of items" supplied for this particular funeral, such as coffin, candles, and gloves followed by another section with space and lines on which to enter debits and credits for the account. In addition, to facilitate the making of an alphabetized index, the record book had a series of blank, ruled pages at the front, with letters of the alphabet thumb-printed at the edge.

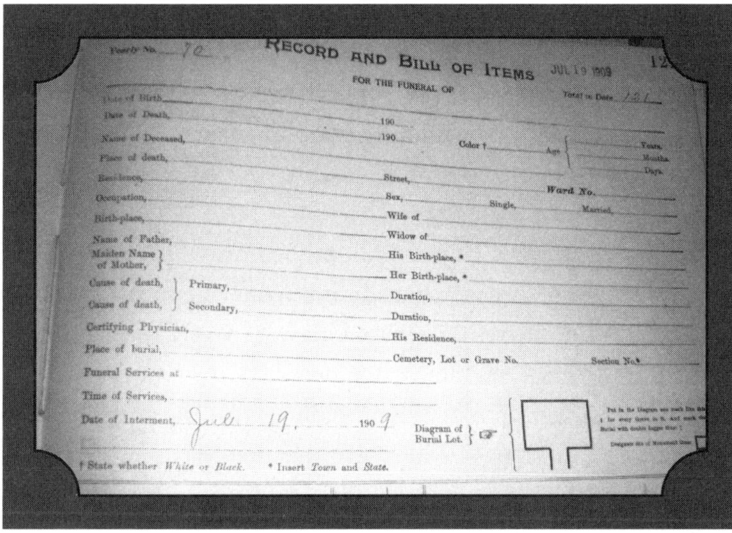

Yearly No. 70 RECORD AND BILL OF ITEMS JUL 19 1909 12
FOR THE FUNERAL OF
Total to Date 121
Date of Birth,
Date of Death, 190
Name of Deceased, 190 Color † Age Years, Months, Days.
Place of death,
Residence, Street, Ward No.
Occupation, Sex, Single, Married,
Birth-place, Wife of
Name of Father, Widow of
Maiden Name of Mother, His Birth-place, *
Her Birth-place, *
Cause of death, Primary, Duration,
Cause of death, Secondary, Duration,
Certifying Physician, His Residence,
Place of burial, Cemetery, Lot or Grave No. Section No.
Funeral Services at
Time of Services,
Date of Interment, Jul. 19. 1909 Diagram of Burial Lot.
† State whether White or Black. * Insert Town and State.

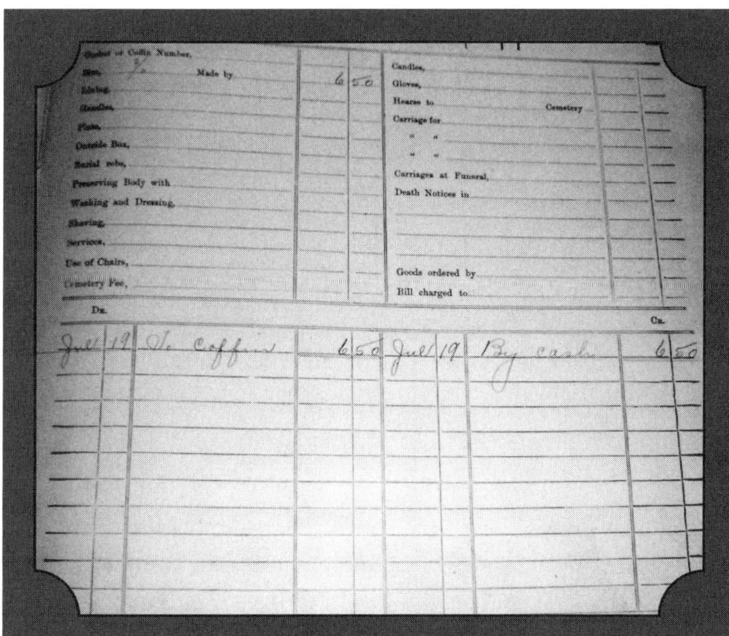

Casket or Coffin Number,
Size, 2/6 Made by 6 50
Lining,
Handles,
Plate,
Outside Box,
Burial robe,
Preserving Body with
Washing and Dressing,
Shaving,
Services,
Use of Chairs,
Cemetery Fee,
Candles,
Gloves,
Hearse to Cemetery
Carriage for
" "
" "
Carriages at Funeral,
Death Notices in
Goods ordered by
Bill charged to

Dr.				Cr.			
Jul	19	To Coffin	6 50	Jul	19	By cash	6 50

Ledger pages from Mr. Dannel's record book

To review the detailed records kept by Mr. Dannel for the 110 funerals he directed in 1909, his first full year in business, is to establish an important reference point for the study of a significant topic in Texas folklore. After considering a few entries in detail, I will comment on patterns and trends that show up in the overall data.

The first funeral of 1909 was for Mrs. N. A. Gray, who died on Jan. 6 at her residence, in the Ida community of Grayson County. She was sixty-eight years old and the primary cause of death was pneumonia. The certifying physician was M. E. Slagle, and the place of burial was Providence Cemetery. The services were held "about 4 p.m." on January 7. A side note indicates she "leaves 6 daughters all married." The coffin chosen was designated "Old Black Couch, 6/3" at a cost of $80. Additional charges were for hose, 50¢, and a burial robe (#1792 Kregel) at $17.50. The charge for sending the hearse to Providence was $15. Thus, the total charges were $113, and these were paid in cash on Jan. 7. On the Internet I found an index of burials for this cemetery (cross referenced as "Burleson") showing a grave for Mrs Nancy Ann Burleson Gray who died Jan. 6, 1909.

The second funeral recorded was for Mr. Joe Logsdon, sixty-six, who died at 9:30 p.m. on January 7. His occupation was listed as "Express man," and the cause of death was paralysis, certified by Dr. Hoard. Funeral service was held at 3 p.m. on January 9. The coffin was "Amer #117 with box, " and there were additional charges as follows: shoes $2.25, hose 25¢, burial robe $12, and shaving and bathing $5. The carriage rentals were: hearse $10, two closed $10 (including one for pallbearers). Total charges were $89.50, paid in two installments on February 1 and February 10. Although no cemetery was specified, I found an Internet listing for the grave of E. J. Logsdon (b. June 29, 1842, d. January 7, 1909) in West Hill Cemetery, Sherman, Texas.

The third funeral recorded for 1909 initiates a tragic series of deaths in one family. It began with the passing of Mrs. Sallie E. Mitchell (also listed as Mrs. J. M. Mitchell) at 9:10 a.m. on January 8, 1909. The primary cause of death was "complications," certified by Dr. Johnson, and she was buried in Sherman's West Hill Cemetery the next day at 10 a.m. She was the mother of twins, both of whom died about ten months later: a boy named Elzie on October 2, and his sister Elsie on October 6. Mrs. Mitchell's funeral cost $100, which was paid by the Sherman Mutual Burial Association on May 17. Each child's funeral cost $20, and $17 was paid in installments on the first one. No payments are shown for the second one, and one wonders if Mr. Dannel chose not to ask for payment. The children were also buried in West Hill Cemetery, but there is no record of their graves, presumably because no marker was erected with their names on it.

In reviewing the overall data from the 110 funerals, I found striking differences from present-day patterns and customs. Embalming, which then cost $25, was rarely performed unless the body was to be shipped to another town, and most funerals took place either the day the person died or the next day. Although graveside services were indicated occasionally, the home of the deceased was most often the site of the funeral, and 3:00–4:00 p.m. was the usual time. Travel by horse and carriage was slow, and late afternoon scheduling allowed sufficient time for relatives and friends who lived in a nearby town to arrive. After the trip to the cemetery, the mourners could return to the home for food and fellowship. The location of the funeral was not always indicated, but only three times was a church specified. Only one funeral was held at the funeral home.

The cost of funerals in 1909 ranged from $1.50 for a pauper case (paid by the county) to $349 for the most expensive one. Most adult funerals cost a bit more than $100, and the fact that the Sherman Mutual Burial Association paid $100 for the funeral of its members suggests that amount was a norm for this period. There were two major costs: (1) the casket and accessories (such as a burial robe) and (2) the rental of carriages. The funeral home's income derived solely from mark-up on these items, estimated to be forty percent by Mrs. John C. Dannel II, the present owner of the funeral home. Only rarely was there a charge for opening a grave (usually $3), providing pallbearers ($5), or a minister ($3). In the rare cases where the funeral home did not provide a casket (presumably because the family made its own), there was a service charge of $5 or $10.

The cost of a child's casket was typically $6.50, with a few at $8.50, and the most expensive being $35. Adult caskets started at $37.50, and $50 to $85 was most common. One physician was buried in a copper-lined casket that cost $150, and one young woman's casket cost $200. One could choose a white or a black hearse, and the cost ranged from $5 to $15, depending on the distance to the cemetery. Carriages rented for $5, and usually one was designated for pallbearers. The rental of a surrey cost only $3.50. There were often few or no carriages rented for children's funerals.

In some cases the Dannel Funeral Home prepared the body and placed it in a casket, which was then shipped as freight to another location, such as Gainesville or a town in Oklahoma. Likewise, Mr. Dannel directed some funerals for a person who died elsewhere (e.g., Fort Worth) but was buried locally.

Perhaps the most surprising finding is the age distribution for deaths that year, as follows:

0–5 years of age: 41 deaths
5–18 years old: 5
19–60 years old: 27
61–78 years old: 24

Clearly, in 1909 infant mortality was high. There were several indications of "stillborn" as a cause of death, as well as others in which the record showed that a child lived only hours or days with no cause of death indicated. In other cases the causes of death included pneumonia, congestion, whooping cough, and stomach or bowel disorders. These same causes of death were shown for adults, as well as consumption, influenza, typhoid, paralysis, cancer, meningitis, old age, and apoplexy. There were two railway accidents, a suicide, a drowning, and one shooting.

Another surprising finding was the number of funerals for "colored" people: fourteen. There was an African-American funeral home in Sherman at the time, and my expectation was that segregation would have meant that a white funeral home did not handle any black funerals.

Finally, the total amount charged for the 110 funerals was $6,509. The total amount collected on those funerals was $6,087.25. Approximately eighty funerals were paid for in cash (including eighteen for which the Sherman Mutual Burial Association paid $100, usually within a few months). Fewer than thirty were paid for in installments, often at the rate of a dollar or two at the time, and usually paid in full within the calendar year in which the funeral was held. The latest that a payment was made was December 1911, and one man made his final payment on December 24, 1909. Another received credit for $1 on his account on two occasions by washing pallbearer gloves for the funeral home. Mrs. Dannel advised me that the general rule today is that any payment they fail to receive soon, they are not likely to collect at all.

In conclusion, my study of funerals that occurred in Sherman, Texas, just after the turn of the century, reminds us of important differences between the lives of Texas folk in 1909 (when the TFS began) and our lives one hundred years later. It also makes me think of the Greek philosopher Heraclitus of Ephesus (c. 535 BC – 475 BC), who was known for his doctrine that change was central to the universe, sometimes paraphrased as "There is nothing permanent except change," or "Change is the only constant." The validity of that doctrine is readily apparent to anyone who peruses this volume on a century of Texas folklore. Looking to the future, people will continue to die and there will always be funeral rites and customs; this paper demonstrates that we need to continue recording and studying those rites and customs.

THE FOLK: WHO WE ARE

AND WHAT WE'VE DONE

Elmer Kelton

HOW THE TFS HAS INFLUENCED ME AS A WRITER, BUT MORE IMPORTANTLY, WHAT IT HAS MEANT TO ME AS A LISTENER

by Elmer Kelton

The Texas Folklore Society meetings have long been a highlight of my year, in small part because I pick up inspirations for my fiction writing, but in much larger part because I simply enjoy the people, the stories they tell, and the songs they sing.

I attended my first TFS meeting in 1976 at Arlington to deliver the banquet talk, "Three Kinds of Truth: Fact, Folklore, and Fiction." I was struck by the broad range of subject matter and the laid-back, informal manner of the presenters. The following year I went again, under the guise of being a reporter looking for a news story or two. Soon, I no longer needed excuses. I went because I wanted to, because I enjoyed the papers, and more than that, because I enjoyed the people I met. I have missed few annual meetings since.

Over the years the papers have inspired me, and they have given me story ideas and obscure details which I have used shamelessly to help bring the illusion of life to my fiction. They have given me an insight into the lives and times of people who came before me, people who never show up in the standard history books. In all the history courses I took in high school and the university, I don't remember one that mentioned Big Foot Wallace or Sally Skull or Ab Blocker, yet those people left a deep imprint on the Texas of their time. They and their anonymous contemporaries have left an imprint on us all.

As a fiction writer I have tried to keep my antenna up for anything that can add color or a sense of reality to my stories. At one TFS meeting a long time ago, someone made reference to the use of madstones to draw poison from bites inflicted by rabid animals.

I was told that J. Frank Dobie had written on that subject in an early TFS publication. At the moment I was having plot problems with a sequence concerning a cattle drive. I had heard about madstones since I was a boy, but this casual comment triggered my imagination. I found an article by Dobie and another by Michael Ahearn. Thanks to them and the TFS, I had a plot twist that lifted my story off high center.

At another time I was writing a novel about boom days in early West Texas oilfields. From my own boyhood recollections of one such boomtown, I knew that bootlegging was of considerable economic importance during Prohibition. A paper at a TFS meeting described in detail the construction and workings of a homemade still. With permission of the author, Janet Jeffery, I worked this into my story to enhance the illusion of reality so necessary in a piece of fiction.

I had long been aware of the great black folklorist J. Mason Brewer and his wonderful stories, like the one of the boys trying to baptize a cat and her kittens. (The punchline: "Jes' sprinkle her an' let her go on to hell.") Jim Byrd's TFS accounts of Brewer were helpful to me in constructing a continuing character I used in half a dozen books based on the early Texas Rangers. (I wish I could have told Brewer the reply my father received from a black service station attendant when Dad asked him the difference between regular and ethyl gasoline. The droll answer: "About two cents a gallon.")

Thanks to Joyce Gibson Roach, I have been able to place several high-toned women in various fictional settings. And thanks to Ernestine Sewell Linck, I learned to avoid any restaurant whose sign proclaims "Eats."

The beauty of folklore is that it is free of restrictions that so often bind the formal historian, who must be able to document every detail. Formal history too often squeezes out the breath of life, leaving only names, dates, and bare statistics. Folklore shines light into the black holes of history. It imparts life to men and women of the past and gives us insight into who and what they really were. It recreates in color and detail events of long ago. It puts flesh on dry bones. This is very much what the historical novelist tries to do—to breathe life back into the past and make the reader feel that, vicariously at least, he or she is reliving events of an earlier time in widescreen and living color.

Formal history gives us the essential basic facts about what and when, but all too often that is where it stops. Folklore can tell us how it was done, why it was done, and often a great deal about those who did it. It addresses the questions of how and why and who.

History tells us that pioneers raised or made most of the goods necessary to their survival, but it seldom gives us the *how*. Folklore, often based on word of mouth information passed down through successive generations, tells us how Grandma made her lye soap, how she kept a quilting frame suspended from the ceiling and used it to make bedcovers from scraps of cloth and bits of cotton. It tells us how Granddad planted his crops and worked his livestock by the signs of the moon, and how he preserved meat without allowing it to spoil. These details are often of little interest to formal history. But to the folklorist and the historical novelist, they are the staff of life.

Folklore tells us much about people of the past, their moods, their motivations, their deeply-held beliefs. A persistent piece of Texas folklore is the story of Travis using his sword to draw a line in the sand at the Alamo. The incident did not come into the public consciousness until decades later, and could well be a figment of an old man's imagination. Regardless of its literal truth, it offers a moral truth of its own. It speaks to the courage and the determination of men in the face of almost certain death. It is an indelible part of the Texas myth, which helps define who we are and why we are as we are. It has given us an ideal to which we as a people have clung through many generations.

Valuable as it is in illuminating the dark corners of the past, folklore cannot always be taken for literal fact, of course. I was born on an Andrews County ranch known as the Five Wells. The commonly accepted story locally is that the place was named for an early settler named Wells who had five daughters. My father and my uncle both told me this story, and I heard it from others. However, Mackenzie's military map from the early 1870s clearly shows the Five Wells, holes the Indians dug into the sands to find shallow water. At that time there were no settlers in the area. The Comanches and Kiowas still held the deed.

When we come into lean times or face personal troubles, family folklore reassures us that our forebears also encountered hard times, yet managed to survive conditions more dire than our generation has known. We draw strength—and I have drawn fictional stories—from experiences of our parents, grandparents, and their contemporaries, from their determination to prevail no matter the obstacles. The Texas Folklore Society has given us many such accounts of hardship and survival that inspire us to face up to the problems of our own time. These have told us much that we might otherwise never have known about our ancestors and their way of life. They have increased our appreciation of those hardy people.

Much of my pleasure in the TFS has nothing to do with my fiction writing. The biggest delight has always been the people, the lasting friendships, the memories we hold of friends no longer with us. The delightful Martha Emmons was still around during the first meetings I attended. I have remembered and borrowed from her recollections of a small-town boarding house, which reminded me of one I frequented during my first couple of years at the University of Texas. And she could tell dialect stories in an innocent manner that would not offend even in this oppressive period of political correctness.

Paul Patterson was one of my high school teachers and remained a lifelong mentor. I always looked forward to a chance to sit with him at the hootenanny, to listen to him tell witty stories of his many misadventures as a cowboy, a hobo, a soldier, and a teacher. It was my privilege once, during a tribute to Paul, to read aloud his account of a family trip to Midland in a wagon, and his terror on being told that Midland's many windmills sucked up all the air. His older brothers convinced him that they would all be suffocated at the city limits. Paul sat in the audience and laughed as hard as anyone there.

Every time I eat a piece of pie, I remember Jim Lee's essay, "God, I Love a Pie," and his declaration that the most satisfying place to eat pie is over the sink.

I am a charter member of the vast right wing conspiracy, resentful of the way some historical revisionists revile our forebears in pursuit of their own political agenda. I still take pleasure in Ab Abernethy's comment that today's revisionists too often practice generational chauvinism.

In my schooldays I learned the old Frank Desprez poem "Lasca," about a cowgirl who sacrifices her life to save her cowboy sweetheart. It has become a tradition at every TFS hootenanny. It always takes me back to the fifth grade and an overheated schoolroom in Crane, Texas, where a teacher solemnly read the poem and made us feel genuine sorrow over the cowboy's loss:

> "And I wonder why I do not care.
> For the things that are like the things that were."

This nostalgic poem and other works like it were early inspirations to me as a writer. They taught me that emotion is a vital part of effective fiction.

Much as we enjoy hearing a paper read, most is soon lost to memory unless it is preserved. The TFS annual publications, therefore, become a treasure trove into which we can dip time and time again. My collection is extensive but not complete. My only trouble with these books is that, like clearing out the attic, I become absorbed in some essay that catches my eye and forget what I was looking for in the first place. These pieces, many written by old friends now gone, are like a brief visit back to what the German settlers called *Die schöne alten Zeit*, the good old times.

I never know when one of them is going to strike a chord and spark a new story idea for me to claim as my own. I won't exactly steal it; I will just borrow it for a while, like a story I heard from the wife of an old Hollywood writer friend of mine. She had been a script girl at Republic Studios, famous for slick, superior B Westerns. She said the writers' room always had a large stack of Western pulp magazines from which plots were often borrowed. One day one of the company writers shouted in delight, waved a magazine, and said, "I've just finished reading one of the best story ideas I ever had."

I have the Texas Folklore Society to thank for a number of my best story ideas.

TEXAS A PARADISE

By the Author of "Hell in Texas"

The Lord said he wished to show
To His erring children here below
That He had plenty in His Store
For those who knocked at Heaven's door,
And hence would give to some bright land
Samples of blessings from His right hand;
And if you think there's Cause to doubt it,
Just listen to how God reasoned about it.
These gifts I can't give to the States in the East
The weather's too damp for both man and beast,
And the Northern States I consider together,
I made a mistake when I put up their weather,
For in blizzards and cyclones, tornadoes and cold,
No one can enjoy good gifts, I am told.
'Tis too cold, hence westward I shall go
To the land where the fig and the orange trees grow
For here it is true is a beautiful land,
But then here's the fogs, the dust and sand;
And those who enjoy these gifts as they must
Can't do it in the sand and the fogs and the dust,
At last reaching Texas, a State of some size
He decided to give her His capital prize:
He opened wide His bountiful hand,
He dispersed His blessing all over the land,
And hence we enjoy as these blessings of ours
Ten months in the year the most beautiful flowers;
And nights most delightful, fanned by the breeze,
That comes sweeping across her from over the seas;
And Italy's skies with our own won't compare;
Nor is her land more fertile nor ladies more fair
And the grasses that grow on the range of ours
Are kept beautifully green by these sweet summer
showers,
And as we know, to enjoy our wealth,
We must first secure the blessing of health.
Thence we declare to the sick in each clime
That health you can have, if you come here in time
And now to our friends in the East, North and West
We want you to come here and with us be blest,
For God never intended that we all alone
Should enjoy all these blessings that He has bestown.

1920s postcard describing some of the state's charms.
Courtesy, Clarence Jay Faulkner

Peggy A. Redshaw

WOMEN IN THE TEXAS FOLKLORE SOCIETY

by Peggy A. Redshaw

Introduction

From the beginning, women have been instrumental in the development of the Texas Folklore Society (TFS) and remain integral and important contributors to the Society today. The roles played have been as varied as required to keep the organization functioning. For instance, women have been in charge of local arrangements for meetings, served as Program Chair and Vice-President, President, Director, Councilor, and Secretary/Treasurer. They have also presented an estimated 420 papers since 1909. Some developed their interest as students and became members; others simply developed an interest in folklore and have been presenting papers for years; others first accompanied a spouse to the meetings and then began presenting papers of their own; and still others have attended for decades without a formal "paper" or "role" but have contributed immeasurably to the vitality of the Society.

Fellows

General guidelines for being selected a Fellow of the Texas Folklore Society are being a long-time member, contributing through paper presentations, and providing service on the board or in other leadership positions and publications. In 2002, Martha Emmons was inducted posthumously as the first female Fellow; in 2006, Joyce Gibson Roach and Fran Vick were selected as Fellows, and a year later, Lou Rodenberger was.

Martha Emmons (1895–1990) was raised in the Mansfield, Texas, vicinity, and her father was a storyteller as well an innovator in peanut cultivation. She had friendships with African-Americans in her childhood that nurtured her interests in folklore and

African-American speech.[1] She was an English teacher at the Waco State School as well as Baylor University,[2] and she was a member of the TFS for sixty-six years. The first meeting she attended was in 1925, where she presented a paper on the "Folk-Lore of Williamson County." While teaching English at the State Home in Waco in 1933, she inherited the planning and organization of the April 1933 TFS meeting when John Streckler, the President of TFS that year, died unexpectedly.[3] She became President of the Society twice, first in 1935–36 and again in 1969–1970.

Miss Martha read some sixteen papers at the annual meetings and her last paper was presented in 1986. Also, she had papers published in seven Publications of the Texas Folklore Society (PTFS) volumes.[4] Furthermore, her *Deep Like the Rivers* was published as Paisano Series No. 4 in 1968.[5] Additionally, *Hoein' the Short Rows* (PTFS XLVII , 1987) was dedicated to her.[6] In 1976, she self published *I Come Runnin'* which contained humorous anecdotes, superstitions, folk sayings, and cures collected from her early days and friends, black and white.[7] Additionally, her oral memoirs are at Baylor University.[8]

In 1979, she received the Grasshopper Library Award; the title of the award was taken from a hymn to universal wisdom that Frank Dobie included in *Coronado's Children.*[9] In 1984, the annual Hootenanny was dedicated to her,[10] and she gave her rendition of "Adulteration of Ole King David." Finally, the 1988 annual meeting was dedicated to her.[11]

On December 3, 1939, J. Frank Dobie dedicated his first *Dallas Morning News* column, entitled "The Flavor of the Soil and the Folklore Society," to a summary of the best of the TFS writers since the publications began in 1912. At the top of his list was Martha Emmons and her skill as the best Negro dialect writer.[12] It is easy to understand why she is considered the grand dame of the society. [13]

Joyce Gibson Roach has lived all her life in the ranch country and has an interest in Western folklore. She earned the B.F.A. and M.A. from Texas Christian University, and taught English at TCU from 1984–1997.[14] She has won three Spur Awards, which are given annually for distinguished writing about the American West:

in 1977, *The Cowgirls*; 1987, *A High-Toned Woman*; and 1990, *Just As I Am.*[15] Joyce's first TFS paper was presented in 1965[16] and she has given thirteen more. She has published articles in eight of the PTFS volumes.[17] Joyce served as Program Chair and Vice-President for the 59th annual meeting (Houston, 1975), and then as President of the Society for the 60th annual meeting (Arlington, 1976). Additional publications include *This Place of Memory* (1992), and she was a co-author with Ernestine Sewell Linck of *Eats: A Folk History of Texas Food* (1988), which won the Best Non-Fiction Award from the Texas Institute of Letters.[18] She is a Fellow of the Texas State Historical Association and a member of the Texas Institute of Letters.[19] Her papers are on deposit at the Wittliff Collections at Texas State University in San Marcos.[20]

If one only looked at the papers read at the annual meetings by Frances Brannen (Fran) Vick (three, the first in 1998) and articles in the PTFS (one), you might ask, what significant role did she play in the Texas Folklore Society? In 1979, Fran offered her fledgling E-Heart Press to Francis E. "Ab" Abernethy, Secretary-Editor, and the Society for publishing the PTFS series.[21] Initially, *Built in Texas* (PTFS XLII, 1979), *Legendary Ladies of Texas* (PTFS XLIII, 1981), *T for Texas: A State Full of Folklore* (PTFS XLIV, 1982), and *Singin' Texas* (LXXVI, Exb 18, 1983) were published by E Heart. Since 1990, the publication program for TFS books has been with the University of North Texas Press, which Fran founded. Additionally, she is one the editors and contributors of *The Family Saga: A Collection of Texas Family Legends* (PTFS LX, 2003),[22] a contributor to *Texas Women Writers* (1997), *Texas Women on the Cattle Trail* (2006), and *Notes from Texas: On Writing in the Lone Star State* (2008). She is a co-author, along with Jane Monday, of *Petra's Legacy: The South Texas Ranching Empire of Petra Vela and Mifflin Kenedy* (2007). Her latest book, *Literary Dallas* (2008), was recently published.

Fran was born in Trinity, a fifth-generation Texan and an East Texan to the core.[23] She graduated from the University of Texas and Stephen F. Austin State University, and holds an honorary doctorate from the University of North Texas. Without her insight into publishing, the Society would not have the publication program it has today.

Lou Halsell Rodenberger, the thirteenth Fellow of the Texas Folklore Society

Lou Rodenberger was the latest woman to receive the Fellow designation. Also, in 2008, she was honored as a Western History Fellow to go along with her Fellow of the Texas State Historical Association. Lou received the Ph.D. from Texas A&M University and was a Professor Emeritus of English at McMurry.[24] She served as Program Chair and Vice-President for the 71st annual meeting (Galveston, 1987) and President at the 72nd annual meeting (Lubbock, 1988). Her interests included rural schoolteacher parents, Texas women writers, and writers of the Southwest. Since 1980, she presented four papers at the annual meetings and placed articles in three volumes of PTFS.[25] Among her other publications were *Quotable Texas Women* (2005), *Writing on the Wind: A West Texas Anthology of Women Writers* (2005), *Jane Gilmore Rushing:*

A West Texas Writer and Her Work (2006), *Her Work: Stories by Texas Women* (2000), and with co-editor with Sylvia Grider, *Texas Women Writers: A Tradition of Their Own* (1997).

Presidents and Vice-Presidents (Program Chairs)

From 1909–1937 there were seven women Presidents of the Texas Folklore Society. From 1938–1962, no women served as President. This suggests that academic male chauvinism was reigning for a couple of decades. Finally, a woman, Elizabeth Brandon, was selected as President in 1962–63. Since that time there has not been such a noticeable "gap" in the presidency.

The first woman to serve as President was Dorothy Scarborough (1878–1935), who was born near Tyler, Texas. She was President at the 5th meeting of the Society (Baylor, 1915), which was the first meeting held outside of Austin. Remarkably, she served as the Local Arranger and Program Chair as well as President for the meeting.[26] She left Texas in 1916 for Columbia University and earned her Ph.D. in 1917. Scarborough presented two papers at the annual meetings, in 1913 and in 1915 (the Presidential Address). Sylvia Ann Grider presented two papers about her in 1985 and 1987, as well as contributed a chapter on Scarborough in *Texas Women Writers.*[27] Scarborough is also published in the first two PTFS volumes.[28] Additionally, she published two novels about Texas, *In the Land of Cotton* (1923) and *The Wind* (1925). *The Wind* was adapted for the screen as the 1928 silent film of the same name and starred Lillian Gish and Lars Hanson. Two additional folklore publications, *On the Trail of Negro Folksongs* (1925) and *A Song Catcher in the Southern Mountains* (1937), continue to be regarded as standard references.[29]

Lillie T. Shaver was a charter member of the Texas Folklore Society in 1909, served as a Vice-President in 1911,[30] and was the Dean of Women at Southwest Texas State Normal College. She presented her first folklore paper on Indian Customs in 1911, at the very first meeting in Austin. Shaver served as President at the 7th annual meeting (San Marcos, 1917). Additionally, she presented four more papers at meetings, the last being at the 11th annual meeting (Austin, 1925).

Julia Estill (1882–1965) was a collector and writer of German folklore of Fredericksburg. She was born in Fredericksburg and received the B.S. in 1904 and the M.S. in 1905 from the University of Texas. She taught school and served as a principal in the Fredericksburg vicinity for forty-seven years.[31] She was the President of the Society for the 10th Annual Meeting (Austin, 1924). She presented three papers at the annual meetings and published eight articles in the PTFS.[32] Topics she wrote about were Sunday houses, Easter fires, Indian rock art, and other landmarks in Gillespie County.[33]

The first two-term woman President of the society was Jovita González (1903–1983); she was also the first Mexican-American woman to be President. Jovita was born near Roma, Texas, and was the fifth generation of a land-grant family.[34] She earned the B.A. in Texas history from St. Mary's Hall in San Antonio and became a pioneer in collecting Mexican folklore in the Rio Grande valley. She used these research skills to earn her M.S. in 1930 at the University of Texas, under the direction of Eugene Barker. Jovita was President at the 17th Annual meeting (San Antonio, 1931) as well as the 18th Annual meeting (Austin, 1932). She read ten papers at the annual meetings, including her two Presidential Addresses. Also, she had five articles published in PTFS volumes.[35] She taught Spanish at St. Mary's Hall in San Antonio as well as Mexican history and folklore, and her Spanish language textbooks were adopted in schools in Texas and throughout the Southwest. Her papers are housed at the Nettie Lee Benson Latin American Collection at the University of Texas in Austin.[36] Martha Emmons is the only other woman to serve two full, regular terms as President.

Mabel Major (1894–1974) was a native of Utah and earned the A.B., B.S., and M.A. degrees from the University of Missouri. She taught in the English Department at TCU from 1919 to 1963, specializing in Southwestern literature.[37] She presented her first paper at the 1932 meeting and then followed with six more, usually on British songs and ballads. She served as Vice-President for the 22nd annual meeting (Austin, 1936), and as President at the 23rd annual meeting (Ft. Worth, 1937). She had one publication in the PTFS series.[38] Her papers are housed in the Special Collections at TCU.[39] Additionally, Joyce Gibson Roach has an article about Major in *Texas Woman Writers*.[40]

During the 1938–1963 time period when no women were President of the Society, women were serving the TFS, but even then, there were distinct gaps in service as Vice-President or Councilor. From 1938–1953, women were serving as Councilors (22) and Vice-Presidents (11). From 1953–1960, no women served as officers. In 1961, Mary Tom Osborne served as a Councilor and in 1962, Elizabeth Brandon was a Vice-President, becoming President the following year. Clearly, it was difficult for women to serve the TFS as an officer during this period.

In 1963, Elizabeth Brandon, a Professor of French at the University of Houston, was selected President of the Society for the 47th annual meeting in Austin. She had served as Vice-President and Program Chair for the 46th annual meeting in Monahans. Her area of interest was Cajun stories from southern Louisiana.[41] She presented two papers at the annual meetings on this broad topic (1957, 1961) and had an article in the PTFS Volume XXXI.[42]

After Martha Emmons completed her second term as President in 1970, Bessie Pearce, from the Department of English at San Antonio College,[43] served as a Councilor for the 54th meeting in Wimberley, Vice-President for the 55th annual meeting in San Antonio (1971) and President for the 56th meeting in College Station (1972). Then she transitioned back to a Councilor for 197–74.

The typical pattern of service now is that individuals interested in serving the Society are nominated and elected to a position as a Councilor or Director. As the term ends, they can be appointed Vice-President of the Society. This role involves serving as the Program Chair (soliciting papers and organizing the program) for the meeting prior to the year they are President. At the next annual meeting, the individual serves as President, and among other things, conducts the business meeting of the society. In most cases, once the presidency is completed, the person becomes a Director of the Society to help ensure continuity and provide guidance to the rest of the Board for the next three years. Also, many officers have served as the organizer of Local Arrangements for an annual meeting as well.

Two women Presidents were selected in just three years: Joyce Roach for 1975–76 (see above) and Ernestine Sewell Linck for 1977–1978. Ernestine (1918–2001) was born and raised in Texarkana, Arkansas, and after graduating from Henderson State Teachers College in Arkadelphia, she began teaching English in high schools in Arkansas and Houston. She earned her Ph.D. in English from East Texas State University in 1968. She taught English at the University of Texas at Arlington from 1963–83,[44] and was a weaver of fine wools and an artist in Indian jewelry.[45] As noted earlier, she co-authored *Eats: A Folk History of Texas Food*, with fellow TFS member Joyce Roach.[46] She was a printer at Cow Hill Press, which her husband and fellow TFS member Charles Linck owned.[47] Ernestine was Vice-President and Program Chair for the 61st annual meeting in El Paso (1977) and President at the 62nd annual meeting in Nacogdoches the following year. She presented her first paper in 1971, and by 1998 had presented a total of ten. Also, she had five articles published in the PTFS books.[48]

In the 1980s there were three female Presidents: Sylvia Grider (1982–83), Lou Rodenberger (1987–88; see above), and Sarah Greene (1988–89). Sylvia Grider received her Ph.D. in folklore from Indiana University's Folklore Institute, and then joined the Department of English at Texas A&M University. With a detour through the Department of History, she is now in the Department of Anthropology.[49] She presented her first paper in 1970 and continued with seven more, including two papers on Dorothy Scarborough. She has three articles in the PTFS series.[50] Additionally, her published works include *Texas Women Writers* (1997) and *Let's Hear It: Stories by Texas Women Writers* (2003) with Lou Rodenberger, and *Haunting Experiences: Ghosts in Contemporary Folklore* (2007) with Diane Goldstein and Jeannie Banks Thomas. Sylvia was Vice-President and Program Chair for the 66th annual meeting (Fredericksburg, 1982) and President at the 67th annual meeting in College Station (1983).

Sarah Greene, owner, publisher, and retired editor of *The Gilmer Mirror*, served as the Vice-President and Program Chair for the 72nd annual meeting (Lubbock, 1988) and the President at the 73rd annual meeting (Uvalde, 1989). Sarah presented a paper in 1972 and has an article in PTFS LVI. In 2004, she received the Emma C. McKinney Award, which is the highest honor given to a working newspaper woman for distinguished service to the community press.[51]

In the 1990s, women continued to take leadership roles, with six Presidents in one decade: Jeri Tanner (1991–1992), Mildred Boren Sentell (1993–1994), Faye Leeper (1994–1995), Margaret Waring (1996–1997), Sylvia Mahoney (1998–1999), and Mary Harris (1999–2000).

Jeri Tanner (1926–1998) taught English at Texas Tech University and was the former President of the Arkansas Society of X-ray Technicians.[52] Jeri was the local arranger for the 72nd annual meeting in Lubbock (1988), was Program Chair for the 75th annual meeting (San Marcos, 1991), and President of the 76th annual meeting in McKinney the following year. She presented seven papers; the first one was in 1966, and the last one was presented with James Byrd on the "Life of J. Mason Brewer." Additionally, she has one article in PTFS XLIX: "Ollie North. Hero, Villain, or Temporary Prince."

Mildred Boren Sentell was born in Post. After the death of her first husband, B. J. Boren, she moved in 1972 to San Angelo to attend Angelo State University, and she taught in the English department from 1976–1993.[53] She has presented four papers, the first in 1990, and has two articles in PTFS publications.[54] She served as Program Chair and Vice-President at the 77th annual meeting (San Angelo, 1993) and as President at the 78th annual meeting in Victoria (1994).

Faye Leeper served as Vice-President and Program Chair of the 78th annual meeting (Victoria, 1994) and President of the 79th annual meeting (Ft. Worth, 1995). In 1956, Faye received an honorable mention award in the student paper contest for her story entitled "Pebble in the Devil's Shoe" at the 40th annual meeting.

She was then a student at San Marcos State College. Since then she has presented six additional papers, had three articles in PTFS books, and served as a Director for the Society.[55] Faye taught English at Robert E. Lee High School in Midland and Midland Community College for over twenty years. Beyond writing about folklore, she is a published poet.[56]

Margaret Waring is the Founder and Head of the Comanche Public Library and served the Society as a Councilor from 1991–1993, then as a Director from 1994–1995, Vice-President and Program Chair for the 80th annual meeting (Abilene, 1996), and President for the 81st annual meeting in Huntsville (1997). She then transitioned back to a Director for three years, from 1998–2000. She was named Texas Library Association Librarian of the Year and Comanche Woman of the Year for 1996.[57]

Sylvia Mahoney serves as the Director of Institutional Advancement at Vernon Regional Junior College and is a former English teacher and rodeo coach at New Mexico Junior College.[58] In 1992, she was selected as the first President of the National Intercollegiate Rodeo Association Alumni (NIRAA, Inc.), a group interested in preserving the history of college rodeo.[59] In 2004, she published a book entitled *College Rodeo: From Show to Sport.* Her papers at TFS meetings have showcased college rodeo, as well. She presented her first paper in 1991, and has followed with two more. She has two articles in PTFS books.[60] She was Program Chair and Vice-President for the 82nd annual meeting (Sherman, 1998) and served as President for the 83rd annual meeting (Midland, 1999).

Mary Harris, a member of the TFS since 1973, earned the Doctorate in Education in 2004 from Nova Southeastern. She serves as Dean of the School of Education at College of the Southwest in Hobbs, New Mexico.[61] She served as Program Chair and Vice-President for the 83rd annual meeting (Midland, 1999) and President for the 84th annual meeting (Nacogdoches, 2000). She has presented three papers at annual meetings and has an article in PTFS LXIV: "Farm and Ranch Entrances in West Texas."

The last decade has seen four more women serve as President with one in the wings: Lora B. Garrison (as Interim in 2002 and a full term in 2002–2003), Phyllis Bridges (2003–2004), Jean Schnitz (2006–2007), and Cynthia Savage (2007–2008). The Vice-President and Program Chair for the 2009 meeting is Lucy Fischer West, who then will likely move up to President.

Lora B. Garrison of Utopia has attended TFS meetings since the early 1970s and is a pioneer storyteller at public schools and at the Texas Folklife Festival. She has collected oral history since 1979, and wrote a column entitled "Stomping Grounds" for the *Uvalde Leader-News*.[62] She presented her first paper in 1985, and has continued with four more, as well as three articles in PTFS volumes.[63] She was serving as Program Chair and Vice-President for the 86th annual meeting (in Victoria) when President John Lightfoot died in 2002. She covered both positions for that meeting. Then, she served as President for the 87th annual meeting in Kerrville in 2003.

Phyllis Bridges is a Professor of English at Texas Woman's University, where she has served for over thirty years. She earned her Ph.D. at Texas Tech and was named a Distinguished Alumna in English.[64] She has presented five papers, the first in 1991, and she has published three PTFS articles.[65] She served as Program Chair and Vice-President for the 87th annual meeting (Kerrville, 2003) and President for the 88th annual meeting (Allen, 2004). She has also served as the President of the Texas Joint Council of Teachers of English and the Southwest American Culture Association.[66]

Jean Granberry Schnitz was born in Spur and graduated from Texas A&I College in Kingsville. She is a retired legal secretary.[67] Jean has presented eight papers at the annual meetings, the first on the hammered dulcimer. She plays the dulcimer and regularly participates in the Hootenanny, as well as represents the Society at the Texas Folklife Festival in San Antonio. She has five articles in PTFS books.[68] She served as Program Chair and Vice-President for the 90th annual meeting in Galveston (2006), and President for the 91st annual meeting in San Antonio the following year.

Cynthia Savage was born in the folklore-rich region of Southeastern New Mexico. She studied folklore at the University of Texas at Austin under Américo Paredes, and has earned an M.A. in education. Following a 1988 conversation with fellow Robert E. Lee High School teacher and TFS member, Faye Leeper, Cynthia began attending the annual meetings.[69] She has presented two papers at the annual meetings, the first one a shared presentation with her sister Sarana. Cynthia has an article entitled "Folklore 101" in PTFS LXII. She served as Program Chair and Vice-President for the 91st annual meeting (San Antonio, 2007) and President for the 92nd annual meeting (Lubbock, 2008). Additionally, she has served the Society as a Councilor, and along with her sister, organized local arrangements for the 83rd annual meeting in their hometown of Midland in 1999. She teaches in the Career and Technology department at Robert E. Lee High School in Midland. She is also a member of the West Texas Historical Association.

Lucy Fischer-West was born in Catskill, New York, but grew up in El Paso. She has done freelance editing in the field of Southwestern history and is a teacher at Cathedral High School in El Paso. She is the author of *Child of Many Rivers: Journeys to and from the Rio Grande* (2005).[70] This memoir received the WILLA Finalist Award from Women Writing the West at their 2006 conference. Also, her book was the finalist for the 2006 Writer's League of Texas Violet Crown Award.[70] She is serving as Vice-President and Program Chair for the 93rd annual meeting in Nacogdoches in 2009. She presented her first paper in 2000, and has two articles in Society publications.[72]

OTHER NOTEWORTHY WOMEN

The list of dozens of women who presented papers and had articles in the Publications of the Texas Folklore Society who were not President is a testament to their involvement in the organization at many different levels. Many women have served as "go-to" individuals for the local arrangements for the annual meetings. Sometimes their names were listed in the meeting programs (as in the

60th meeting in Arlington, 1976) and other times there is no mention of this important role (the 76th meeting in McKinney, 1992). Additionally, many have served as Councilors for the Society. Others have made presentations at meetings of the Texas State Historical Association, the East Texas Historical Association, the West Texas Historical Association, the Texas Book Festival, or Texas Folklife Festival on behalf of the TFS. And how many women have played instruments, sung, recited poetry, or told stories at the annual Hootenanny?

Selecting a few representative individuals who have presented papers at the annual meetings or had articles in the PTFS series and did not serve as President was difficult. However, I wanted to highlight individuals from different decades who made the meetings and publications more informative and interesting because of their papers. Adina Emilia De Zavala (1861–1955) was born in Harris County and moved to San Antonio about 1873. She graduated from Sam Houston Normal Institute in Huntsville in 1881.[73] One of her contributions to Texas was the preservation of a portion of the old San Antonio de Valero Mission, better known as the Alamo. She even barricaded herself in the north barrack of the Alamo in 1908 to protest its destruction.[74] She presented her first paper in 1911, at the first meeting of the Folklore Society, and she served as a Vice-President for the second meeting. She presented a total of four more papers, the last one in 1936. Additionally, she had an article in PTFS Volume I ("Religious Beliefs of the Tejas, or Hasanias, Indians") and was the author of *History and Legends of the Alamo and Other Missions in and Around San Antonio* (1917).

Mrs. John Q. (Loraine) Anderson pieced a quilt in July 1969 that she named the "Texas Folklore Society Paisano" quilt, and Sylvia Grider won it in a lottery at the next meeting.[75] Undoubtedly she attended meetings with her husband John Q., who was very active in TFS, but she did not present any papers at the annual meetings until three years after his death in 1975. But after she started, eleven papers were presented, from 1978–1994. She also had two articles published in the PTFS books.[76]

In the recent decade, several women have presented several papers and published articles in volumes of the PTFS. Mary Margaret Dougherty Campbell is a published author and poet, and in November 2008 became the Executive Director of George West Storyfest.[77] She has presented three papers since 2004 and has three articles in recent PTFS volumes (LXIII, LXV). Margaret Cox grew up in Eden and is the fourth generation of 1886 Concho County pioneers.[78] She has presented two papers and has an article in PTFS Volume LXV. Becky Carnes Matthews, of San Antonio, has presented three papers and has two articles in PTFS books, volumes LVIII and LXII. Mary Joe Clendenin has taught school from elementary students to college students and is the author of a dozen books.[79] She has delivered two papers at the annual meetings and has an article in Volume LXIII of the PTFS. Gretchen Lutz of Houston has presented three articles at the annual meetings and has an article in PTFS Volume LXIV. Gloria Duarte, of the English department at San Angelo State, has presented two articles at recent meetings and has articles in PTFS Volumes LXI and LXIII.

Intergenerational presentations—Mother and daughters—are another paper combination that has been a very positive development of recent meetings. Karen Haile and daughters Acayla and Sierra presented at the 87th annual meeting (Kerrville, 2003): Karen on "Folk Art . . . It's Everywhere" and Acayla and Sierra on "Once Upon A Time . . . Storytelling Adventures of Acayla and Sierra Haile." Their papers were in a Special Plenary Session for the Young and Young at Heart. Another mother-daughter duo, Tierney and daughter Miché Untiedt, presented papers at the 86th annual meeting in Victoria (2002) on "Day Care Oral Traditions and School Yard Games" and at the 88th annual meeting in Allen (2004) on "First Generation Texan," respectively.

SECRETARY/TREASURERS

Fannie E. Ratchford (1887–1974), a native of Paint Rock, earned the B.A. in 1919 and her Masters in 1921 from the University of Texas.[80] She was associated with the Wrenn Library from 1919 until she retired in 1957. She became the recording secretary and Treasurer of the Society in 1925 and served in this capacity for four years. In 1929, she received a Guggenheim Fellowship and spent 1929–30 studying in Europe. She presented two papers at Texas Folklore Society meetings in 1925 and 1926 and had three papers published in PTFS volumes.[81] She achieved prominence as a Charlotte and Branwell Bronte scholar of miniature manuscripts.[82] Interestingly, recent scholarship on the Brontes has emphasized the rise of folklore as a subject of study in England during their careers. Ratchford's significance as a librarian, literary detective, and scholar are addressed in an article by Clara Sitter.[83]

Marcelle Lively Hamer (1900–1974) was born in Whitewright and earned the B.A. in English in 1921 from University of Oklahoma.[84] She served as Treasurer for the Society for seventeen years, from 1934–1951. She took over when Byron Shipp, whose records were "incomplete and indefinite," was replaced. As a matter of fact, he left the Society with a debt of $300–400 and a cash balance of only $8.30.[85] From 1932–1955, Marcelle was the director of the Texas Collection at UT Austin. She was indispensable and served the Society as the "general factotum," and when J. Frank Dobie was off a-wandering, she was regularly left in charge of the business of the Society.[86] Additionally, her job description included editing book publications, handling book distribution, and keeping the financial records of the Society. While she was Treasurer, she earned her M.A. in 1939 from the University of Texas with a thesis on anecdotes as they revealed truths in history, and this scholarship was published in PTFS XV.[87] When she resigned, the Society gave her the typewriter that she had used for years, and the organization had $652.29 at the time.[88]

When Francis E. "Ab" Abernethy assumed the Secretary-Editor position of the Society on August 16, 1971, he hired Martha Dickinson as his secretary and she worked with him for ten years. She kept the books, handled society correspondence, edited manuscripts, and was "irreplaceable." Ab recalls that she "knew more than I did."[89] In 2000, at the 84th annual meeting in Nacogdoches, Ab recognized three of his secretaries: Martha Dickinson (1971–81), Carrol Daniels (1985–1989), and Carolyn Satterwhite (1989–2001). Also in that year, the office secretary position added a Treasurer function as well, and Carolyn Satterwhite assumed that position, as well as continuing her work as an assistant editor for publications and office secretary.[90] In 2005, Ken Untiedt assumed the position of the Secretary-Editor of the Society and the latest volume of the PTFS series (LXV) is dedicated to Janet Simonds, the current office secretary and Treasurer of the Society. Janet has an article in PTFS Volume LXIV. Each of these women has made the Society office run smoothly and kept Ab and Ken sane.

CONCLUSIONS

The record speaks for itself: women have served TFS in innumerable ways. Likewise, the TFS has enabled women to use their many and varied talents and be recognized as valued contributors to the collection and study of the lore of Texas and the Southwest.

ACKNOWLEDGMENTS

This paper would have been impossible to complete without the three volumes of the Texas Folklore Society history compiled by Francis E. "Ab" Abernethy, as well as the Folklore society web site. Additional information was gathered from the PTFS volumes and author information sections. I thank Jerry Lincecum for reading and commenting on this paper.

ENDNOTES

1. http://contentdm.baylor.edu/cdm4/item_viewer.php?CISOROOT=/08oralhist&CISOPTR=2084&CISOBOX=1&REC=7 [Accessed 12.26.08].
2. Francis Edward Abernethy. *The Texas Folklore Society, Volume I, 1909–1943*. PTFS LI. Denton: University of North Texas Press, 1992. 244.
3. Ibid. 57.

4. Emmons titles from the PTFS publications are as follows: VII:119–134, "Confidences from Old Nacogdoches"; X: 55–61, "Dyin' Easy"; XI: 94–100, "Cats and the Occult"; XIII:130–136, Walk Around My Bedside"; XXXVIII:157–165, "Green Flags over Texas"; XLIV: 23–30, "A Place Against the Sky"; LXIII:199–203, "The Long Arm of the Law."
5. Martha Emmons. *Deep Like the Rivers, Stories of My Negro friends.* Austin: Encino Press, 1969.
6. Francis Edward Abernethy. *The Texas Folklore Society, Volume III, 1971–2000.* PTFS LVII. Denton: University of North Texas Press, 2000. 100.
7. http://contentdm.baylor.edu/cdm4/item_viewer.php?CISOROOT=/08oralhist&CISOPTR=2084&CISOBOX=1&REC=7 [Accessed 12.26.08].
8. Ibid.
9. Abernethy. *Vol. III.* 72.
10. Ibid. 88.
11. Ibid. 102.
12. Abernethy. *Vol. I.* 254.
13. Ibid. 244.
14. Abernethy. *Vol. III.* 30.
15. http://www.westernwriters.org/spur_award_history.htm#1977 [Accessed 12.26.08].
16. Francis Edward Abernethy. *The Texas Folklore Society, Volume II, 1943–1971.* PTFS LIII. Denton: University of North Texas Press, 1994. 234.
17. Roach titles from the PTFS publications are as follows: XXXVII: 65–72, "Revive Us Again"; XLVII: 1–10, "A High Toned Woman"; XLVIII: 220–223, "Toys in the Frontier"; XLIX: 63–76, "A Sense of Place," with Robert Flynn; LII: 87–94, "Pistol Packin' Mamas: Gun Code for Western Women"; LV:10–15, "Defining Folklore for My Students"; LVI: 44–50, "Prescriptions for Ailments Did Not Always Find a Cure" and "Dyin' Easy and Several Other Ways of Crossing Over and Departing This Life"; LVIII:106–121, "Baby Lore: The Why and Wherefore of It."
18. Kenneth L. Untiedt. *Inside the Classroom (And Out): How We Learn Through Folklore.* PTFS Volume LXII. Denton: University of North Texas Press, 2005. 304.
19. Francis E. Abernethy. *2001: A Texas Folklore Odyssey.* PTFS Volume LVIII. Denton: University of North Texas Press, 2001. 336.
20. http://www.thewittliffcollections.txstate.edu/swwc/archives/writers/roach.html [Accessed 12.26.08]
21. Abernethy. *Vol. III.* 40.

22. Francis E. Abernethy, Jerry B. Lincecum, and Frances B. Vick. *The Family Saga: A Collection of Texas Family Legends.* PTFS Volume LX. Denton: University of North Texas Press, 2003.
23. http://franvick.com/aboutfran.html [accessed 1.3.09].
24. Untiedt. PTFS LXII. 303–304.
25. Rodenberger titles in PTFS: XLIV: 85–94, "Texas Country School-teachers: Living Proof of a Legend"; LVI: 80–84; "Tales of a Rural School Teacher"; LXII: 46–55, "It All Depended on the Teacher: Classroom Resources in Texas Country Schools."
26. Abernethy. *Vol. I.* 42.
27. Sylvia Ann Grider. "Dorothy Scarborough," pp. 134–140, in *Texas Woman Writers: A Tradition of Their Own.* Tarleton State University Southwestern Studies in the Humanities, No. 8 edited by Sylvia Ann Grider, and Lou Halsell Rodenberger. College Station: Texas A&M University Press. 1997.
28. Scarborough titles in PTFS: I: 50–54, "Traditions of the Waco Indians"; II: 52–66, The 'Blues' as Folk Songs."
29. http://www.library.unt.edu/rarebooks/exhibits/women/20th.htm [Accessed 12.29.08].
30. Abernethy. *Vol. I.* 7, 13, and 54.
31. http://www.tshaonline.org/handbook/online/articles/EE/fes9.html [Accessed 1.6.09].
32. Estill titles from the PTFS publications are as follows: II: 67–74, "Customs Among the German Descendants of Gillespie County"; III: 24–27, "Lost Mines of the Llano and San Saba"; III: 153–156, "The Enchanted Rock in Llano County"; IV: 103–114, "Indian Pictographs near Lange's Mill, Gillespie County"; IX: 130–132, "Grandfather Wiley and His Dream"; XXII: 231–236, "Children's Games"; XXVI: 207–212, "Children's Games in Fredericksburg"; XXXVIII: 145–150, "Customs Among the German Descendants of Gillespie County."
33. http://www.tshaonnline.org/handbook/online/articles/EE/fes9.html [Accessed 12.29.08].
34. http://www.tshaonline.org/handbook/online/articles/GG/fgo34.html [Accessed 12.29.08].
35. Gonzalez titles from the PTFS publications are as follows: VI: 7–22, "Folklore of the Texas-Mexican Vaquero"; VIII: 86–116, "Tales and Songs of the Texas Mexicans"; X: 99–108, "Among My People"; XII: 107–114, "Bullet Swallower"; XXVI: 19–24, "Stories of my People."
36. http://www.tshaonline.org/handbook/online/articles/GG/fgo34.html [Accessed 12.29.08].
37. http://libnt4.lib.tcu.edu/Spcoll/www/finding%20aid_files/Major%20-%20MS3.pdf [Accessed 1.6.09].

38. Major title from the PTFS publication is as follows: X: 131–168, "British Ballads of Texas."
39. http://libnt4.lib.tcu.edu/Spcoll/www/finding%20aid_files/Major%20-%20MS3.pdf [Accessed 12.29.08].
40. Joyce Gibson Roach. "Mabel Major," pp. 82–86, in *Texas Woman Writers: A Tradition of Their Own*. Tarleton State University Southwestern Studies in the Humanities, No. 8 edited by Sylvia Ann Grider, and Lou Halsell Rodenberger. College Station: Texas A&M University Press. 1997.
41. Abernethy. *Vol. II*. 191.
42. Brandon title in PTFS: XXXI: 108–118, "Superstitions in Vermilion Parish."
43. Abernethy. *Vol. II*. 281.
44. http://www.easttexashistorical.org/membership/resolutions/linck.html [Accessed 1.06.09].
45. Abernethy. *Vol. III*. 35.
46. Untiedt. PTFS LXII. 304.
47. Abernethy. *Vol. III*. 37.
48. Sewell titles in PTFS: XLIV: 167–176, "Folklorish Remnants of Peyote Ceremonialism," with Charles Linck; XLV: 22–25, "The Rural Mailbox," with Charles Linck; LV: 235–245, "Punching Sticks, Flannel Wrapped Bricks, and Pink Powder Purgatives: Spring Rituals"; LVI: 37–43, "Bois d'Arc Recollections," with Charles Linck; LXII:134–147, "'Jes Sir, 'Meester Patternson': The Legendry of a Master."
49. http://anthropology.tamu.edu/faculty/directory.php?ID=225 [Accessed 1.06.09].
50. Grider titles in PTFS: XLII: 141–146, "Shotgun Houses and Shacks"; XLIX: 96–103, "The Folksong Scholarship of Dorothy Scarborough"; LVIII: 74–89, "Epics of Defeat: Texas' Alamo and Scotland's Culloden."
51. http://www.sallygreen.org/mirror925.html [Accessed 12.31.08].
52. Abernethy. *Vol. III*. 147.
53. Untiedt. PTFS LXV. 262–263.
54. Sentell titles in PTFS: LXIII: 161–172, "The Trials and Tribulations of a Dirt Road Country Doctor"; LXV: 79–88, "Most People in Texas Don't Die."
55. Leeper titles in PTFS: XLI: 137–146, "Talking and Touching: A Function of Storytelling"; XLIX: 163–171, "Storm Cellar Wisdom: Tall Tales from the Down Under"; LXV: 247–253, "Super Reality."
56. The web site for Faye Leeper's poetry is http://www.upli-wcp.org/poetryinenglish/fayleeperusa.html [accessed 1.1.09].
57. Abernethy. *Vol. III*. 166.
58. Untiedt. PTFS LXII. 302.

59. http://collegerodeoalumni.com/history/default.htm [Accessed 1.06.09].
60. Mahoney titles in PTFS: LII: 221–230, "College Creates a New Breed of Cowboy"; LXII: 200–211, "College Rodeo Cowgirls: From Queen to Contestant to Coach."
61. Kenneth L. Untiedt. *Folklore in Motion: Texas Travel Lore.* PTFS Volume LXIV. Denton: University of North Texas Press. 2007. 275.
62. Jim Harris. *Features and Fillers: Texas Journalists on Texas Folklore.* PTFS Volume LVI. Denton: University of North Texas Press, 1999. 224; and Kenneth L. Untiedt. *Folklore: In All of Us, In All We Do.* PTFS Volume LXIII. Denton: University of North Texas Press, 2006. 284.
63. Garrison titles in PTFS: XLVII: 141–150, "Hog Drovers: The Why and How of Hog Drives"; LVI: 66–69, "The Ol' Red Rooster Learns a Hard Lesson"; LXIII:215–226, "Cactus Jack Garner as Folk Hero, Vice President of the United States 1933–1940."
64. Untiedt. PTFS LXIII. 331.
65. Bridges titles in PTFS: LII: 95–104, "First Thing We Do, Let's Kill All the Lawyers"; LVIII: 154–163, "La Quinceanera: A Hispanic Folk Custom"; LXI: 150–161, "Clementine Hunter: Folk Artist."
66. Francis E. Abernethy and Kenneth L. Untiedt. *Both Sides of the Border: A Scattering of Texas Folklore.* PTFS Volume LXI. Denton: University of North Texas Press, 2004. 293.
67. Ibid. 295.
68. Schnitz titles in PTFS: LII: 159–174, "Hammered Dulcimers and Folk Songs: The Musical Heritage of the C. A. Lee Family"; LVI: 187–194, "A Collection of Poems"; LXI: 175–205, "Same Song, Second Verse"; LXII: 92–113, "School Yearbooks: Time Capsules of Texas Folklore"; LXIV: 193–201, "Driving Across Texas at Thirty-five Miles Per Hour."
69. Untiedt. PTFS LXIII. 304.
70. Abernethy and Untiedt. PTFS LXI. 296.
71. http://plumafronteriza.blogspot.com/2006/10/chicano-liturature-francisco-lomali.html [Accessed 1.02.09].
72. Fischer-West titles in PTFS: LLXI: 42–55, "Growing Up on Both Sides of the Border"; and 92–99, "A Tortilla is Never 'Just' a Tortilla."
73. http://www.tshaonline.org/handbook/online/articles/ZZ/fzafg.html [Accessed 12.30.08].
74. http://www.tamu.edu/ccbn/dewitt/adp/history/bios/zavala/zavala.html [Accessed 12.30.08].
75. Abernethy. *Vol. II.* 259 and 269.
76. Anderson titles in PTFS are as follows: XLIV: 31–42, "My Favorite Texan and Folklore"; XLVII: 151–160, "A Key of Golden: Brief Encounters Remembered."

77. Kenneth L. Untiedt. *Death Lore: Texas Rituals, Superstitions, and Legends of the Hereafter*. PTFS Volume LXV. Denton: University of North Texas Press, 2008. 255–256.
78. Untiedt. PTFS LXV. 256.
79. Untiedt. PTFS LXIII. 281–82.
80. http://www.tshaonline.org/handbook/online/articles/RR/fra42.html [Accessed 12.20.08].
81. Ratchford titles from the PTFS publications are as follows: III: 57–59, "Native Treasure Talk up the Frio"; III: 104–108, "Moro's Gold"; XIV: 174–184, "Legend Making on the Concho."
82. http://www.tshaonline.org/handbook/online/articles/RR/fra42.html [Accessed 12.20.08].
83. Clara Sitter. "Librarian, Literary Detective, and Scholar: Fannie Elizabeth Ratchford" pp. 135–162, in *Reclaiming the American Library Past: Writing the Women In*. Contemporary Studies in Information Management, Policies, and Services. Edited by Suzanne Hildenbrand. New York: Ablex Publishing, 1996.
84. http://www.tshaonline.org/handbook/online/articles/HH/fhadv.html [Accessed 12.29.08].
85. Abernethy. *Vol. I.* 196.
86. Abernethy. *Vol. II.* 64 and 70.
87. Hamer title from the PTFS publication is as follows: XV: 59–74, "Anecdotes as Sidelights to Texas History."
88. Abernethy. *Vol. II.* 70.
89. Abernethy. *Vol. III.* 9 and 79.
90. Ibid. 164–165.

Joyce Gibson Roach and her mother, Ann Gibson

BETWEEN A ROCK AND A HARD PLACE: REFLECTIONS ON THE TFS AND A WRITING LIFE

by Joyce Gibson Roach

[This work is dedicated to my mother, Ann Gibson, whom I dub the Patron Saint of Only Children, and who, since the Laredo meeting in 1972, has kept an eagle eye on me; her grandchildren, Darrell and Delight; and now her great-grandchildren, Trey and Hollyann.—*Roach*]

Prologue—wherein the author explains herself

It will come as no surprise that I'm not a well-known author and there isn't time left to become one. One among us is considered, arguably, the greatest and best known Western novelist of all times—Elmer Kelton. Every person in the Texas Folklore Society who calls himself or herself a writer stands in Elmer's beneficent shadow. It was a distinct honor to write the Afterword for the TCU Press reprint of *Honor at Daybreak* (2002), and to be asked to write it because of long membership in the TFS and acquaintance with Elmer, and probably because Jim Lee, serving as acquisitions editor for TCU Press, instigated the invitation.

Charles Leland Sonnichsen, chronicler of more than forty books and tomes and scores of articles about the American Southwest, was my mentor, my best friend, and sternest critic. One of my books was about him (*C.L. Sonnichsen*, Boise State Western Writers Series, 1979). Jim Lee had a part in that book, too. He was the first person to *ask* me to write anything—this in 1971 for the defunct Steck-Vaughn Southwestern Writers series that went that-a-way right after Hermes Nye, somebody else, and I submitted assignments and signed contracts.

What Sonnichsen knew about himself as a writer is exactly what I learned, and so I offer his words as prologue. He said that he was a grassroots historian, preferring to talk to old-timers about old times, poke around in old court house records, read old letters, journals and diaries, investigate historic places and events, and consult fiction as a guide to the past, knowing that what people have agreed to believe about the facts is a fact in itself and just as important. He explained, "I play second fiddle in the grand orchestra of history, but, still, the music wouldn't be complete without me. I sit below the salt; not on the level of the high king, or of the first order of writers, but still a part of the court—an author with a respectable body of works published and an audience who reads my work."

With some substitutions, I am that kind of writer, too, although on a much less productive level—his output was substantial; mine is not.

Sonnichsen wrote about the American Southwest—all of it. My vision never reaches far beyond West Texas, small-town, country culture, cattle and horses, and those who people such places; and, most important for me, the fact, fiction, and folklore of time and place, whether writing non-fiction books, articles, short fiction, humorous prose, a little music, drama, or poetry.

I could never have become a writer of any kind if not for the Texas Folklore Society. Some of the membership have nurtured me, inspired me, grounded me, criticized me, and informed my style even as the Society itself has changed over the years—my writing along with it. I'm preachin' to the choir here, but there's never been a better audience. *JGR*[1]

* * *

Between a Rock and a Hard Place

I knew I wanted to write before joining the Texas Folklore Society in 1964; I had wanted to ever since the age of about ten, after discovering that penmanship might be my calling. I loved the rhythms of cursive writing, the scrolls and curves, ovals and push-pulls—and the grade that came with it. Developing a fine style—large, expansive, visible, just like me—I was rewarded with an A+ every time. Who wouldn't want to write? And write I did, copying poetry, sayings, song lyrics, quotations from great speeches, recipes, scriptures from the King James Bible—anything. While reading all that stuff to my mother, who surely hadn't read any of that for herself in spite of the fact that she was providing the copy, I fell in love with the sound of my own voice reading other people's works, and thereby took the rhythms and writing patterns of others unto myself, especially the Bible—developing what Beowulf described as his "word hoard." Don't think any of these exercises in vanity foreshadowed a writing career. But the era of my birth—the Depression, World War II, life and times in Jacksboro, Jack County—certainly did foreshadow what I would write *about* much later.

And, because of everything I sopped up like a sponge at an early age, I was placed squarely between a rock and a hard place when it came to real writing later on—I had developed a style that was too "popular" for the serious, academic journals and books including TFS publications in earlier years, and too academic for the popular publications. Both eventually took my work but, for some years, I had to "fix" everything to suit both audiences. Most important of all, I had to get over my glorious penmanship and use a typewriter to copy what I had written by hand, then become proficient on a word-processor, which proved technically challenging. That's where I began to re-write a lot and actually learned to write.

Now, back to the beginning. In the year of my birth, the tail end of 1935, the nation was drowning in the Great Depression, the Great Plains whirling itself into oblivion along with its inhabitants, and the Lone Star fixin' to celebrate its centennial as Amon

G. Carter proclaimed Fort Worth—"Where the West begins"—superior to Dallas—"Where the East peters out."

Meanwhile, in West Texas . . . there lay the ranching kingdom—the wild and wooly, droughty, windy, tornado-prone, torrid, flower-strewn region of blistering sun, starry nights, wide vistas, but narrow viewpoints. It is a place of thousands of square miles crammed with fabulous folklore, tales, songs, and stories, and populated with stubborn, hard-headed, gentle, smart, stupid, mean, generous, stingy saints and sons-a-bitches—a place that hung like an artist's canvas in the blue, cloudless West Texas sky anywhere west of Forth Worth. That was the world into which I was born and where my heart will ever be.

At that time, the Texas Folklore Society was twenty-six years old, J. Frank Dobie was the editor, Martha Emmons was president, followed in 1936 by Mabel Major, who would, twenty years later, become my favorite professor and introduce me to Shakespeare, Browning, and Dobie (up to that time I thought all three were contemporaries) and the Texas Folklore Society. It was also she who begged me leave-off scholarly literary criticism of Medieval Camelot (my master's thesis was in Middle English literature) and return, hence, to the Cowlot of my youth and write about that. Charles Leland Sonnichsen followed Mabel as president, and it was he who, in 1971, schooled, cajoled, criticized, and encouraged me as a writer—but more of Major ("No s at the end, please") and Sonnichsen later. It violates the ethics of good paper writing to jump the gun.

In the year of my birth, the TFS presented Carl Sandburg in a program at Hogg Auditorium on the UT Campus. The Society met in Dallas at none other than the Adolphus Hotel, with John Lee Brooks presiding. Serious business was conducted wherein the question of raising dues from $1.50 to $2.00 was discussed. The publication for the year was *Puro Mexicano.*[2]

I was born in late December at the hind-part of the year, 1936, which was also of some importance to my birth. The entire state wallowed in fable, fact, legend, and lore of the Alamo Epic and, at the same time, took in such popular culture as Sally Rand in Fort

Worth, who fanned the flames of more than history at the newly-built-for-the-occasion, Casa Mañana. Centennial! Other celebrations and acknowledgments were going on in other places, but that never became part of my history.

Being born on the tail end of the Depression was fortunate for me. In Jack County we all had plenty of nothing in equal proportions; no one had more of nothing than anyone else. The Depression was followed by World War II, and the war was even better. That the history books considered both occasions major catastrophes made me suspicious of historians ever after.

The reason for my pleasure in World War II was that I knew where everyone was and what we were all supposed to do. The entire National Guard unit from Jack County, Battery F, 131st Field Artillery was lost—the Lost Battalion. I remember thinking it was strange that men from Jack County should be lost anywhere, any time. My Uncle Glen was on a tank chasing a fox named Rommel in Africa. Uncle Fred was in a big ship, the USS Blackhawk, somewhere in the Pacific Ocean. They were there, we were here. My daddy was butchering beef at the grocery. My mother was in the kitchen. Mama Hartman was down on her knees asking God to smite the enemy. The citizens were on the square having parades or war rallies, saving coupons for sugar and such, collecting tinfoil in big balls to make bombs, buying U.S. Savings bonds to help lick the Axis, and giving the V-for-Victory sign. Yes, I knew where everyone was and what they were doing. I was safe in the bosom of family, neighborhood, church, and town and beloved by one and all, or so it seemed, who made me—and every other child—feel safe.[3]

It's time to note that I was an only child. Only-children look at the world differently than others. We know from an early age that we are special; everybody likes us, wants us around; we don't have to be like everybody else; we never have to abide by the dictates of what someone else wants us to be. I did exactly what I wanted to do—by myself, of course. Such children are incredibly naïve and being born into a naïve time and place—well, that's called double naïveté, if not double jeopardy.

The place of my dry, rocky, thirsty, oak trees/grassland genesis and personal historical time frame of the 1930s through the 1960s—somewhere between the music of "The Old Chisholm Trail" and the "dawning of the age of Aquarius," free love and hippies—made all the difference in what I am and am not. It has inspired, confused, helped, and hindered me; given me great confidence and terrible insecurity; pushed me way ahead, and held me way back from all sorts of notions. The stage and setting were provided, almost supernaturally it seems, appearing without my summons, and populated with all the supporting cast—the personal family ancestry who came to Texas in the 1880s to Bell County, remaining ever present in the recounting of the family saga by my grandmother: life in Jack County absorbed from home, neighborhood, church, and around the square of a county seat. (You just can't trust a town that isn't built on a square.)

There was the countryside complete with ranches with Hereford cattle and Quarter horses, and Fort Richardson where William Tecumseh Sherman arrived at almost the same time the Warren Wagon Train Massacre occurred, thereby assuring the first Indian trial for the transgressions of Satanta, Satank, and Big Tree. The Coca Cola Ranch and Fort Richardson were my playgrounds, where historical scenes in one form or another were rehearsed again and again, and absorbed with the rhythm of a horse. Cowboys and Indians were themes embedded in my psyche and cemented in my thinking at the Saturday afternoon picture shows where Roy, Gene, Hoppy, and later, John Wayne, Randolph Scott, and Gary Cooper held sway. Dale didn't impress me much, but Trigger did. I thought even more of Roy after learning that he had Trigger stuffed after the horse's demise.

Add to that a red brick school house and a city set on a hill located sixty-five miles away so that to get there seemed like a long journey—Fort Worth, the center of my small universe. Yes, everything encompassed in less than 100 miles. You can guess just how short the play and how small the stage, but understand, too, that exploring every trail, furrow, fork in the road, creek, and river, knowing intimately the land and the people, absorbing speech patterns and cadences, becoming imprinted with sayings, philosophy of range country, and Biblical vocabulary and plots, and yearning to tell about it has all taken a lifetime.

Real writing, sort of, began in high school. Penmanship got old by the time I learned to take notes on note cards, write a research paper, and navigate footnotes and bibliography, although good handwriting still counted. And, I was ready for college—TCU, the Only University for me.

Meanwhile, back in other parts of Texas . . . While I was busy growing up, Mabel Major and C. L. Sonnichsen had landed in Texas—Mabel at TCU, Sonnichsen at El Paso School of Mines before it became UTEP—and took up with TFS.

Mabel grew up in Mark Twain country in Hannibal, Missouri, and was squarely ensconced in the Victorian Era. Wishing to escape the female restrictions imposed by the times, she applied for teaching jobs as far away as possible and was accepted in the garden spot of Texas—Big Spring. From there she went to TCU where she spent the rest of her teaching years.[4]

It's unclear just when Mabel joined the TFS, probably in the early 1930s, but following her presidency in 1936, she invited the society to meet in Fort Worth in 1937. F. E. Abernethy noted in Volume II of his three-part history that "Mabel was a feisty and formidable maiden lady on one level, but smiling warmth on another. She put the big pot in the little one and accompanied the whole of it with music . . . the most notable of which was the Kentucky dulcimer played by Josiah Combs, author of the classic *Folk Songs of the Southern United States*, which was first published in French." J. Frank Dobie's minutes were complimentary: "The Twenty-Third Annual Roundup . . . was in some ways the best meeting the Society has ever had. The credit is all due to the president, Mabel Major, and to her able assistant Rebecca Smith. The whole meeting was carefully arranged."[5] Abernethy's remarks as well as those of Dobie allude to the times—still under the banner of the Victorian Era when independent women were not much tolerated, except for kind remarks when they performed their duties well. Mabel published little in the TFS but her contributions were written with scholarly seriousness, using the Turabian method.[6]

Mabel explored the Southwest often in the company of Rebecca Smith Lee, a friend and teaching companion at TCU. One of the most important trips was to the Taos pueblo in the 1930s where she met Mary Austin, the brightest female writer in the Southwestern skies.[7] She also visited and enjoyed a squash blossom omelet prepared by D. H. Lawrence's widow sometime in the 1940s. Other than one paper, "British Ballads in Texas," published in the TFS publication *Tone the Bell Easy* (1932), Mabel published little else.[8]

Sonnichsen arrived in El Paso in 1931, with a new Ph.D. from Harvard and a dissertation on Samuel Butler. After noticing the library was short on *Hudibras* materials and being informed by President Dosie Wiggins—who claimed to have hired his teachers as if he were buying mules who could perform all kinds of services—in 1935 that he would be teaching a course about Life and Literature of the Southwest, the Border apprentice started looking around. There was *no* literature he could find, and besides that, he was told to teach the course because Dobie was teaching it at UT. In spite of the fact that he later went to Austin to teach the course for Dobie one summer, he wasn't interested in wearing another man's mantra. There was plenty to do in the hinterlands of Border Country, and so he went to work.[9]

When the Texas Folklore Society met for the first time in El Paso in 1936, Sonnichsen joined, and became President Elect. He insisted such a meteoric rise to presidency was because he was the only one in that part of the world to organize and put on a meeting. New Mexico—it was to be a joint meeting—had "the best artillery," as he put it, with such names as Paul Horgan, Alice Corbin Henderson, and others of their stature. Under difficult circumstances involving difficult personalities, Dobie among them, all went well.[10] After that, Sonnichsen participated fully in meetings but began publishing prolifically about events, characters, life, and times—everything pertaining to that region encompassing El Paso on both sides of the border.

I entered TCU in 1954 and embraced education and campus life whole hog, joining the band and the debate team. I didn't last long on the debate team—you weren't supposed to quote poetry or offer maxims, and had to be able to concede there were two sides to any argument. Speech/Drama was my declared major. My freshman year I tried out and was cast as the aged English madam in *Ladies in Retirement.* At the tryouts I was able to pull off a perfect upper crust Brit accent. During the run of the play, however, the accent disappeared (where?) and the madam strode about the stage speaking some strange dialect, a combination of West Texas and English English: "Gawd! It's non a' yore bloody bidness." The play called for the madam to get bumped off early and her body stuffed in a brick oven in the wall. The director, cast, and audience looked forward to—even prayed for—my demise. I never tried out for another play, but it only took one role to remain forever devoted to footlights.

English literature captivated me from the beginning. And I was an excellent reader of Shakespeare, getting the phrases and rhythms just so, although in Texas dialect. Called upon often to read by my favorite professor, Mabel Major, she seemed perplexed about my ability to get the phrasing right, the rhythms precise, and the expression and emphasis on the nose. She wondered, Why? How?—especially when it became obvious from tests that I barely knew what was going on. Such matters as themes, literary devices, and the meaning didn't mean a thing to me. This went on a pace until one day Miss Major asked me if I read the Bible much. Of course; I read it until most of the important parts were memorized, feeling conscience stricken to do so as a fully, immersed, born guilty, Southern Baptist Convention Baptist who read the Holy Baptist King James Bible. I had even heard Billy Graham, in person, for Christ' sakes. That King James, Shakespeare, and Jesus spoke the same English was an epiphany for me! It will come as no surprise that not only Shakespeare but also the Medieval period of Arthurian legend and lore were my favorites, and, as I would discover later, the stuff of westerns and the foundations of more than just West Texas life. Hearing that it rained in England all the time caused me to long to visit someday. I did, and it did—rain all the time. Loverly!

Mabel Major. Photo courtesy of Joyce Roach

About the time I was really getting good at research (had figured out the Dewey Decimal system and wrote in an acceptable footnoted style), the same professor who asked me to read Shakespeare as an undergraduate asked me to take her class, Life and Literature of the Southwest, and if my by-then husband, Claude (we married in 1957 just before I completed a BFA in 1958) and I would like to be her guests and give her a ride to a meeting of the Texas Institute of Letters. There I met part of the triumvirate—Walter Prescott Webb, J. Frank Dobie, but not Roy Bedichek—and we later accompanied Mabel to a meeting of the Texas Folklore Society. The rest may not be history, but for the purpose of my life as a Texas writer, it's the most important part.

Miss Major—I never did call her Professor—made one other illuminating suggestion to me as I was writing my thesis in Chaucer studies (MA, 1965). "Why don't you turn away from England and look in your own backyard when you want to write again?" Frankly, it was a relief. Training to be a scholar was instructional and much needed, but confining—fenced in. She had also discovered that I yearned to write, trying short stories, poetry, and personal narrative to enter in TCU's creative writing contests, which she helped found and organize. Subject matter for these entries was always the same—life and times in small-town West Texas. Mabel was the first to let the gap down, rescue me from myself, and save England from me. She also caused the publication of my first work, "A Hat Is Still a Hat," in TCU's literary journal, *Descant*, in 1963.

Joining the TFS in 1964, I jumped in head first. Full participation in the Folklore Society meant giving papers—a chance to speak, to render with feeling, to expound on topics, and that I did, beginning in 1965. In the beginning I went at it in true scholarly form: outlines, footnotes, and such with the expectation of being published in a TFS book. But the topics leant themselves to a popular style. I was "caught between" from the beginning, and the writing was a peculiar mix, but the voice came through in ways that covered my lack of skill on paper. I learned that a speaker does not a writer make, but finding one's voice can help. And the voice? Speech patterns, gospel songs, scripture, maxims, jokes, tales, religiosity, and the philosophy of dry, rain-starved West Texas.

My first paper was given in Austin. It was a rehash of "A Hat Is Still a Hat," and I was sure that Wilson Hudson would publish it. Not! Wilson still adhered to old school topics—digging up bones, as some put it, C. L. Sonnichsen included—and the more formal style of footnoting. Granted, folklore topics and papers never lent themselves to the rigid standards of rigid research; nevertheless, one was supposed to back up everything possible with references linking Texas folklore to American and international folklore, if possible. Noting motifs and themes was important. There were not many family stories then, referred to as how-grandpappy-fit-the-war tales. It may be duly noted that in 1963, Margaret Hartley, editor at SMU Press that published TFS volumes then, was known as one who "demanded correctness and consistency" and pushed for *Chicago Manual of Style*.[11]

If change was in the air regarding style, it also affected subject matter. In looking over the contents of TFS publications, I notice an increase of papers on folklore in literature, exploring themes and motifs in everything from Dime Novels to literature and film. In 1967, Jim Byrd gave a paper on "The Outhouse in Lore and Literature." I remember hearing the paper and comments from two—Mabel Major among them—that decried the investigation of the scatological as worthy of folklore study. I was thoroughly entertained but kept a solemn demeanor in the presence of her remarks. Also, I didn't know what scatological meant.

Change was also occurring in the world at large, including the US of A. It was the jumping off place from the good-old-days of the Fifties after World War II—the feminist movement revved up with bra-burning; free love abounded; new folk music of social comment appeared; dance styles evolved, not to mention everything else under the sun, or so it seemed. Even Wars with a capital W took on a new and horrific image. "People just won't behave anymore," was a phrase that comes to mind, and although the expression found more sophisticated syntax and vocabulary, the folk had it right.

My first piece appeared in *Hunters and Healers*, 1969—"Diesel Smoke & Dangerous Curves: Folklore of the Trucking Industry"—given as a paper in 1967 in Nacogdoches. It wasn't easy. Hudson questioned every statistic, causing me to look up everything again, and he made me rewrite a lot of it, letting me know how little he thought of my work. Taking it as my due as a female without a Ph.D. in an organization heavy on the side of college professors, I accepted his constructive criticism and got on with it.

At the Dallas meeting in 1967, I gave a paper entitled "The Legends of El Tejano, the Texan Who Never Was," making use of a shorter version of a term paper written for George Hendricks' graduate folklore class at NTSU, now called UNT. TFS didn't publish it, but *Western Folklore* did in 1968. It was serious stuff. The story was told to me by my Uncle Carl Hartman, who lived in Tucson and knew the desert folk—in this case, his friend Alejandro, whose last name was unknown—and their tales. Uncle Carl found other stories and did exhaustive research; I added the folk motifs and themes, documenting it all. The story had never been told in print before; it also was published in a pulp, *Treasures*, in 1972, that paid a little money, which I sent to Alejandro through my kin.

In 1971, at the San Antonio meeting I rendered "Hallelujah Thine the Glory" with gusto. It wasn't serious, but got some laughter—dangerous stuff and habit forming. It was also the year that James Ward Lee asked me to do a monograph on C. L. Sonnichsen. I'd never met him but fell under his spell immediately. Not acquainted thirty minutes, we started singing—me the melody, he the tenor harmony. From that moment on we started to sing, wherever we were, the minute we spied each other. By then I had two children, Darrell and Delight, and was at home on a very small piece of range, along with a few cows and horses near Keller.

Continuing my acquaintance with Sonnichsen—he taught at the University of Texas at El Paso for forty-one years and served another fifteen as editor of the *Journal of Arizona History*—led him to ask me what my next project was. I told him it was about cowgirls, ranch women, and others of their ilk. "Why?" he wanted to know. Because I'd grown up observing and admiring at a distance the Worthington sisters of Jack County, who lived on horseback, roping, riding, working cattle, and rodeoing for entertainment. They didn't seem to be cut out of the same piece of cloth as pioneer women who got by, made do, walked behind a plow, and such. These cowgirls rode everywhere—they didn't walk—and they worked just as hard as men, talked tough, acted tough, were tough, and had an air of confidence about them that was hard not to notice, if not admire. Discovering stories about others of their kind from the frontier to the then present made me want to write a book detailing characteristics that represented an authentic American folk heroine. Sonnichsen predicted, "You're on to something. Let me see an outline, look at chapters, give you some advice." He did. One piece of advice was especially helpful. Mentioning that there was a lot more research yet to do before really getting down to writing—there were scores of women not yet investigated—Sonnichsen insisted that the writing should begin with the examples in hand. "If you wait until you have all the women gathered up, you'll never write. Use the ones you have that make your point and move on." Taking what he said as really good news and a radical departure from the kind of researching I'd been taught to do—don't leave a leaf unturned—I wrote full speed ahead, through 1974–75.

The western novel was still in vogue, in fact riding high in 1975 when *The Cowgirls* started making the rounds. Non-fiction wasn't. But still I sent the manuscript to Doubleday. We all want New York to tell us no first. The editor was a man known to like westerns a lot, but this wasn't fiction. It took a long time for the rejection to come back, but the editor said something important: "If your work had been written by someone with a 'name' we'd take it in a minute. But you're an unknown. Sorry." I saved all my rejection notes and letters just as Sonnichsen said ought to be done, because if editors send more than form letters, they have really read your submission, even if they tell you it's trash. I was disappointed and didn't waste any more postage east of the Mississippi, but approached Bob Gray, editor of *Horseman Magazine*, having heard they sometimes published longer works about western subjects. They took the manuscript and published it without changing a word or a footnote—footnotes which appeared at the bottom of each page, Turabian style, with the bibliography at the end of the book. For taking the book as it was, I will always be grateful, but, at the same time, I wished for a good editing and some rewriting. *The Cowgirls* won a Spur Award from Western Writers of America in 1978, the same year C. L. Sonnichsen was president of that organization. The book stayed in print with some five more printings from 1977 until 1988. It couldn't be bought in bookstores but ordered from Cordovan Press through half-page ads and blurbs in *Horseman Magazine*.

It would be easy to claim that a writing life began because of the WWA award and the little known subject of cowgirls, ripe for the picking. The truth is that association with Mabel Major, the TFS, and, above all, C. L. Sonnichsen opened that door. To this day, I am still asked to speak and write about those real and unreal stereotypes they represent. Then in 1991, Fran Vick, new at the helm of UNT Press, took the book, cleaned it up, put footnotes as chapter notes, added an index and bibliography, and a smashing color cover designed by Fred and Barbara Whitehead. Sonnichsen's Preface from the 1977 edition was repeated and an Afterword by Elmer Kelton added. And it's still in print—appearing at a time when the whole world got interested in Cowgirls. One reviewer called me Revisionist Historian and although the review was flattering, I had no use for the Revisionists then. Fran, among other talents, knew how to get UNT's books publicized. She went to numerous book events, even to New York City. And it was there she arranged a book signing at the Cowgirl Hall of Fame Café. Her family, my son Darrell, and I dressed Texas and stood the New York press people on their ears. The title was listed in the *New York Times* book section for a time.

Sonnichsen continued to impact my writing life and confirming what I wanted to write about and how I wanted to write it. He was as familiar with the Bible as I and put it to use by quoting, misquoting, and misapplying the Scripture, knowing how to bend it to humorous use. He was familiar as well with literature, which he also quoted and bent. He wrote history in a creative, readable, unbiased way, perhaps because he was an English professor and not a history scholar.[12] If there was more than one way to interpret the facts, he did. During the years between the 1950s and 80s, Sonnichsen was frequently out of favor with the "pure" historians who put down his work. He often went back over subjects the historians had already passed judgments on, making some of them critical of his writing. His explanation was that scholars didn't like "another rooster crowing on their dung heap." He continued to counsel me, insisting that I not be fenced in by any one historical school of thought, method, or view of history—that the facts could and should be presented in a variety of ways without violating the truth; folklore was as important to history as history was to folklore. His philosophy adhered to a paraphrased poetic ethic: "Call no man historian unless he makes you *feel*." Sonnichsen was, himself, caught between a rock and a hard place.

After *The Cowgirls*, there were articles, essays, and short pieces published in newspapers, Western magazines, historical and literary journals, and books. Every single piece came out of papers written for the TFS meetings, published in TFS books, or related to topics and ideas inspired by other TFS members.

By 1975, matters were still evolving, changing in the Texas Folklore Society. At the 1975 meeting in Houston, where I was program chair and made what I thought was a coup by persuading Stanley Marcus to speak—*Minding the Store* was newly published and Stanley was speaking everywhere, but I didn't think about that—Sonnichsen delivered the banquet address. His title was "Poor Wayfaring Stranger," and, with stinging humor, he accused the Society of continuing to dig up bones. F. E. Abernethy, who became editor in 1971, noted: "Sonnichsen had accused folklorists of ignoring the modern folklore, the poplore and popular culture that was circulating all around them."[13] The story goes that some of the membership cornered Sonnichsen, pointing out that timely folklore was being published. *What's Going On In Modern Texas Folklore* appeared in 1976 as a response to his observations and criticism.[14]

Yes, such topics as "Cobras in K-Mart" (Ann Carpenter), "A Bumper Crop of Modern Epigrams" (Jim Byrd), "The Folklore of Marijuana" (Robert Russell), and "Zydeco" (Joseph Lomax), were indeed current—modern. The program of 1975 included a paper by James Ward Lee titled "Mommanem: Some Notes on Mothers and Others" that blew the door open to raucous humor mixed with serious folklore exploration of stereotypes of the past. Lee and Byrd had given some mildly humorous pieces before and so had others, but nothing like Mommanem—"Mama and them."

Certainly, laughter opened the way for me, and "A High Toned Woman," rendered in Jefferson at the 1986 meeting, brought acceptance and, in some cases, notoriety. Kent Biffle heard the piece, literally grabbed it out of my hand afterward, then published it in the *Dallas Morning News*. It appeared in *Hoein' the Short Rows* in 1987, was submitted in the short non-fiction category of WWA, and won a Spur Award in 1988 for myself and the TFS as publisher. The piece was combined with an earlier TFS paper, "Revive Us Again" (published in *Observations and Reflections on Texas Folklore,* 1972), into a short story entitled "Just As I Am," published by Doubleday in 1990 in *Women of the West: An Anthology of Short Stories by Contemporary Western Women Writers,* which won a Spur from WWA in 1991.

Other changes were occurring with Abernethy at the helm as editor. On a personal note, he accepted my kind of writing and published it, and he was open to others whose work included very creative family stories—Al Lowman and his delightful elephant ears series, Kenneth Davis's tales of Bell County, more of Jim Lee's rich stuff and nonsense, and then Robert Flynn's tragic-comedic perspectives that moved us to tears alongside laughter. Robert Flynn and I did duets for TFS programs wherein we traded information and insults about religion and our hometowns, Chillicothe and Jacksboro. With Jim Lee, I traded stories about characters who lived in imaginary towns of Bodark Springs in Eastis County and Horned Toad, Texas, in Caballo County. It amounted to playing straight man for both of them and some of the work was published, but because of their reputations, not mine. One of Jim Lee's papers, "Eats," provided inspiration and the title for a book Ernestine Sewell Linck and I teamed up to write, *Eats: A Folk History of Texas Food*, which won the TIL non-fiction prize in 1989.

Texas Folklore Society sessions for TSHA brought the organizations together for what were considered popular and well-attended programs, one of which included Jim Lee, Bob Flynn, and myself: "Laughing All the Way." They are both silly, brilliant writers, have the impeccable timing of the best of comedic actors, and differ in style but not in theme. They are both known as the funniest men in Texas, and deservedly so. The three of us were considered as a trio to hold forth for a national meeting of Merrill Lynch clients. Lou Dobbs and Robert Redford were also in contention. We agreed to a conference call-interview with a group in New York, as in City. They asked questions; we went into our very best banter back and forth with each other over the wires. Complete silence on the New York end. They asked if we had ever bombed. Confessing that individually we had all bombed, we discovered that we also bombed as a group. Robert Redford got the nod and, for our efforts, we were sent a copy of some magazine autographed by Redford—or somebody. Redford was paid $3,000.

During this time frame, Ab began developing books around a theme: titles were intriguing, covers were attractive, and design was skillful—*Folk Art in Texas*, 1984; *Dance Across Texas*, Betty Casey, 1986; *Mexican-American Folklore*, John O. West, 1988; *Texas Toys and Games*, 1989; *Hecho en Tejas: Texas-Mexican Folk Arts and Crafts*, Joe Graham, 1991; *Juneteenth Texas: Essays in African-American Folklore*, 1996; *Features and Fillers: Texas Journalists on Texas Folklore*, Jim Harris, editor, 1997; and a reprint, *The Best of Texas Folk and Folklore, 1916—1954*, 1998. The reprint is mentioned because Ab was always aware of the importance and quality of voices from the past, and sometimes included a piece or two in volumes. The reprint, however, marked the occasion of looking back in time, knowing that times, they were a'changin', and recognizing, perhaps, that his tenure was drawing to a close, but only by his own choice. The history of Texas Folklore Society in three volumes appeared beginning in 1992, from editor Abernethy; Charles Shaw designed the cover. The volumes are the most important contributions from Abernethy.

As to the Society itself, it may, and should, be noted that women were in stronger positions much due, I think, to the influence and reputation of Fran Vick, who, over many years supported the TFS with her time, talents, and tithes, as the Methodists are wont to say. *Legendary Ladies of Texas*, published under Fran Vick's E-Heart name in 1981, marked a publication of such popularity and demand that it was reprinted. Fran became publisher of TFS books (UNT Press) in 1990. Because of her intensive approach to marketing and willingness to pitch TFS books anywhere and everywhere, titles from the past were reprinted and new titles always prominent. In 2000, Editor Abernethy reported that "Fran Vick and UNT Press is experimenting with a way to bring out-of-print books back in print through a new book distribution program by Lightning Print, Inc. LPI loads the out-of-print books into a database and can then electronically print books on demand to customers who order them. The books can be printed in about forty-eight hours. Lightning Books then ships the printed and bound book directly to the customer."[15] Fran remains on the cutting edge of what is good for the TFS, but also for TSHA and the entire state of Texas, for that matter.

Other powerful female influences and voices were added—Lou Rodenberger, Margaret Waring, Phyllis Bridges, Mary Harris, Sylvia Mahoney, Lucy West—and are forces to be reckoned with outside the TFS as well as in.

Beginning in 2000, new Fellows were elected—an occasion occurring very few times before. Membership had shifted dramatically even before the '90s and the majority were no longer university professors, but *us*: retired from teaching or various other professions, members who were interested and supportive; and we were into the time known as the wise years—old age. Yes, a few young ones helped—Patrick Vick and Delight Roach gave papers—and we were glad, and yes, proud. The membership of the organization now is mature to elderly, but those in charge keep moving—we now have a presence at the Texas Folklife Festival in San Antonio, for instance.

As for me, I was beginning to come out from under a rock and a hard place. During the period of the '90s, Fran Vick allowed me the opportunity of editing an anthology that featured several TFS members. *This Place of Memory: A Texas Perspective* (1992), was dedicated to the TFS and featured pieces in poetry, non-fiction and fiction by Ernest Speck, Tony Clark, Jim Harris, Paul Patterson, Ernestine Sewell Linck, F. E. Abernethy, and Elmer Kelton, respectively.

Another anthology, *Collective Heart: Texans in World War II* (Eakin Press, 1996), included Fran Vick, and by association, her brother, Joe Pat Brannen, Elmer Kelton, F. E. Abernethy, Hazel Shelton Abernethy, James Ward Lee, Jim Harris, and Robert Flynn. Both books revealed some of the finest writers in the state, bar none. Both anthologies had good reviews with the only criticism being that I included some of my own work in both books.[16]

I began to write fiction about 1990. Because almost all works of non-fiction, papers given at TFA and various conferences, and later, personal narratives, humorous prose, a musical play or two, were connected in one way or another to my time and place, I felt the need to invent a town and county—Horned Toad, Texas, in Caballo County—West Texas—where almost everything I'd ever said or written in other genres was fictionalized.

Toad, for short, is one of those plain, no-nonsense names such as Texas is full of: Muleshoe, Levelland, Hereford, Prairie View, Plainview. Such places are marked by unpredictable weather, men, and beasts, as well as hard-nosed religion, peculiar politics, curious customs, clubs and rituals, some of them having to do with games on horseback. It is ranch country, dry-land farming country, oil country, King James Bible country. West Texans compare themselves favorably with the Wilderness of Zion that Moses knew for sure wasn't the Promised Land. The characters, male and female, have their crosses to bear and gospels to proclaim, and they are various mixtures of saints and sons-of-bitches. They take God's name in vain, swear expertly, pray mighty prayers, sing gospel tunes at the drop of a stained Stetson, and quote the scriptures, Edgar A. Guest, and Shakespeare in the same breath. The litany of brown places is always supplication for rain and their colloquy of praise is ever for it.[17]

There are heroes and heroines among the males and females of Toad. Real heroes in West Texas are mostly football players who've gone on to great college careers or even to the pro ranks. Writers, scientists, politicians, entrepreneurs, and even gangsters, hucksters, and crooks had to move on to a larger arena if they were ever going to get ahead. School teachers occasionally qualified as heroines. Most never wanted or needed to be important people in any of the aforementioned categories. Such people were heroes and heroines to me because they didn't or couldn't go anywhere else; they stayed put and made the most of life on earth as it is, not as it is in Heaven. One hero, Joe Don Wheelright, and heroine, Annie Laurie Rogers, are typical of mine. Jesse Earl is short, fat, sloppy—"I swear his momma must'a put a nipple on the ketchup bottle when he's a baby"—has a college degree, and is the smartest man in town. He is also kin to the meanest and most dangerous man in town who is running unopposed for the sheriff's office. Annie Laurie is six feet in her stockings. "She was nice enough, but you know, typical ranch woman—bronc buster, roper, shrewd cattle dealer—even rodeoed some. She didn't put a rifle in her pickup. She kept it about her at all times. Talked Spanish real good and hired mostly Mexicans." The unlikely pair team up to elect a write-in candidate and end up falling in love in the process. The narrator muses at their wedding, that he couldn't "understand how such as them two could have married one another. But my wife said at the wedding in her sentimental voice that she figured they both fell in love with the better parts of each other that nobody else could see."[18] Discovering in an article in *Texas Monthly* that the first woman sheriff was elected in 1947 in Mentone, Texas, it was easy to transport the basics to the radical '60s and '70s, adding the kinds of characters I knew well—good old boys, ranch women, and underdogs.

There have been no stories from me about blacks. Yes, in the Fifties I worried more about needing rain than I did about segregation. The closest thing to a racial joke was from a Jacksboro native who recounted a tale about flamboyant citizens, John Moore, a lawyer, and Roy Cherryhomes, a land and oilman whose ancestors helped found Jacksboro. The story goes that John went into Eckman's Café—the only place to eat besides the legendary Green Frog Café—saying that integration was not a legislated fact and Negroes could not come in and sit down and eat with "us." Without missing a bite, Roy's reply was, "Yes, and it will serve them right, too." I know that with changes in time and place, the "serves 'em right, too" motif is a folk-traveler, appearing in anecdotes the world over.

As to Mexicans—the term Hispanics was not even a word then and Mexican American wasn't in use, either—I knew only one and not personally. The moving picture show portrayed them as fabulous swordsmen and horsemen, even if they were bandits. Who could resist the Cisco Kid—"Ah, Cisco! Ah, Pancho!" The one known to me was the handsomest man I ever saw and he had blue eyes. Such a character appears under the nickname of Fudge, a little boy who comes to live with his daddy, a ranch cowboy. In true Western tradition, nobody asks anything, certainly not who his mother was—nothing. It's obvious that the little boy is Mexican but has blue, blue eyes—his daddy's eyes. Ma'am, the owner's wife, takes the child under her wing, and it is she who must teach him how to shoot her small pistols. One night Fudge gets her guns off a peg on the wall, goes outside in the dark, practices the draw, fires by mistake and kills Ma'am's cat; then the rest of the ranch is shot up pretty bad by cowboys firing back—at someone: "Gathering back the horses, digging bullets out of the bull, mending the corral, scalding dead chickens for plucking and cooking, repairing Manuel's wagon, cleaning the chicken yard off Fudge, ordering more glass for the house windows, and scraping what was left of the cat off the outhouse wall took . . . time."[19] The idea for the story came from hearing Paul Patterson's tale about a little boy named Fatty who practices drawing his gun in front of a mirror with such intensity that he accidentally fires by mistake, breaking the mirror and scaring everyone half to death.

Although there was limited practice of personal racial prejudice, I didn't hold back from religious prejudice against any denomination that wasn't mine. There were excellent reasons for not liking other denominations, having to do with serious matters such as hymns, length of sermons, preachers, their wives, who could or could not take the Lord's supper as well as when and where, baptism (infant, immersed, or sprinkled), the plan of salvation, once saved always saved, blacksliding, falling from grace—the essentials. Two groups, not even classified as denominations, were the Catholics (who had too many children, drank wine instead of Welch's grape juice as God intended, and had services in a foreign language) and the Pentecostals. Both were considered secret organizations. Nobody would have visited either church, although the invitation was always open. The rest of us were in one accord on that matter. We were Christians, for Jesus sake. All such nonsense was covered in "Just As I Am," but was framed in the dilemma of what happens to a young girl's convictions when her friend, a prostitute, comes to a revival meeting.

Pentecostals, at least in many back-prairie towns, caught the worst of it. There was a negative feeling that amounted to discrimination. For one thing, they didn't look like us—women wore their hair different, and the skirts and sleeves on their dresses were too long. Services were mysterious: glorious music in four-part harmony that echoed all over town, and fiery sermons that caused the congregants to shout in some other foreign language—tongues, they called it. I lived not two blocks from the church and, so, had a front row seat. I longed to go to that church. It was mostly because of the music and their prayers for rain. Their religion was stubborn, hardheaded. They believed in some God that seemed stronger than mine, more demanding, and my denomination was plenty demanding. When the Pentecostals prayed for rain, as did every church in the summer, our supplications were weak compared to theirs. "Won't Somebody Shout Amen?" pays homage to a group who, like trees planted by the water, shall not be moved.[20] Once again, hearing and reading papers about such groups—including the art of snake handling—through the TFS reinforced my own experiences.

One other book, *Horned Toad Canyon*, a children's fantasy about horned lizards, owes something to a 1959 TFS publication, *And Horns on the Toads,* the title of which was taken from a paper by the same name by John Q. Anderson. The last section of the book talks about the folklore of horny toads, some of it taken from John Q's piece.

In conclusion—as every piece of writing must have, no matter the genre or style—I am a West Texas writer successful in a very small puddle, a dried up puddle at that. It's as much as I've ever aspired to, to know and be known here. My work is nothing more than voices speaking and behaving appropriately to their time and place. The motif and theme of drought and the need for rain is ever present, underscoring and explaining attitudes, behaviors, and relationships—good and bad. The thirsty land itself is a character, and

I'm certainly not the first writer to notice. Not a few TFS papers over the years address heat conditions in West Texas—the fact, fiction, and folklore of drought and those who live with it. That salient feature, exclusive above all others, resides in my mind and in the pores of my skin. After studyin' on it, as Paul Patterson would put it, I believe this to be true:

> In those days when God created heaven and earth and saw that it was good for West Texas to be parched, scorched, hot as hell, and without rain much-to-most-of-the time, His people feared Him, bowed down before Him. Their religion was narrow as dusty furrows, deep and dark as the cracked earth for falling into, jealous as Joseph's brothers in the years of famine, dry as the stone on which Moses and Charlton Heston received the Ten Commandments, and blind as nomads without sunglasses. But, lo, sometime in the Twentieth Century, somebody discovered how to harness the winds, gather air in a box, disperse it through water, and blow it through blades—conditioning the air. And, lo again, Jehovah's folks were relieved and comforted, and saw that it was not only good, but great. After that time, the Great I Am was no longer feared but known as a God of love, nicer, and not so stern. There was reinterpretation of the Word, now that groups gathered in the comfort of refrigerated air, and each interpret-tated and prophe-cated [to interpret; to utter prophesy; NBD (*New Bush Dictionary)*] according to, and leaning on, his or her own understanding, which the Scriptures say one ought not do. God's people seemed less afraid of Him. Worship services were more relaxed, even happy. Soon matters were in a mess and haven't been the same since, and all because West Texans cooled off.

> No one but me figured this out, but now you know. Further, there is a global lesson here. I am of a mind to believe that citizens of dry, droughty places on the face of the earth are more warlike, contentious, mean, fractious, and hard-headed. And if we could just get those folks cool—with air conditioning and such—they wouldn't want to study war no more.

That's my final thought, and it's probably not original, either. I'm now like Elmer Kelton: a thief and a liar—and all the fault of the Texas Folklore Society.

ENDNOTES

1. All names in this piece are identified with the TFS or otherwise identified.
2. Francis Edward Abernethy. *The Texas Folklore Society, Volume I, 1909–1943.* PTFS LI. Denton: University of North Texas Press, 1992. 204.
3. "Jacksboro Goes To War." *1941: Texas Goes to War.* James Ward Lee, ed. UNT Press, 1991. 186.
4. "In Memoriam: Mabel Major." *Some Still Do: Essays on Texas Customs.* F. E. Abernethy, ed. Encino Press, 1975; also "Benjamin Capps, Mabel Major, Charles Leland Sonnichsen" [bibliographic entries] *Southwestern American Literature: A Bibliography,* eds. John Q. Anderson, Edwin W. Gaston, Jr., and James W. Lee, Swallow Press, 1980.
5. Francis Edward Abernethy. *The Texas Folklore Society, Volume II, 1943–1971.* PTFS LIII. Denton: University of North Texas Press, 1994. 212.
6. "British Ballads in Texas" by Mabel Major appeared in *Tone the Bell Easy,* 1932, SMU Press; reprinted 1965; "Texas Versions of Some British Ballads," collected by Mabel Major, Fort Worth, sung by Melvin Dacus and accompanied by Keith Mixon, Texas Christian University was on the 1942 program in Denton, held at Texas State College for Women; "Frank Deperez, an Englishman Who Remembered Texas," Mabel Major, Baylor University (she taught there briefly after TCU retirement) appeared on the 1966 program in Austin. Lou Rodenberger and Sylvia Grider edited a major work

about those less than halcyon days for women writers, *Texas Women Writers: A Tradition of Their Own,* Tarleton State University Southwestern Studies in the Humanities, TAMU Press, 1997; I wrote the entry on Mabel Major.

7. Abernethy. *Volume II.* 243.
8. Major wrote a biography of Susan Elston (Mrs. Lew) Wallace which was never published. I did, however, read it in its entirety along with copious notes made in longhand and letters to and from various sources when cataloging her papers for Special Collections at TCU in the '90s. In 1929, Rebecca Smith appeared as her co-editor in *The Southwest in Literature: An Anthology for High Schools.* T. M. Pearce, of the University of New Mexico, was added as co-editor for the 1938 and 1948 editions of a survey entitled *Southwest Heritage: A Literary History with Bibliographies.* The 1972 edition appeared under the names of Major and Pearce only. *Early Times in Texas, or, The Adventures of Jack Dobell* (1936) by John C. Duval, contained a preface and commentary on the life of Duval by Major and Smith. *My Foot's in the Stirrup,* by W. S. Bartlett as told to Major and Smith, appeared soon after. An edition of *The Adventures of Big-Foot Wallace* by John C. Duval was edited by Major and Smith. In 1949, an anthology of southwestern poetry, *Signature of the Sun: Southwest Verse 1900–1950,* listed Major and Pearce as co-editors.

   I taught on the adjunct English faculty from 1984 to 1997. In 1992, Fred Erisman, then chair of the department, asked me to revive Mabel's course, Life and Literature of the Southwest. It became part of the regular curriculum, moved into graduate studies under an altered title, and is still being taught in some form today. Erisman turned over his course in the Western Novel to me, and I taught a one-time Folklore course in 1995. Each course allowed me to make use of work and books by TFS members, including F. E. Abernethy, Elmer Kelton, Bob Flynn, and Jim Lee.
9. Joyce Gibson Roach. *C. L. Sonnichsen,* Boise State Press, Boise State University Western Writers series, No. 40, 1978.
10. Abernethy. *Volume I.* 220.
11. Ibid. 192.
12. Sonnichsen was president of Western Literature Association twice, Western History Association, and Western Writers of America.
13. Francis Edward Abernethy. *The Texas Folklore Society, Volume III, 1971–2000.* PTFS LVII. Denton: University of North Texas Press, 2000. 32.
14. It was also the year I served as president of the TFS, and Elmer Kelton admitted to being a thief and a liar—taking others' information and turning it into made up stories—during his banquet speech, "Three Kinds of Truth: Fact, Folklore and Fiction."

15. Abernethy, *Volume III.* 177.
16. "The Best Time" in *This Place of Memory*, UNT Press, 1992; and "The News of War" in *Collective Heart, Texans in World War II*, Eakin Press, 1996.
17. "The Chronicles of Toad," *Writing on the Wind: West Texas Women Writers.* Lou Rodenberger, ed. TTU Press, 2007.
18. "In Broad Daylight," *Texas Short Stories.* Billy Hill, ed. Browder Springs Press, 2000; finalist for Spur Award, 2001.
19. "A Two-Gun Man." *New Trails: 23 Original Stories of the West.* John Jakes and Martin H. Greenberg, eds. Doubleday, 1994.
20. *Texas Short Stories II.* Billy Hill, ed. Browder Springs Press, 2000.

F. E. Abernethy, back in the Ought 'Sixties

BACK IN THE OUGHT 'SIXTIES

by Francis Edward Abernethy

I (an English teacher whose academic field was Renaissance drama) became a folklorist in the 1960s, and I am going to tell you about a few of those dear souls who stood in loco parentis and showed me the way.

This all started over coffee and moon pie—at five cents apiece, I might add—in the Lamar Tech faculty lounge, in 1959. The subject of the Texas Folklore Society came up, and a colleague told me that I should join up with that group. And fifty years ago I did. The following Easter, in 1960, I took the Greyhound from Beaumont and went to present a paper at my first meeting in San Antonio.

I was much <u>im</u>pressed with the Menger Hotel, but I was much <u>sup</u>pressed by the boisterous jollity of that Thursday evening's TFS gathering at Casa Rio, when I lately arrived. After dinner, people sang. I sat in the last tier, hugging the shadows. Members were in full cry when I crept out and went back to the hotel to go over my paper for the fiftieth time.

I was probably still going over my paper Friday morning at 8:45. Soon after nine, I made my first appearance before the Texas Folklore Society with "East Texas Josey Party Songs." I was pleased that the audience did not go to sleep, walk out, or throw things. I was warmed by their reception. But, the high point of the session—and of many sessions and of many years thereafter—occurred when Hermes Nye, whom I had never heard of, passed me a note that read (I still have that note!), "Delightful! Let's get together this evening."

And we did!

After the banquet that night, Hermes, Américo Paredes, Roger Abrahams, and I and three or four others congregated in a dim corner of the banquet room. Everybody else had gone. Hermes had his guitar, and we circled up our chairs and began to sing, usually singly but sometimes in duet harmony or as a group. We quickly worked it out that each of us would sing two songs and then pass on the guitar. A soldier from Arkansas wandered in and joined us, and a bunch of folks wandered by and sat in the darkness around us. We loved it. Nobody hogged the guitar. Everybody enjoyed everybody else. I remember singing "Precious Jewel" and "Little Green Valley," neither of which anybody knew. It was a close encounter of the very best kind, and I felt a sense of belonging with them and the Texas Folklore Society that I have never gotten over. I have missed only one meeting, last year at Lubbock, since 1960.

Actually, during those morning and afternoon sessions, I enjoyed meeting a whole host of TFS folks, one of whom was Joe Doggett, a long-lost and distant cousin, and Hudson Long whose name was famous on an American lit textbook—and Jim Lee continually confused Hudson Long with Wilson Hudson. Ironically, later generations got confused between Jim Lee (He of Many Households) and Jim Byrd, and they called both of them "Jim Byrd Lee." I met the poet Everett Gillis from Texas Tech and Brownie McNeill, who was famous because he had cut a folk song LP with his picture on the jacket and was to become president of Sul Ross, and John Q. Anderson with the tiny guitar that knew a thousand songs, and many who would become integral parts of my life. That is who I am remembering and celebrating herein, those TFS members of my parents' generation, Back in the Ought 'Sixties, the ones who planted the vines from which I harvested the grapes, the richest part of my academic life—my years with the Texas Folklore Society.

And I also secondarily celebrate those that came into the fold about the same time, because we were on the watershed, and we were the new generation. Jim Lee and Ed Gaston had come a year earlier in 1958, but we all—James Ward and Edwin Jr., Jim Byrd, John O. West, Paul Patterson, Jim Day—came about the same time. And later in the 'Sixties, the much younger Joyce Roach, Sarah Greene, and Sylvia Grider came on board. We were the new TFS generation in the 'Sixties. We were the kids! believe it or not, still wet behind the ears!

And Hermes Nye, he of the generous welcome, was the beginning for me.

Hermes was a fashionably-dressed, would-be hippie lawyer who gave papers on hot rods and armadillos and "hangin' ten." He had come down from the Midwest and married a rich Southern belle. I don't know how much law he practiced, but he was the Society's Counselor until the day he died. During that folk music explosion of the 'Sixties, Hermes sang at all the Dallas cabarets and emceed and performed on his own Big D radio show. During the Society's Thursday night hoot (I had never heard the word "hootenanny" until I came to the TFS.) Hermes was the interlocutor and was the best we ever had, always fully focused on the participant, never stealing the light. Hermes knew how to make first-time performers confident and comfortable. His own annual presentation was a melodramatic and interminable recitation of "Lasca" and/or a musical rendition of the pecadillos of Aimee Semple MacPherson. Hermes wrote the meetings' resolutions in purple Victorian prose and read them in stentorian tones with flourish and gesture. In the 'Seventies, Hermes wrote a semi-fictional autobiography detailing his AC/DC sexual escapades, among other adventures, for which wife Mary Elizabeth forgave him (she said!) but Martha Emmons would not. The title of Hermes' opus was *Sweet Beast, I Have Gone Prowling*, which should give you some idea of the nature of the content. Hermes was a jewel!

Martha Emmons read Hermes' *Sweet Beast* and was *not* amused. Miss Martha, from the heart of Baylor Bible-Belt Baptistry in Waco, was the moral arbiter for the Society even then. The meeting papers were liberal in topic and delivery, during those chaotic transitional times, when the world was turning upside down. Martha handled the sexual and social revolution of the 'Sixties with mature sophistication, but she was also not amused by religious flippancy. At the Waco meeting she received Robert Flynn's first presentation of "Growing Up a Sullen Baptist" with pursed lips and tightened eyes. On the other hand, her presentation of "The Adulteration of Old King David," both religious and sexual, was an all-time hootenanny classic: "Sister Uriah, what chu doing with that wash tub on yo' front po'ch?" "Why, Ole King David, it's Satidy, and I'm fixin to take a bath." "Woman, ain't you got no shame? Take that tub inside!" "I would, Ole King David, but I'm just a pore little weak woman, and I cain't tote it inside all by myself." "Well, here, Miz Uriah, let me help you."—And that was the last they seen of Ole King David till come Monday!

And speaking of young—and old!—liberals, during one Driskell Hotel-Austin meeting we had a passionate and protracted integration discussion supporting Emmett Till or the Freedom Riders or something similar. We were to the point of passing resolutions to send to the Capitol and all Texas newspapers—or maybe we were going to march to the Capitol!—when ultra-liberal Hermes Nye informed us that, satisfying though it might be, such a political outpouring could jeopardize the Society's academic tax-exempt status. Such topics regularly arose thereafter during those parlous times, but they were in softer tones and kept in house.

Another indication of the TFS spirit of the times: Martin Shockley, the impeccably dressed Virginian with the aristocratic Tidewater accent and the strikingly grand white moustache, had the distinction of being fired from the University of Oklahoma in the 1940s for inviting a Negro to speak to an on-campus academic meeting. Martin later resigned as English Department head in Indiana when the president fired a colleague for supporting Henry Wallace of the far-left-wing Progressive Party. Fortunately for Texas and the Folklore Society, Martin spent most of his career at North Texas in Denton. One could not out-liberal Martin Shockley.

Another memorable elder member and episode was Judge Charles Francis II's getting drunk at the 1966 Monahans banquet and Mody Boatright's directing Jim Lee and me to take him back to his motel room. Dutifully we loaded the Judge into his car, poured his honor into his bed, and proceeded to take his long, shiny, black Cadillac on a midnight tour of the Monahans' honky tonks. I watched Lee cut an impressive swath that night, and I have ever since deferred to James Ward's sophistication and worldly ways.

On another evening of alcoholic enlightenment, one of the Society's grande dames took umbrage with one of my folkloric

Martin Shockley, TFS President 1959-60

pronouncements and baptized me with a full glass of scotch and soda (It was a Baptist total immersion.) as a group of us discussed "professional matters" in the banquet room of the Shamrock Hotel. Jim Byrd promised to write a sonnet to suit the occasion but he never did.

Mody Boatright was the Secretary-Editor, the Alpha male, and the paterfamilias of the Society. With the forever cigar and a slight stoop, Mody moved with quiet authority among the members, closely trailed by young aspiring writers and presenters ever mindful of their need for upward mobility and the unwritten "publish or perish" clause in their teaching contracts.

Stith Thompson, the editor of PTFS # 1 and the venerated producer of the six-volume *Motif Index*, was a hero of that generation of folklorists, and John Q. Anderson imported him at least twice to TFS meetings, once in the 'Sixties to A&M, John Q.'s academic base. He was much welcomed by his peers, almost fawned upon. I am afraid that my peers were more involved in the night's hoot and where one could get booze in College Station.

Frank Dobie sometimes showed up at the Austin meetings to visit old friends, but he seldom stayed long. Most of us stood around in awe of this Texas icon and dared do little more than try to get a handshake and a howdy. Mr. Dobie and I had corresponded once, and we visited briefly at Mody's house one evening, but I am sorry to say that I never made a solid and personal connection with Texas folklore's Man of the Times. By the 'Sixties Dobie had become a member of the national (or international) folkloric pantheon and was out of the sphere of us ordinary assistant professors of English.

My warmest impression of Frank Dobie came on the night that he was made a Fellow of the Texas Folklore Society in Austin at the Driskill in 1961. (J. Frank Dobie, who was responsible for the early resurrection and the vigor and vitality of the Texas Folklore Society, was made a Fellow twenty years after he retired as Secretary-Editor. That distinction did not come lightly.) Dressed in his white linen suit, Dobie cut an imposing picture at that evening's banquet. He gratefully accepted the Fellowship scroll, briefly thanked the Society and sat down. Martin Shockley, as splendid an orator as Hermes, paid Frank Dobie his tribute, which concluded thusly (What I wouldn't give to orate this in Shockley's mellifluous tones!):

> A Texan not by birth but by choice, I came to Texas with about the average ignorance and prejudice. I had always considered the coyote a pesky varmint, a cunning chicken thief, a sneaky villain best seen over the sights of a .30-30; then I read a book by Frank Dobie and learned that the coyote is a noble creature with a proud and independent

> spirit and a fierce love of freedom. I had always considered the longhorn to be a stupid cow critter, all bone, gristle, and stringy meat, mean, vicious and hard to handle; then I read a book by Frank Dobie and learned that the longhorn is a noble creature with a proud and independent spirit and a fierce love of freedom. I had always considered the mustang the sorriest specimen of horseflesh, hammer-headed, wall-eyed, ewe-necked, sway-backed, bushy-tailed, ornery and dangerous; then I read a book by Frank Dobie and learned that the mustang is a noble creature with a proud and independent spirit and a fierce love of freedom. Now they tell me Mr. Dobie is writing about rattlesnakes, and I anticipate another agonizing reappraisal.

Frank Dobie laughed out loud, hugged Martin, and spent the rest of the evening going around and visiting with members. That was a grand night, and Dobie was a grand man.

So many others of our, or "my," sainted elders were on stage Back in the Ought 'Sixties. Leland Sonnichsen, famous author-historian of El Paso, was a fine singer and piano player. He was also a charmer, and the ladies flocked around him like birds at a seed feeder. Allen Maxwell, Director of SMU Press, was there, and this was during a time of troubles between the TFS and the SMU publishers, because of late books and unanswered correspondence. Ralph Houston of Southwest Texas and the dearly loved Mabel Major of TCU, who had been a part of the Society since the 'Thirties, were regular presenters.

The most important elder in my professional life was Wilson M. Hudson. Wilson was a UT Phi Beta Kappa with four years in the Air Corps during WWII. He was also a scholar, who did his best to lead the TFS to higher academic levels with use of motif index numbers. He was a serious academic with a Victorian sensitivity and morality that made Miss Martha's standards almost bacchanalian, and he was my guide and mentor during the early years of my membership. Additionally, I shall ever be indebted to Wilson and Gertrude because they rescued Hazel and me from five o'clock Dublin traffic and restored us with brandy. To Wilson M. Hudson I owe the most.

And let us not forget John Lomax, Jr., a son of the Society's founder. John was a regular and bore his Lomax plaid-shirt mantle with due regard to his family's folklore heritage. John loved to sing acapella, and he could carry a tune, but it was in a rusty bucket. However, what he lacked in musical texture he made up for in volume and vitality. He loved to lead a singalong of "The Rivers of Texas," but John is best remembered by some of us for a one-time rendition of "Take This Hammer."

At a Houston folk singing soiree, we noticed at singing time that a six-foot, fifteen-inch-dbh, red-oak log lay half way between the audience's front row and the singers' table. Its presence aroused a flurry of speculation until Big John got up to sing "Take This Hammer." He reached behind the table and pulled out a shiny-sharp, double-bit axe, and stepped up to the log. After a few words explaining that "Hammer" was a work song learned from "Lead-belly" and used to coordinate axe or sledge hammer work, Big John began to sing: "Take this hammer (Whop! The axe bit into the log!) Give it to the Captain (Whop!) Take this hammer (Whop! This time a chip of wood went sailing toward the far end of the front row.) Give it to the Captain (Whop! We could tell, to our dismay, that John flat knew how to chop wood.) Take this hammer (Whop! Chips—Big chips!—were flying by now, and the first two rows were cleared, the previous occupants hugging the wall.) Give it to the Captain (A long pause, then a ferocious Whop! And a chunk of wood the size of a brickbat whizzed into the sheetrock wall and stuck.) Tell him I'm gone, Lawd (Whop!) Tell him I'm gone (Whop! Those of us left were ducking behind chairs.).

The audience was pretty well thinned by then, but Big John had two more verses to go and by golly, he was going to sing his song and chop his wood if it hare lipped the governor. He did. We all crept back to our seats and to a room carpeted with wood chips.

John Avery Lomax, Jr. singing a cappella

Big John, grinning in self-satisfaction, accepted our scattered applause as his due, and took his seat, convinced that Old Daddy John Lomax was somewhere heavenly, applauding his demonstration of reality folklore. John Lomax, Jr., was a hard act to follow.

They were all hard acts to follow—Frank Dobie, Stith Thompson, Mody, Wilson, Sonnichsen, Shockley, Hermes, John Q. These members of the 'Sixties were the TFS builders of their time and their future, and they put the marks of their personalities on this organization. We honor these our ancestors who kept the Society's circle unbroken through their years to ours. We would not be here had they not kept the faith in the Society's future.

A different generation is now building our time and our future, and I can tell you when I look out over this membership of the Texas Folklore Society in its *one hundredth year of existence!!!* (Can you believe it!?) that the Society is larger, stronger, richer, filled with more vitality and imagination and folkloric expertise than it had Back in Ought 'Sixty and much of the time before. I can remember times in this past half-century of the Society's life when its sessions were held in a college classroom and we had empty chairs, times when we had so few acceptable papers on hand that we had trouble publishing an annual, times when we had to wait 'til the year's dues were paid to get money enough to pay for the publication of an annual. *But* I can also call to mind presentations and personalities that thrilled and excited me with their revelations, that were the greatest parts of my education—folkloric, academic, and personal. The richness of the Texas Folklore Society's coming together in this discipline made me rich with understanding of ways of life I would never have learned to see without the Society and its members.

We have come a long way in this last half of the Society's lifetime, and I have complete faith in the Society's future and in Ken Untiedt's and Janet Simonds' management and leadership as the Society heads into its next one hundred years.

Now, as then, our future and the Society's future depend on its members' continued interest and involvement in Texas folklore and in the energy that they—you and I!—invest in the collecting, preserving, and presenting of our folklore. I am convinced that beyond the good fortune the Society has had in its membership, the reasons for its success are that it has loved and preserved folklore without embalming it in academic pedantry and *with* presenting it in ways palatable to public tastes and interesting to the eyes and ears of the general.

Folklore classes in colleges and universities have thinned out in the last two decades. Folklore centers at The University and throughout Texas and the U.S. have dwindled or disappeared. The American Folklore Society has diminished in membership and production and is seldom heard from. But the Texas Folklore Society has grown larger and stronger. We have, therefore, an even greater obligation and responsibility to dance with the partner who brung us.

I am convinced also in the good fortune that the Texas Folklore Society has had in its membership. We are a solid bunch of folks, children of many parents and many professions and many cultures, but rich and poor, we have always been kin. No matter what our ways of life and living, we come together as loving kinfolks bound together by our pride in our present and our past, cherishing the same songs and learning new ones, hearing the same stories and learning new ones, joined by the same traditions and beliefs—and learning and understanding and growing into new ones. We folks of the Texas Folklore Society are always learning and always growing, along with people who share with us the love of family and country and the native soil from which we grew.

Long live the Texas Folklore Society! Let us live another hundred years!

A dogtrot worth saving

THE ALFORD HOMEPLACE: DECONSTRUCTING A DOGTROT

by Sue M. Friday

When I got back from Hemphill with the barbeque sandwiches from Fat Fred's Grocery, husband Tom and cousin Troy Pfleider had already stopped work and were sitting on what was left of the front porch. Tom's camo T-shirt blended to the same khaki brown as his pants, the pattern barely discernable. The T-shirt that Troy wore under his overalls would never be white again. Both seemed to have a dusty aura, beginning with their caps and moving down to their boots.

"You are the two dirtiest men in Sabine County," I said, shaking my head.

"Sue," Troy answered, "we've been slithering around under this house like snakes!"

It was October of 2001, and the house they had been slithering under is our 100+ year-old dogtrot that was on the verge of falling down. Never painted or modernized beyond electricity and rudimentary plumbing, it sits on land outside of Hemphill that has been in my family for five generations. My grandparents, Adron and Ada Alford, lived there, and my mother and her twin brother were born in it in 1916. Vacant since my grandparents' death thirty years ago, the house has always been "home" and snuggles into that spot in my heart reserved for the place that welcomes and gives comfort. It preserves special childhood memories of barefoot summers, watermelons on the porch, hugs, and hymns. Although we live a two-day's drive away in North Carolina, by virtue of being retired and experienced remodelers Tom and I were the only family members willing to undertake its rescue. Troy is also retired, and like Tom has a unique ability to problem solve and improvise—essential qualifications for this type of project.

The house is simple. It is built of the virgin longleaf pine that once covered Sabine County. The main boards are 1" × 12" × 15' and rough sawn. Battens cover the seams between the boards and because there are no studs, the outside wall is also the inside. My late uncle, Sabine County historian Cecil McDaniel, told me it was a box house, a type once common throughout the county. There are two main rooms sixteen feet square, backed by two shed rooms eight by sixteen feet. The open hall in the center and porch across the entire front are each 8' wide. They form a "T" shaped extra living area that catches every stray summer breeze.

The original kitchen was a log structure attached to the north shed room. Grandpa hitched a team of mules to it and dragged it

Ada and Adron Alford in front of the house with Pearl and Ruby, early 1960s

into the pasture in the '20s. In its place he built a larger board and batten kitchen. By the time we started work, parts of that kitchen were on the ground and severely termite damaged. On the advice of a friend with a backhoe, we filled the kitchen with everything we couldn't use, cut it loose from the main house with a Sawz-All, pulled it away with the backhoe and disposed of it. We were able to salvage the doors. Troy later rebuilt one that still had a latch string and installed it on the back of the main house. Tom used another as the headboard for our bed when we began camping out in the house.

Longtime fans of the TV show *This Old House,* we quickly realized that Norm (Abrams) doesn't tell you everything you need to know about old houses—like the filth that accumulates from the rats and mice that move in when the people move out. The kitchen was used to dispose of all the bedding, clothing, fiberboard, linoleum, and furniture too far gone to re-use. We spent the first few days in gloves and masks.

The house sits on large iron ore rocks spaced under sill beams. Since the tin roof was in reasonable shape, Tom and Troy began with this foundation. The floor was springy and we were in danger of falling through certain parts. They found that over the years the pine sill beams had cupped around the tops of the rocks, causing the floor to sag. Two beams were on the ground. They crawled under the house with a car jack and lifted it corner by corner. To help bring it to level and firm it up, they added forty-five additional cement block supports under the sill beams and the sixteen-foot floor joists that had no support under the span. They tore up floorboards and installed three more sill beams.

Among the parts that had to be torn away and disposed of were the remains of the mud daub chimney on the north side. The sticks used for the framework of the chimney had served as a super highway for termites. They even made inroads on a few of the pine boards around it, although they avoided most of the old wood as it is still rich with resin. The only curve in the house was a decorative arch over the hearth. We found that the arch had been made by a crosscut saw nailed at each end and covered with a mud/cement mixture.

The two dirtiest men in Sabine County, Troy Pfleider and Tom Friday

Other discoveries were under the three layers of linoleum "rugs" in the fireplace room. The original pine floorboards had several rat holes with flattened tin nailed over them. We also found the perfectly round hole where Grandma's shotgun accidentally went off as she rested the barrel on the floor while peering out the door at a vanilla extract salesman who was making his rounds—her form of homeland security. Cousin Earnest McDaniel, then in his late eighties, told me that before linoleum the old houses had floor cracks wide enough that "you could see the color of the chickens underneath."

Dating the house was interesting. I knew my grandparents married in 1912, and thought that was when the house was built. When we analyzed the building process, it became apparent that one side was older than the other. The north side has a window and a door on the front instead of the traditional two windows. The boards of this older side have the swirls of a circular saw and those of the newer side were sawn with a band saw. The floorboards of the porch were wider on the north side, and the roof was obviously spliced together. We concluded that on their marriage they moved into the north side—a shotgun house, and then Grandpa converted it to a dogtrot. Our conclusions were confirmed by "dirt dobber dating." When Tom and Troy cleaned out the two attics they counted the bucketfuls of dirt dobber nests on each side. The north side had so many more that they extrapolated the difference and concluded that part was built in the late 1800s.

How do you get everything straight and square and strong enough to last over a hundred years without studs? Even the cousins in their nineties didn't know. The corners are butted together and nailed and there is a one-board-wide band at the top and bottom of each box. Construction must have started with the floor and these corners. Then the bands provided a base for nailing the wall boards. One size nail—big—was hammered through and bent down. Except for the front, windows are not uniform and appear to have been added as they became available. Grandpa hacked out a hole with an ax and framed around it for a couple of them. Screens nailed to the outside frame kept out bugs and small nails held in the glass.

Several times, I commented on the gentle quality of the light streaming through the wavy old glass in the windows. Then Tom washed them. So much for romantic notions.

The next spring, before we went back to finish the rescue, a friend paid $4 for a used book called *Built in Texas* (Publications of the Texas Folklore Society # XLII) at a Charleston, S.C., library book sale and presented it to me. There on page 30 was a description of our house and the words, "the house form which perhaps more than any other means Southern folk housing to the cultural geographer and the culture historian—the open central passageway or 'dogtrot' house." Eureka! We now had an historical context for what we had thought was just a labor of love. The book led to emails and eventually a meeting with editor F. E. (Ab) Abernethy. Ab spent an afternoon with us discussing dogtrots and other East Texas lore, and we came away with a much better feel for what we had. He helped us justify going on and doing what we wanted to do anyway but felt was impractical.

It is still impractical, but we now have a working bathroom in the north shed room, a snug place to sleep in the fireplace room, and across the hall in the south box we have a kitchen/gathering room. Family and friends from throughout the county congregate there when we come back, and food and yarns fill the place just as I remember. Thomas Wolfe was wrong—you can go home again.

Yolanda Chávez Leyva, a contemporary traditional healer

MEXICAN AND MEXICAN-AMERICAN FOLK HEALERS: CONTINUING TO NOURISH OUR SENSE OF HUMANITY INTO THE TWENTY-FIRST CENTURY

by Meredith E. Abarca

Traditional holistic healers guide their lives by four principles: faith, compassion, respect, and reciprocity. According to folklorist John O. West, these same values are embedded in all aspects of folklore and folk life. Yet, because many people in our society are suffering from *sustos*, these concepts are disappearing into oblivion. *Susto* literally means "fright." *Susto* "occurs when a person has experienced an emotional shock, an accident or a great fear."[1] In its more severe cases, *susto* manifests itself in soul loss, "a state in which we . . . feel that 'something is missing' because our spirit, the energetic aura that surrounds us, has been violated."[2] *Susto*, therefore, is a form of imbalance that causes physical, mental, emotional, and spiritual illnesses. A society populated with individuals suffering from *susto* can diminish our sense of humanity.[3]

Within Mexican and Mexican-American folk healing traditions, a *susto* is combated with a *limpia,* "cleansing where the body, mind and spirit are brought into balance, as the negative is removed and replaced with that which is healthy."[4] Holistic healers strive to bring into balance the entity of our total being. Through their *limpias*, we can claim our humanity and enrich our soul. We can also obtain a *limpia* through the power of inspiration. Reading about people's life stories has the power to awaken the desire to strive for a healthy, balanced life and a stronger sense of humanity. For example, one of my students, after reading Lucy Fischer West's *A Child of Many Rivers*, wrote in his journal that he felt blessed, inspired, and hopeful to know that ordinary people can do extraordinary things for their community.[5] Perhaps, reading about the lives of holistic healers and understanding that being physically, mentally, emotionally, and spiritually in balance is an on-going process, we can be exposed to the benefits that a society provides when it is guided by faith, compassion, respect, and reciprocity. Members of the Texas Folklore Society continue to actively research and document such folk healing traditions.

The accounts of folk healers usually come to us in two forms: anecdotes from people's experiences with folk healers, and from the healers themselves. In the Texas Folklore Society's annual publications, which date back to 1916, we find primary anecdotal sources of Mexican folk healers. Ruth Dodson's "Folk-Curing Among the Mexicans," which appeared in *Tone the Bell Easy*, edited by J. Frank Dobie (PTFS X, 1932), provides vital historical perspective on Mexican healers. In this article, Dodson introduces Doña Lupe's journey as a healer, her methods and skills, as well as her commitment to make her knowledge a benefit to her community. Through this description, we can identify three of the ethical values that guide the practices of *curanderismo* (folk healing)—faith, compassion, and respect.

Faith is demonstrated in at least three different ways. First, there is Doña Lupe's own faith in her natural inclination towards learning the ways of folk healing; second, in her belief in God to help her develop her knowledge; and, finally in the faith that clients have in her healing ability. Doña Lupe was a "Mexican woman with a . . . taste for the study of *remedios* and the human ills to which they may be applied." She became "so efficient that her services [were] sought more and more until she [was] automatically, raise[d] to the profession of *curandera*—one who cures."[6] The title of *curandera* comes with great responsibility towards the community, and most traditional healers accept this duty as one given by God.

While Doña Lupe learned her skills through long periods of being a practitioner, her ability to ascend to the level of official *curandera* was a result of a *don* (a gift) from God. Contemporary traditional healer Yolanda Chávez Leyva, who is also an associate professor of History at the University of Texas at El Paso, explains this *don* in terms of a person's faith and discipline to develop the gift of healing. Chávez Leyva says:

> I believe that everyone has the ability to be a healer. Everyone is born with the ability to help others . . . but not everyone has the discipline to learn and not everyone has the compassion to help others. . . . Even though I have seen people with great talent, [they] will never be healers because they don't have the compassion yet, or they don't have the openness for humanity. . . . They are very judgmental; they feel better than everyone else.[7]

Chávez Leyva's views indicate three things: we all have the ability to be healers, compassion is needed to nourishe our humanity, and Doña Lupe was a nonjudgmental soul always willing to help others.

Healers often say that it is the power of God working through them which helps people heal from their illnesses. Patients need to share in the same faith if their illnesses are to be healed. This was the case for Doña Lupe. Once "a little girl, not of Doña Lupe's race, but not lacking confidence in her *remedios*, had a toothache as a result of a decayed molar. She went to Doña Lupe and ask[ed] her to [cure] her."[8] With the use of snake oil, the girl was cured. Faith in Doña Lupe's healing ability worked to overcome racial differences that could have kept people from ever forming a sense of community.

Doña Lupe showed her compassion for her fellow human and her desire to alleviate their pain in a number of different ways. One involved overcoming great distances. She "waded the creek [at night] to go to a neighbor who had acute indigestion." Her compassion, combined with her knowledge and faith, worked to reveal the shortcoming of modern scientific medical opinions. [When] her son-in-law was thrown by a horse and hurt so badly that the doctor they had with him said he could not live, Doña Lupe hastened to him. Among other *remedios* she made him blow into an empty bottle with all his might to expand his broken ribs, and worked with him so successfully that he made an amazing recovery.[9]

Doña Lupe's compassion also led her to understand that human emotions are often the cause of people's illness, which at times are manifested as *embrujo* (bewitching). When Doña Lupe arrived at the house of a woman believed to be bewitched, the woman greeted her by saying "*Buenas tardes* Doña Manuela." This was enough for Doña Lupe to know who was responsible for causing the *embrujo*: Doña Manuela, the neighbor.

Doña Lupe went to work. "In the patient's stomach she located—so she says—something like an iron bar. This she grasped with both hands and, with what must have been a Samson-like twist, broke it in two. The patient recovered."[10] From Dodson's descriptions such as "so she says" and "Samson-like twist," we can infer that Dodson does not personally believe in the concept of bewitching. Maybe neither did Doña Lupe.

If so, they are not alone. Elena Avila, a registered nurse with a master's degree in psychiatric nursing and a practicing holistic healer for over thirty years, does not believe in people being cursed. She goes to the extent to suggest that most of what we read about black witchcraft is a result of academic misunderstandings of basic human psychology. Physical and emotional illnesses generally accepted as a result of *embrujo* come from the human follies of envy, greed, revenge, and jealousy, known in Mexican folklore discourse as *mal de ojo* (evil eye), *mal puesto* (a hex or curse) or *mala suerte* (bad luck). "When we send negative thoughts to someone, it does harm to [such person] and it comes back on us."[11] People's evil attempts to harm others are consequences of negative intentions. If the attempts are effective, it is because of the recipient's own low self-esteem and fragile soul.

Respect for elders and for nature shaped Doña Lupe's life as a healer, and it helped her nourish a strong soul. In indigenous traditions, the elders are seen as the wise members of the community, as the *abuelas* and *abuelos* (the grandparents) who embody ancestral knowledge. Dodson acknowledges this principle by stating that if four women of different generations are gathered, and they all know a remedy for a particular illness, the younger will always defer to the older out of respect. Knowing nature is a way of respecting it. Dodson states that to "the unmodernized Mexicans, especially the women, every tree, shrub, and plant in their environs holds an inherent interest . . . [such as] its probable or known medical properties, its curative powers."[12] This knowledge comes from an intimate connection with the natural environment, which is maintained through a lifetime and passed down from the *abuelos* (grandparents).

Modern society has taken all of us, not just Mexicans, away from an intimate connection with nature. But this bond can be restored if we recognize the generosity of our natural environment, something folklorists attempt to do. For Chávez Leyva, creating such a bond can be as simple as going into our yards, literally. Speaking of plants she says:

> [Plants] we think of as weeds are really very useful plants. I was thinking about what is growing in my yard the other day. There was a plant to rinse your hair with, *yerba del negro o yerba de la negrita*; there was a plant to make *asadero* cheese, *tronpillo*; there was a plant for arthritis. There was *verdolaga*, which is very nutritious, and *estafiate*, good for stomach problems. Oh and *amarato*, which you can eat the leaves, and it is almost perfect protein. The plants that grow near you are all the plants that you need.[13]

Familiarity with weeds is just one way for us to develop a respectful, intimate, and appreciative relationship for and with nature.

Familiarity with Doña Lupe's life shows us how respect for nature filters to people, and for her this influenced her commitment to her community. In Dodson's description of Doña Lupe's life, the values of faith, compassion, and respect are clearly outlined. The principle of reciprocity, Dodson makes most obvious in her description of Pedro Jaramillo.

In 1951, Ruth Dodson wrote a major article about Pedro Jaramillo, which became the central focus of the Texas Folklore Society's 24th volume, *The Healer of Los Olmos and Other Mexican Lore*. Pedro Jaramillo was known among his community as Don

Pedrito, a faith healer, and his tombstone honored him as The Benefactor of Humanity. He was born in Guadalajara, Jalisco, México, and he died in Paisano, Starr County, Texas, July 3, 1907. Since Don Pedrito was already in his "early nineties, in 1893," he lived at least to be 100 years old.

The article on Don Pedrito was actually a translation of Dodson's original 1934 Spanish version, published by Casa Editorial Lozana in San Antonio, Texas. The Library of the College of Physicians in Philadelphia, "the oldest medical school in the United States," requested a copy of the Spanish version.[14] The request represents a shift from a long-standing attitude by scientific-based medical institutions to discredit the faith healers. Dodson alludes to this point when she writes how Dr. J. S. Strickland, who worked in the same country and covered the same territory as Don Pedrito, responded to a request to prohibit the *curandero* from doing his work. The doctor replied: "No, how do I know that Don Pedrito's prayers don't do more good than my pills?"[15]

Don Pedrito discovered his *don* (gift) through a personal misfortune. While living in Mexico, "he suffered an affliction of the nose." Dodson writes how one night, he was "suffering so much that he went out into the woods to a pool of water. He lay down and buried his face in the mud at the edge. This relieved him. He stayed there treating himself with mud. At the end of three days he was well. . . . He returned to his house and lay down and slept. After a while a voice awakened him and told him that he had received from God the gift of healing."[16] According to Chávez Leyva, the idea of a healer suffering a personal misfortune is often what helps healers become compassionate towards others' sufferings. She says that sometimes the best healers are those who have gone through significant personal losses, mistakes, and/or traumas, because these experiences help healers to not be judgmental.

Perhaps Don Pedrito's level of compassion was initially put to the test when he received his first call as a healer. His "master," who compensated Don Pedrito's labor with "only a bushel of corn and the equivalent of five dollars a month," got sick and it became Don

Pedrito's moral duty to heal him. He did so by prescribing the first thing that came to his mind, "a tepid bath daily for three days."[17] Because his remedies came to him, and most dealt with drinking water in a specific ritualistic manner, Don Pedrito became known as a faith healer. Don Pedrito "claimed that God had bestowed on him the power to heal the sick; to say which prescriptions, given in the name of God and executed with faith and in the name of God, had power to heal."[18] Even now, people who believe in Don Pedrito's healing power often take their medication evoking not only God, but also Don Pedrito. People's faith in his healing abilities is such that in Laredo, Texas, a "firm . . . that supplies curative herbs uses his picture and the trademark, 'Don Pedrito.' "[19]

The Benefactor of Humanity was born a humble man and remained humble throughout his life. Following the traditional belief within healers' practices of not charging for their services but simply accepting donations, Don Pedrito's essential needs were always more than met. A man by the name of Antonio Hinojosas gave Don Pedrito a present "of a hundred acres of land. This he developed into a farm. He fenced it, put a small house and a well on it, and set someone to work it. Here he raised corn . . . watermelons, cashews . . . peppers, garbanzos . . . and garlic."[20] All of these were given away.

Don Pedrito often purchased groceries and left them in a special room in his home called the "store." These groceries were left for those people who came to see him from far away places and might miss him because he was attending to clients elsewhere, such as Corpus Cristi, San Antonio, or Laredo. Don Pedrito would "buy four or five hundred dollars' worth of groceries at a time" to stock his store where "nothing was sold." For Don Pedrito, "where need existed, food was given."[21] Another remarkable action that illustrates his deep understanding of the need for reciprocity—as a healing aspect in and of itself—is reflected in his commitment to his community in desperate moments of need. "When Don Pedrito had been at Los Olmos about ten years a most terrible drought visited the country. It began in 1893 and lasted several years. . . . Don Pedrito practically fed the northern part of Starr County."[22] Reciprocity for Pedro Jaramillo simply meant that what we receive with one hand, we give away with the other.

Don Pedrito, as well as Doña Lupe, gave much to their communities, and their communities, and the offspring of such communities, through their anecdotes have given us the stories of these two Mexican folk healers. Another way to learn about folk healers is to hear them speak about their own stories and views on healing. This is the case with contemporary folk healer, Elena Avila, a native from El Paso, Texas, who in 1999 published her autobiography, *The Woman Who Glows in the Dark: A Curandera Reveals Traditional Aztec Secrets of Physical and Spiritual Health.*

Avila is a fascinating modern Mexican-American *curandera* who combines over thirty years of traditional healing practices with her knowledge as a registered nurse with a master's degree in psychiatric nursing. Her journey as a healer reveals how Dr. J. S. Strickland's assumption in the late 1800s was correct, that his pills as well as Pedro Jaramillo's prayer assisted in the process of healing. Avila's life path emphasizes the need for scientific medicine and spiritual healing to come together in the process of curing a person, because science and technology alone cannot heal a person.[23]

Avila has worked in many different medical institutions, from Thomas Hospital in El Paso, Texas, to the Neuropsychiatric Institute at the University of California, Los Angeles, to a Rape Crisis Center in Albuquerque, New Mexico. She spent her career meeting "many compassionate healers among the nurses, doctors, and staff. These individuals confirmed [Avila's] belief that loving attention was often the best medicine that anyone could offer."[24] This realization took Avila from the world of modern medicine and led her to become solely a traditional *curandera*. Modern medicine, says Avila, often lacks soul because it does not understand people's souls. To understand soul, Avila says, "we have come full circle and [have] begun to look back towards our past and towards those cultures that have preserved their holistic, nature-based healing traditions."[25] Avila is aware of this shift, as numerous medical schools and hospitals have asked her to give *pláticas* on *curanderismo.*

Avila has taken a "vow to be of service" to help people in their own healing process through self-empowerment. At the center of *curanderismo* we find not the healer, but God, the Creator, or universal spiritual energies. Therefore, self-empowerment means that Avila's main responsibility is "to educate and empower people" by teaching them "to call upon divine guidance, saints that are meaningful to them, and to the protective spirits of their ancestors."[26] To accomplish this, Avila's sessions begin with a *plática*, a counseling session, which allows her to learn about a person's spiritual and cultural beliefs. *Pláticas* allow a person to *desahogarse,* which means a person "speaks until everything has been released from the body, soul, and heart."[27] A *plática*, in many ways is a *limpia* (a spiritual cleansing). As a professor, I do not have clients but I have students. By sharing our stories through *pláticas* that take the form of discussions, journals, and research papers, my students and I create venues of *desahogos* (of opening up and letting go), and in the process convert the classroom into a space of *limpias.*

Avila offers a useful distinction between the soul and the spirit. It demonstrates how important the well being of both is for us to maintain a healthy and balanced sense of self. The soul, she says, "is the part of us that includes all that we are: our talents, our hopes and dreams, our true voice, our nature, our identity, . . . [and our] seat of creativity."[28] Our soul is sacred. The spirit, on the other hand, is "the envelope that protects [the] soul from harm." What makes this envelope effective or ineffective as a seal of protection is that the spirit contains "the sum total of our nutritional habits," whether they are "good or bad." The spirit also keeps "the energy generated from our feelings" as well as our thoughts, whether they are positive or negative.[29] The nature of our spirit affects our social relationships, making them healthy or destructive. If this protective envelope rips easily, then our soul, the core of our being, gets violated. A wounded soul, or soul loss, never fully leaves our body, otherwise we would be dead. However, depending on the severity of a physical, emotional, or psychological abuse, we can become like the walking dead. As a result of *sustos*, an injured and violated soul can live within us.

The origin of *susto* as soul loss comes from a Mexihka philosophy, which also offers the remedy to maintain the vitality of a healthy soul. The Mexihkas, the indigenous people whom the Spaniards renamed Aztecs to mean "people who created technology,"[30] divided a person's energy into four parts. The first part requires fifty-two percent of our total energy to maintain the health of our physical body. Only twenty-six percent is necessary for us to "feel the full range of our emotions, [while] . . . maintaining them in a healthy way." The desirable amount to sustain the health of our minds is only thirteen percent. The final nine percent is the amount needed to feed our spirit. When our energy follows this distribution "we have a healthy soul, based on a healthy body, mind, emotions, and spirit."[31]

There are several steps to make the envelope that protects our soul stronger. The first step, Avila says, is to take responsibility for our own health, to see the interconnection between our body, mind, emotions, and spirituality. The second step is to work at forming "proper balanced relationships with ourselves, our partners, our families, our community, and the universe."[32] Because Avila has studied with a number of Mexican teachers whose ancestors go back to the Mexihkas, her method of healing follows the energy distribution set forth by the Mexihkas' philosophy.

Healer Yolanda Chávez Leyva has also studied with Mexican teachers and, not surprisingly, some of her views on healing are similar to Avila's. As mentioned above, Chávez Leyva is both an associate professor of History at the University of Texas at El Paso and a traditional healer. Our acquaintance and friendship began through a writing circle where a few Chicana professors come together to help and support one another as we travel through the world of higher education. The writing circle, in and of itself, creates a healing space for all of us, and Chávez Leyva's presence adds much to such healing. Through these meetings I learned about Chávez Leyva's work as a healer. In order to learn about her journey of becoming a healer and her views on *curanderismo,* I began to gather and record her story.

When our conversation began in my home in El Paso on August 5, 2008, the first thing Chávez Leyva did was correct my assumption that she already holds the title of *curandera*. She told me, "I guess I want to say that my teachers have taught me not to call myself a *curandera* until I have thirty more years of experience. So when I am in my eighties, I can call myself a *curandera*. What I call myself is *promotora tradicional*. To be a *curandera* does take years of studying."[33]

Even though Chávez Leyva has been studying and practicing healing since her late teens, she still does not hold the title of *curandera* because her studies have had decades of interruption. Empathy is what kept her from fully pursuing her studies. According to many

Chávez Leyva with a raramuri staff

of her teachers, Chávez Leyva is blessed with the *don* (the gift) for healing through the channeling energy and a strong sensitivity to other people's energies. As she says, "I had to be very careful not to pick up people's illnesses, not to pick up whatever negative things were happening to them . . . [For many years] I didn't know how to protect myself." By the time she reached forty, she finally met teachers who taught her how to protect herself and use her *don* to help others. In May 2008, I had the privilege of attending the ceremony where she officially became an Elder at the age of fifty-two, and where she celebrated more than a decade "of pursuing, learning, and doing healing work."

Before I knew Chávez Leyva as a traditional healer, I knew her as Dr. Leyva, a Public Historian. The combination of a history professor and a traditional healer is one that deserves special attention. First of all, with Chávez Leyva's story, as well as with Avila's, the generally accepted notion that Mexican and Mexican-American folk healers lack formal university studies ceases to be a given assumption. The story of Chávez Leyva's journey as a healer and her healing practices are often framed within historical contexts, which illustrate the deep cultural roots of *curanderismo*. Finally, her story can offer us, "logical, rational-minded" people, a way to integrate the two worldviews often presented as separate: the intellectual and the spiritual.

Chávez Leyva admits that for a long time she struggled with these two views by which to engage in the world. When I asked her how being a traditional healer and a professor of history interconnected, she responded with this story:

> A few years ago I was studying, just for the weekend, with this man who could see energy really clearly. He could see colors. He was training me how to see energy. He didn't know me; we were total strangers. But he came up to me and said, "Over your head I see two paradigms. You struggle with them because you don't know which is true." I knew exactly what he was talking about because I

> have the whole academic world on one half and the healer on the other half. At the time I was really struggling [as to] how [to] combine both.[34]

The same empathy that kept her from fully exploring the knowledge and practices of traditional healing has allowed her to see the connection between the two worlds.

Chávez Leyva speaks about *susto* with her students by exploring what she calls historical trauma. The causes of historical trauma are largely the effects of colonization. In her effort to interconnect the intellectual and the spiritual world in her classroom, Chávez Leyva talks about the need for healing because "as individuals, as a people, as a community [we all] have been injured." She lectures about the atrocities committed to "our ancestors," and on how many of us "still carry that emotional, spiritual, and physical" *susto* within the memory of our soul. When Chávez Leyva speaks to her students about the wounds many of them carry within their soul, "they get it; they understand it. Sometimes they had not heard about it or thought about it, but they really get it once we start talking." In the context of the classroom, dialogues about historical trauma become *limpias.*

The combination of her deeply felt empathy, her knowledge of history, and a strong sense of responsibility to give back to her community have drawn Chávez Leyva to make El Paso her home. Through her ability to sense a place's energy, she feels how in El Paso "there is more pain because of poverty" than in Austin or San Antonio, other places where she has lived. Chávez Leyva tries to connect to the energies of Pedro Jaramillo and Teresita Urea because "they were on the border and understood what this place really did to people. When [she] lived in San Antonio, [she] would go to Don Pedrito's grave to pay [her] respects." Chávez Leyva explains her final decision to live in El Paso in this way:

> I guess it is a responsibility that I feel to this place. I think it is because so many generations of my family have been here. I often think about how

> some of these generations of my family are buried here. I have a connection to the land. This land is special because my [identical twin] sister is buried here, in Júarez. Sometimes I think that maybe she pulls me back because I have tried to leave, but I keep coming back.[35]

This personal connection translates to a high respect for the land, as she has accepted it as sacred. She often connects to the earth's sacredness by participating in sweat lodges, a way to "renew" herself.

Chávez Leyva teaches her four-year-old granddaughter about the sacredness of the land. When they go to the desert and gather herbs, she explains how important it is to always give something back. She tells her granddaughter, "You have to give something to the *plantita*. You can't just take it because it's giving part of its life for you." They offer things like cornmeal or tobacco. Also, they always remember to say "Thank you *plantita*," for its assistance in healing work.

Reciprocity for Chávez Leyva must reflect our connection to the earth. If this form of reciprocity and respect truly becomes part of our daily lives, Chávez Leyva feels it would "really change our so-called modern society." It would help all of us move away from thinking that "humans conquered the earth, [that] humans dominate the earth, [that] the earth is here to provide whatever we need." If we overcame the mentality that suggests human superiority over the earth, and instead, suggests Chávez Leyva, "had a relationship that said, 'we are connected to the tree out there; we are connected to the bug out there,' we could see how we are interconnected." Understanding our interconnection with the earth translates to our interconnection with people, and with universal spiritual energies. Such an understanding, says Chávez Leyva, "would change how we live our lives, the decisions we make as a society."

The answer to a strong and healthy body, mind, emotions, and spirit is within our own hands, yet what makes this process difficult to achieve, according to Chávez Leyva, is that we live in a society that promotes fragmentation of the self. We go to "school to develop our minds" and "we go to church" to become "spiritual beings." This fragmentation does not allow us to see ourselves as a whole being. But through *pláticas*, Chávez Leyva, just like Avila, can sometimes feel the energy that lets her understand how or why a person is off balance. Because her healing ability is through channeling energy, sometimes during these *pláticas* she can transmit to a person an image of "a different way of life." To make the image a reality, we must understand that to maintain a healthy, balanced life is an on-going process, which needs to be kept alive. Eating well for just one week, studying for just one test, taking our elderly neighbor's garbage out for just one week, and going to church or meditating just once a year will not help us have a balanced life. Chávez Leyva explains how a balanced life is an on-going process by showing that "it needs a constant [booster] of energy. It constantly needs nurturing."

Suffering from a *sustos*, whether caused by colonization or other forms of traumas, erroneous assumptions of our superiority over nature, or a fragmented sense of self, does not have to dictate our paths and keep us from developing a harmonious and balanced life. Chávez Leyva believes that the process "of getting in balance," begins by taking responsibility of truly looking at ourselves and asking: 'Am I taking care of my body? How about my spiritual side? How about my emotional side? How about my mental side?' [This does] not say that you don't go and ask people for help, but that you are ultimately responsible for taking care of yourself." If these four parts of our being—body, mind, emotions, and spirit—are fully connected and functioning in harmony, if they follow the Mexihka's philosophy of energy distribution, then our souls and sense of humanity become strong. If we care to live in a culture where faith, respect, compassion, and reciprocity are the rule and not the exception, we can try to emulate traditional healers' ethics by remembering that we are all born with the ability to heal ourselves and others. If we want to be surrounded by people who strive to have a physical, mental, emotional, and spiritually balanced life, then we have to begin with ourselves. Change, as Chávez Layva says, "begins at home."

I'm glad the Texas Folklore Society continues to include Mexican and Mexican-American lore in its meeting presentations and publications. Studying all types of culture in Texas and the Southwest is important to understanding how the various peoples who inhabit this area interact with one another, and also to maintaining the folk traditions of long ago, traditions that bring balance into our lives in the twenty-first century.

ENDNOTES

1. Rafaela G. Castro. *Chicano Folktales: A Guide to the Folklore, Traditions, Rituals and Religious Practices of Mexican Americans.* New York: Oxford University Press, 2001. 216.
2. Elena Avila. *Woman Who Glows in the Dark: A Curandera Reveals Traditional Aztec Secrets of Physical and Spiritual Health.* New York: Tarcher/Penguin, 1999. 69.
3. It does not take long when reading the newspaper to find examples of our lack of humanity: parents killing children, children killing each other and adults, and abuse of drugs and alcohol that leads to violence.
4. Yolanda Leyva. "The Revisioning of History Es Una Gran Limpia: Teaching and Historical Trauma in Chicana/o History." *La Voz de Esperenza.* Part I & II. San Antonio, Texas. Sept. and Oct. 2005. 5.
5. Lucy Fischer-West. *Child of Many Rivers: Journeys to and from El Rio Grande.* Lubbock: Texas Tech University Press, 2005.
6. Ruth Dodson. "Folk-Curing Among the Mexicans." *Tone the Bell Easy.* J. Frank Dobie, ed. Dallas, TX: Southern Methodist University Press, 1932. 83.
7. All of the quotes here from Yolanda Chávez Leyva come from two interviews with her conducted in my home in El Paso, Texas. The first took place on August 5, 2008, and the second on September 16, 2008.
8. Dodson. 1932. 84.
9. Ibid. 84.
10. Ibid. 85.
11. Avila. 27.
12. Dodson. 1932. 82.
13. Leyva interview.
14. Ruth Dodson. "Don Pedrito Jaramillo: The Curandero of Los Olmos." *The Healer of Los Olmos and Other Mexican Lore.* Wilson M. Hudson, ed. Dallas, TX: Southern University Press, 1951. 11
15. Ibid. 16.
16. Ibid. 12–13.

17. Ibid. 13.
18. Ibid. 12.
19. Ibid. 17.
20. Ibid. 14.
21. Ibid. 13.
22. Ibid. 14.
23. His Holiness the Dalai Lama brilliantly makes this point in *The Universe in an Atom: How Science and Spirituality Can Serve Our World.* London: Little Brown, 2006.
24. Avila. 107.
25. Ibid. 21.
26. Ibid. 28.
27. Ibid. 78.
28. Ibid. 182.
29. Ibid. 172.
30. Ibid. 29.
31. Ibid. 64.
32. Ibid. 33.
33. *Promotora tradicional* translates to promoter of traditional knowledge.
34. Leyva interview.
35. Ibid.

MEETINGS, MEMORIES,

INTERIOR OF MUNICIPAL AUDI

AND MORE

A TFS Hootenanny (1976), an important part of every annual meeting

KEEPING THE FLAMES BURNING AND PASSING THEM ON: HOOTS AT TFS MEETINGS

by Kenneth W. Davis

Probably long before recorded history our ancestors gathered on various occasions for communal singing about various events—significant or insignificant. Near the turn of the twentieth century, Professor Francis Barton Gummere of Harvard hypothesized in *The Beginnings of Poetry*[1] that narrative poetry and story telling began as tribal chants when warriors returned from a hunt for necessary food and stood around chanting about highlights of the day. Gummere suggested a hunter would step now and then forward to inject a colorful detail that would be repeated by the circle of hunters and the assembled villagers. In a short time, a narrative of the hunt with its high points would be imbedded in the memories of the tribe.

Among the folk for millennia following the times of hunters who provided food, getting together for listening to singers and for communal singing has been common. Folklorists and anthropologists from all over the world have collected many songs, poems, and favorite narratives from whatever sources are available. In Texas, from the time of the earliest colonists people have delighted in gathering in homes for singing events, usually done with fiddle or guitar accompaniment on verandas or under sturdy oak trees. This customary activity flourished in Central and West Texas during World War II when gasoline and tire rationing made trips into town just for fun out of the question.

In Salado, the Norwood family hosted each Sunday night on their capacious east porch what were called "musicales." The descriptive terms "hoot" and "hootenanny" were not used then. The family had a well-tuned upright piano. There were usually guitarists and fiddlers present. At these events, their children and friends sang popular songs from what is now called the country and western tradition as well as songs by Bing Crosby and his peers.[2] In O'Donnell, at the home of Dan Blocker (best known as Hoss Cartright from TV's *Bonanza*), musicians gathered on Sunday afternoons to sing mostly gospel hymns but also to do some folk tunes. At these events, there were usually brief narratives recounted of local history and/or of current events. The folk do like a good story.

In the hootenannies that are so popular a feature of Texas Folklore Society annual meetings, there are abundant survivals of the ancient characteristics of gatherings of the folk for singing and telling stories in verse or prose narration. The TFS "hoots" are true exemplars of the living folk traditions that have been with humans for countless centuries.

A typical TFS hoot is a splendidly seamless production. The laid back informality of these events adds to their abiding popularity. The hoot begins with someone standing up at the front to give a brief welcome and perhaps to lead a few songs, as Ab Abernethy did for so many years. The unwritten but usually closely observed code is that each succeeding performer will limit his or her presentation to three songs or the equivalent. As time permits, a performer may do an additional stint. The person in charge asks for volunteers to succeed each presenter. Sometimes, specific individuals are called upon. The singing of songs is usually done to the accompaniment of a string band but may be done a cappella. A singer may also do a solo, accompanying himself or herself with a guitar, and then act as song leader for other songs.

The members have come to expect certain songs from specific individuals. "Customary repetition" is one of the phrases used by folklorists to describe transmission of lore. Many members of the Society will recall with delight Martha Emmons' spirited renditions of a temperance song perhaps titled "Down with the Demon Rum, by Gum" and John West's vigorous continuation of that tradition after Miss Martha went on to the Glory Land where she is now surely in charge of the Celestial Collections of folk songs and tales. Familiar also is Lee Haile's singing the glories of "Fried Green Tomatoes." For many years Hermes Nye entertained the audience with his somewhat raunchy and irreverent "Good God, How the

Lee Haile, Hootenanny emcee and popular performer

Money Rolls In." This song and others appear in Nye's book about how to be a folk singer. There are, of course, far too many songs transmitted to the TFS members' collective memories by Ab Abernethy to mention all of them. But no one who heard these songs at a TFS hoot can hear now "Beautiful Brown Eyes," "Farther Along," "Jimmy Crack Corn," "Froggy Went A-Courting," "Foggy, Foggy Dew" or others without having the mind's iPod reproduce the sounds of Ab's voice and guitar.

Some songs are remembered as much for their instrumentation as for their lyrics. "Wild Wood Flower" is a sterling example. Any really good Texas dance hall guitarist or fiddler can play this popular tune and not bother with the familiar lyrics. At TFS meetings various members have often given charming variations of this tune. John Q. Anderson and some of his friends did exceptional renditions. John Q. also did "Salty Dog" in a fashion that yet echoes in the corridors of the minds of loyal TFS members from a long time past. The redoubtable James Ward Lee once did a solo guitar "Wild Wood Flower" at a hoot. Fiddle tunes such as "The Devil's Dream," "The 12th of January," and as done by Joyce Roach,

"The Canadian Waltz" are part of the repertoire of music that TFS members cherish. Of course, many renditions of "Cotton Eyed Joe" must be in even a short listing of favorite tunes that are a part of the heritage TFS members cherish and keep alive. In the later hours of some hoots there has been and continues to be dancing to good music from string bands.

Hosts for TFS meetings sometime recruit local amateur and/or professional musicians to present "sets" and at times to accompany other individuals or groups. These presenters invariably add to the quality of the hoots. One individual, Jean Schnitz, often accompanies the musical groups or individuals with spirited playing of the popular folk instrument, the hammered dulcimer. Her playing is a welcome complement to the sounds from guitars, occasional pianos, and fiddles, banjos, French Harps, and tambourines.

Jean Schnitz playing the autoharp

Hymns are much beloved by TFS members. No hoot can be considered full and complete unless several old time favorites are done. Over the years George Ewing has led a cappella many grand gospel hymns. And with or without instrumental accompaniment, Melvin Mason leads in singing favorites such a "How Great Thou Art," "On Jordon's Stormy Banks," [Jordon should, of course, be pronounced "Jerdon"!] and "I'll Fly Away." Stamps-Baxter songs and others from the popular gospel song traditions are frequently sung by the group as a whole. Comic songs by living authors have also been popular with TFS hoot attendees.

Hoots at TFS meetings occur on Thursday nights and on Friday nights after the banquet. These hoots are surely ordained in Third Corinthians somewhere, perhaps 12:14–15. They are well attended and they are not limited to singing and picking. Two other types of

George Ewing, leading TFS members in a hymn

R. G. Dean reciting "Lasca," a tradition begun by Mabel Major and continued by Hermes Nye

traditional folk entertainment are prominent at the sessions. First, poems are recited from memory—as is the genuine folk tradition in poetry presentation. At least three celebrated members of the Society have kept Frank Desprez's "Lasca" alive. Mabel Major, the Texas Christian University Professor of English who did much to bring respectability to the study of Southwestern Literature, gave a moving presentation of this sentimental poem at the Society's meeting in Austin at the old Driscoll Hotel in the Sixties. Hermes Nye picked up the tradition of reciting the poem sometime after Mabel's death. And now that Hermes is no longer here, R. G. Dean charms TFS audiences yearly with his sensitive delivery of the familiar lines of the long poem. Other and shorter poems are sometimes recited with gusto and vigor, but "Lasca" is the favorite.

Tall or short tales, and what Mody Boatwright called "windies," are key components of TFS hoots. In the true folk tradition, some of these tales or yarns or out-right lies are repeated often enough to cause the audiences to begin giggling before the punch lines are given. Other tales have the similitude of newness, but most are happily refurbished items from the rich heritages of this multi-ethnic state that boasts an amusement park named Six Flags Over Texas. Anyone who attended meetings of the Society during Paul Patterson's reign as tale spinner-in-chief will remember his colorful stories replete with authentic dialects about the cowboy life he lived and knew so well. Lew Schnitz regales the group with anecdotes of the petroleum industry and Charlie Oden keeps alive invaluable railroad lore. I have been known to share news about Old Bell County. Numerous other members do what the folk are best at doing—talking about themselves in oral narration just as the pickers and grinners tell our stories with singing and instruments.

Some folklorists argue that once a song or poem or yarn is reduced to print, it ceases to be pure folk. I can't agree with this notion even if I understand the reasoning behind such an assumption. In their work as collectors and recorders of folk material, the Lomax clan with printed works did priceless service to the study and perpetuation of folklore. (Some TFS long-time members will remember John Lomax singing work songs at our Austin meeting in the Sixties. And Americo Paredes was splendid in his singing in Spanish of Mexican love songs at that meeting.) In the high-tech age, tapes and CD/DVD discs preserve folk songs, poems, yarns, and even out-and-out windies for future generations. The long-lived songs such as "Barbara Allen" will be popular forever, whether sung by Ab Abernethy or some yet unborn talented person who will love the music and stories from what the collective heart and soul of the folk may be and who will record such material on some perhaps yet to be invented electronic marvel.

Our TFS hoots need no apologia. But I will say anyway that they must be continued for as long as humans gather to rejoice and wonder about themselves in song, poem, and story. What we so enjoy in our hoots is really the manifestation of the traditional oral transmission so dear to folklorists—even those of us who are grateful for tapes, CDs, DVDs, and good 78 rpm records of Vernon Dalhart singing "The Prisoner's Song" or "The Wreck of Old '97." When George Ewing sings with his yet magnificent voice a

Kenneth Davis sharing the latest news from Old Bell County at a Hoot

temperance song, TFS members hearing him become a part of an ongoing, traditional oral emphasis that makes the study of *folklore* so meaningful and essential.

The same principle is found in the storytellers who stand before their peers in the TFS to keep alive the customary telling of our collective stories. Fiction writer and ranching industry historian John Erickson, most famous for his Hank the Cow Dog stories, lamented at a TFS meeting in Abilene that when he drove through the Texas countryside and saw a satellite dish in the front yard he knew that family's body of saga lore was either dead or moribund. I do not disagree with Erickson, but I take heart each year at TFS meetings when in our hoots I hear old family lore stories as well as many other sorts recited by people who, for the most part, lived through the times and events they so skillfully and colorfully recreate for all the members to enjoy. And performances by children at the TFS hoots are not only delightful, they are also heartening in that they offer hope for the future of the Society. Whether the children sing songs, recite stories, or just stand before the audience looking cute, they are earnest of the Society's sure survival.

As a coda, let me encourage all Texas Folklore Society members to pass on the torch of picking and singing, reciting poems, and telling yarns of whatever kind to the coming generations whose lives need to be as enriched by folklore as have been ours, long-time TFS hoot attendees and participants. Each year when I see teenagers at our meetings, I rejoice and I delight in seeing young families with lap, porch, or yard kids. And it is always splendid when someone under the age of twenty reads a paper. We who are now becoming smooth of tooth must not only keep the torch lit, we must also pass it on. We can do so by encouraging our children and grandchildren to sing songs and tell and retell stories from the vastly varied body of what we call folklore.

Jan Seale said at a TFS paper session some years ago that when a man dies, a library goes. So it is with our Society; if we falter, we lose riches untold. We can't know who we are unless we know what we have been. With our hoots and with the many and varied papers we so enjoy at our yearly gatherings, we can be conservators as well as perpetuators of the grand traditions of folklore. We can help future generations know themselves by handing along lore transmitted to us that helped us define who and what we are. As Paul Patterson would probably have said, "We jest need to be right study about it."

Endnotes

1. Gummere, Francis Barton. *The Origins of Poetry*. New York: Macmillan Company, 1908, 1–10.
2. The patriarch of the Norwood clan usually had a story or two to tell while the musicians took needed but short breaks. Others at the events would then join in during successive breaks. I wish I had had a tape recorder at the time.

The Haile Family

THE TEXAS FOLKLORE SOCIETY: GETTING THERE IS HALF THE FUN

by Lee Haile

One of the things that I have always liked about being a member of the Texas Folklore Society is the fact that the annual meetings are always in a different place within the state each year. Ever since our family's first meeting in 1982 in Fredericksburg, we have looked forward to the TFS meeting in the spring. But for us, getting there is half the fun—or challenge—depending on how you look at it.

That first meeting I was still in college at A&M in College Station. I was asked by Dr. Silvia Grider to present a paper on folktoys. This stemmed from a demonstration of folktoys that I gave to the folklore class I was in the year before that Dr. Earnest Speck taught at Sul Ross in Alpine. Even going to that first meeting had its challenges. I missed a big lab test in my major (entomology) on that Friday. I had OK'd it with my grad student lab teacher, but that didn't fly with the professor whose reputation as a hardnose was legendary in the entomology department. When I came back, I found out I was in trouble with the prof. I was told to go meet him in his office. Everybody wished me luck in the "lion's den" and off I went. Man, I was nervous; this guy had never shown any quarter whatsoever. But when I informed him why I had missed the lab test, providence was with me. It just so happened that he was from Fredericksburg and had kin there as I do. He also had a big interest in folklore and had collected "insect folklore" for years. He even talked about some of the toys he had played with when he was young!

After an amiable discussion for most of the period I went back to the class. After being gone so long everybody assumed I had really been chewed up and spit out and would get a zero on my test. I told them no, we had a nice visit and talked about toys, bugs, and folklore. The prof. came in and informed the class that it

Lee and Karen Haile with baby Acayla

would not be fair for me to take the test by myself, so everybody would have to take it again. The test was identifying insect specimens from the collection. We found out later that no one had passed the first one, and I always wondered if I wasn't just a good excuse for the professor to save face!

The next meeting that stood out was because we missed it altogether. It was in Huntsville, on Easter as always. We left Thursday in plenty of time and got to College Station and visited with friends. Somehow in my mind I thought the meeting started Friday night, and ran Saturday and Sunday. Well, we stayed in College Station Thursday night and all day Friday visiting with friends. We showed up about 7:30 Friday night just in time for the banquet. We didn't have tickets or money for the banquet, so we just went back out and went to bed in the camper shell on my Toyota and froze all night long. I never forgot that the meeting starts on Thursdays from then on!

Next was the long trip to Lubbock. We started out from Hondo on Thursday, about noon. It was me, Karen, and her aunt Eloise from Georgia. Her kids called her "tick" because she got under your skin. We called her "Aunt Tick." Some TFS members may remember her, as she came to quite a few meetings with us. Karen was pregnant with Acayla and Tick was about sixty-five years old. Well, I am a backroads kinda guy and, let's face it, there is no direct way to Lubbock. We started north along the backroads in Karen's Datsun B210 (44 mpg—boy I wish I had that now!), and somewhere along the way we started having car trouble. I am a pretty good mechanic out of necessity and I knew it was probably just a partially stopped-up fuel filter. There was no place to stop for repairs and nothing to do but push on until it stopped up; then I would take it out and blow it clean.

It eventually turned dark and the car was losing power. Then it started to snow! We had only sixty miles to go but we couldn't see where the road was, only a carpet of white. Then we ran onto some eighteen-wheeler truck tracks. He obviously didn't know where the road was, either, and he had meandered from bar ditch to bar ditch, apparently driving by Braille. We could see where he had crossed the center stripe in his tracks, and so we had something to follow. Onward we pushed along at twenty miles per hour. The filter was allowing less and less gas to get through and I was going only 20 mph with the pedal floorboarded. I knew that if I let off the gas the car would die and it would not start again and I would be outside, under the car, in the cold, in the snow, in the dark, in the road, trying to fix it. Luckily, there were no other vehicles in sight.

It was about midnight when we finally saw the lights of Lubbock. We were all anxiously leaning forward just willing the car to go on. We had just got into town where the interstate splits for the loop and when we came over the overpass, we encountered traffic. I let off the gas, and the car died. I immediately put it in neutral, took the exit, and we started to coast through the cloverleaf. We made it to the bottom of the underpass but didn't make it very far up the other side. Now, there was just a guard rail on one side and a wall on the other side of this single lane access road. There was no place to pull off. So there we were: the car wouldn't start, and we were in the middle of a single lane road, in the middle of a curve, at the bottom of a hill, in the snow, at midnight, in

Lubbock. Yea! I jumped out, and Karen got behind the wheel, but I couldn't push it uphill in the snow. Now what? I told Karen and Aunt Tick to get out and away from the car. I was afraid that someone would hit them from behind.

I noticed a cop pull into a pancake house restaurant across the freeway, and I told them I would go for help. I jumped the guard rail, crossed two lanes, climbed the median fence, crossed two more lanes and went to the IHOP restaurant. I found the cop sitting at a booth with some non-cop friends. I explained my situation and asked for help. He explained that they were not allowed to tow vehicles with their police cars. Okay. I asked if he would help me push my car to a safer place. He said they were not supposed to help with stranded motorists. I was exasperated! So I asked in a very loud voice if he would please "at least get behind our car with his flashing lights so no one would run into us while my pregnant wife and her sixty-five-year-old aunt and I pushed our car to safety?" Everyone in the place got quiet and looked at him. After some hesitation—and a look that could kill—he agreed. He wouldn't give me a ride, so I ran back across the freeway. By then, some men had stopped and already hooked up to our car, so I got behind the wheel and they pulled us to the hotel next to the IHOP. There was an auto parts store within sight, so the next morning I walked over, got a new filter and in less than an hour we left for the meeting and all was well.

A few years later, we were once again heading north. I don't remember exactly where the meeting was that year. Karen's mom, Doris Reinartz, was with us that year and we were in their Ford truck. We had left after work and so we had a later start. We turned north at Junction toward Menard at twilight. Just out of town I turned on the lights, and as it got darker I noticed the lights were not very bright. I realized the alternator was not working and the battery was just about dead. Before I could do anything about it, the engine stuttered and died. The battery was dead and it was twenty miles back to Junction. There is not a lot of traffic on that stretch of road, but after a while a rancher stopped to help. He had an extra battery in the back of his pickup. It looked about the same age and shape as mine, so we traded even and we got back to Junction and a hotel. The next morning, I found a shop that was open until noon and I begged the old guy to work on my truck. I knew what was wrong and how to fix it, and I thought I was just being helpful. But after getting chewed out and being told not so nicely that "if I knew what was wrong and how to fix it, I didn't need him and I could fix if myself," I apologized quickly and profusely and backed away. That is when I learned you do not go into somebody else's business and tell them how to do it. We made the meeting in time for part of the afternoon session.

Then there was the big snow in Abilene. There was not much to the trip until a little past Coleman when we first hit snow. It kept getting worse until we came into Abilene. We pulled into the parking lot of the hotel where the meeting was to register, and that was it. We were not moving from there, the snow was too deep. This was the first time we stayed in the same hotel as the meeting. Up until then, we had always slept in the car in the parking lot or found the cheapest hotel in town. It was not that our finances were any better this time, we were just stuck! That was Acayla and Sierra's first real look at snow. I remember swimming in the heated pool with the kids and then running outside and rolling in the snow. We still have pictures of the kids in the pool next to the snowman I built inside on the edge of the pool. That year Tim Tingle and Doc Moore did the same thing I had done years earlier in Huntsville. After traveling all day Friday through the snow, they got there Friday night to find out that the meeting starts on Thursday. With everybody being stuck in the hotel with two feet of snow outside, it felt really cozy—like we were in a snug country lodge.

Probably the funniest and most amazing trip event was when we were on our way to Nacogdoches. Now my wife, god bless her soul, has the most amazing lack of sense of direction, so I usually drive unless we are on a simple straightaway. And another thing (okay guys, you know this), when we are in the car, she *hears* things and *smells* things. You know . . . "What's that sound?" "What sound?" "*That* sound, it sounds *bad*." Or, "What's that smell—something's burning!" Well, after enduring about five hours in a Toyota Corolla with me, Karen, and her mom, both little girls and, to me it seemed, an endless number of "sounds," "smells," "are you sure that is ok?" and "are we on the right road?"—I was a little testy. At the next to the last town before Nacogdoches, I let Karen take over. It was a straight shot with only one town between us and our destination. I was going to try to take a nap.

I got her on the road and we were just leaving this little town in the pines and I had leaned back the seat and covered my eyes when she yelled, "WHAT'S THAT SMELL?"

"Oh Karen it's nothing."

"SOMETHING'S ON FIRE!"

"No, I saw some people back there burning leaves."

"Are you sure?"

I sat up miffed and started to lecture her. "Every time you hear something or smell something you automatically think there is something wrong with the car. Come on now, the car is not going to just spontaneously catch on fire!" And I swear, just as I said "fire" a big white puff of smoke came out of the air vents and filled up the inside of the car! "QUICK. Pull over. Everybody out. Grab something and get it out." Fire drill: pop the trunk and throw everything out on the ground. Karen and the girls started hollering and dragging stuff over to the fence away from the car and road. Then, I went back in and started to analyze. No sound of any more fire, no smell of burnt plastic. I couldn't see any more smoke coming out or feel any heat under the dash. Hmmm. So I got out my tools and I took the dash apart. I couldn't find anything.

"Well let's go on," I said.

"No we can't do that," said Karen.

"Okay, what do you suggest?" No answer. After about twenty minutes we loaded up everything and started on, only, Karen drove and I sat in the passenger side with the dash in my lap and a towel

Sierra Haile sharing her storytelling skills, 1999

ready to put out any more fires and everybody ready to jump out for another fire drill.

We made it without anymore mishaps. The next day, I finished taking the dash apart and continued my investigation. I had my suspicions. Sure enough, a mouse had built a nest in the vent next to the fan (it happens all the time in the country—especially with Toyotas), and it had overheated and caught the nest made of cedar bark and cotton on fire. Luckily, there was enough condensation from the air conditioner coil that the nest was wet on the outside so it did not burn completely. I took the nest out and put everything back together and things were fine.

Although the trips just described were some of the highlights, all the trips have been interesting and enjoyable. Over the years we have been to El Paso, Lubbock, Denton, Sherman, Jefferson, Nacogdoches, Galveston, Kingsville, Laredo, Uvalde, and many points in between. Each host city has added interest to the meetings with either local musicians or trips to some of the local places of interest or even an interesting and historical place for the meeting to take place. With the meetings coming in the spring, the blue bonnets and wildflowers are in full swing. We have many fond memories of beautiful sights along the way. I remember Sierra's first meeting at San Marcos when she was six days old! Karen recalls that while she was pregnant with Acayla, the first time she felt her move was at a Folklore meeting, and the first person she told was Ab. I remember traveling to El Paso and for five hours driving through one continuous yellow blanket of flowers as far as the eye could see. And traveling back with the Coxes and Deans from the meeting in Midland, and stopping and taking pictures of us in acres and acres of blue bonnets in central Texas. Great times.

Each year, after being hunkered down for the last few months for winter, we start to look forward to the first big road trip of the year, knowing we are going someplace interesting and are going to have fun and will once again have a wonderful reunion with all our fellow folklorists and good friends.

What's so great about Texas Folklore Society meetings? Well, there have been ninety-three of them, and they've been held in over thirty different cities all over the state. We haven't gone to all of the meetings (obviously) or all the cities where they've been held, but part of the excitement is getting to travel to a different part of this great state each year and experience the local attractions and culture that each unique area has to offer. That's why getting there is half the fun. BON VOYAGE Y VAYA CON DIOS!!

The Haile women sing for the crowd

Archie McDonald with Ab and Hazel Abernethy, exploring folklore around the world

FOLKLORE SOCIETY MEMORIES

by Archie P. McDonald

My dilemma is that I have never known precisely what folklore is. I have attended a bunch of meetings of the Texas Folklore Society, and its program chairs have been kind enough to allow me to make presentations on a number of occasions. Even the American Folklore Society let me come to Philadelphia to talk about the contemporary Citizens Band radio phenomenon and to Los Angeles to speak on the "B" Western movie heroes of my youth. But I was never sure any of it was actually folklore, and my association with F. E. Abernethy only exacerbated my dilemma. The reason for that is that in a bitter dispute over the acting ability of my all-time favorite movie hero John Wayne, Ab told me that my taste was all in my mouth. So maybe if I don't have good taste in movie heroes, I don't know what folklore is, either.

That's all right, though, because I do know something about the folk. I grew up in Beaumont, Texas, the child of refugees who fled southwest Louisiana's Depression-era poverty for the glittering, big-city prospects of Beaumont, that Baghdad of the Neches, with its oil fields, refineries, chemical plants, Crockett Street attractions, and nouveau riche pretence. In those days before television, with only Mr. Roosevelt on the radio to tell us that everything would come out alright in the end—of the Depression, then World War II—the grown folk visited of an evening and we little folk listened to their stories and tall tales and learned about life in their rural world before four-cent cotton, possum stew, and Pearl Harbor.

The Opportunity of Education let me wiggle out of a life much like these grown folk in those same oil fields and refineries, a life that I hope would have been industrious and fruitful and noble anyway, in exchange for one in academe that has been easier on the muscles and sweat, and, on the whole, still gratifying. And one of its principal consequences and rewards has been knowing Frances Edward Abernethy.

Our paths crossed in Beaumont, probably in 1957 or 1958, my last year as an undergraduate at Lamar College and I reckon Ab's second year there as a teacher of English. I didn't take his class, but I saw him in the halls of the Administration Building, home to the English and history departments, and where, as was apparent from subsequent conversations, we both fell in love with one of the best actresses we ever knew, Camille Alexander, forever our Ado Annie from *Oklahoma*. This infatuation did not interfere with Ab's marriage to Hazel or mine to Judy, two tolerant helpmates who understood, in their Lorena Bobbitt fashion, that looking was okay, but touching forbidden.

Then I went away to the Rice Institute and after that to LSU, where Ab had been before me, and ended up with a brand new Ph.D. and an assistant professorship at Stephen F. Austin State College in Nacogdoches in the fall of 1964. Ab showed up the following year, coming home. Nacogdoches and SFA became a home for us, too—anyway we've been here nearly half a century—but it was always home for Ab, even though he never saw the place until Talbot Abernethy moved his family there the summer before Ab's senior year in high school. It wasn't love at first sight on either part—for Ab or Nacogdoches—but the two grew on each other and learned to love each other to the point that the town's Chamber of Commerce named him their Citizen of the Year in 2008, despite his curmudgeonly letters to the editor of *The Daily Sentinel*, the town's newspaper. The City Commission even named a trail for him beside Lanana Creek that he required me, Carol Schoenwolf, John Anderson, and sometimes Fred Rodewald (and many more) to help him build. That was before Ab convinced the City of Nacogdoches to help him maintain his trail.

Anyway, by 1971, we both had sinecures at SFA, he to serve the Texas Folkore Society as secretary-editor of its annual publication and me to work for the East Texas Historical Association as editor of its *Journal* and director of its affairs: same jobs, different titles. Over the years many people came to confuse us, despite the great and obvious difference in our ages, especially with cross-delivered mail and telephone calls. A precious moment came when I did something or the other that the newspaper noted and someone congratulated Ab. When he corrected my good intentioned well-wisher, she responded, "Oh, you're the other one." So, Ab went around saying, "I'm the *OTHER* one" for a week. I had to stifle a belly laugh into a modest grin until later, but it was a memory to cherish, nonetheless.

Ab and I worked well together for nearly four decades, each always supportive of the other with just the right intensity of testosterone-driven competition to keep us on our toes. It helped my request to drop to a six-hour teaching load in view of accelerating office duties when administrators remembered that Ab had already done the same, and I'm pretty sure it helped him persuade them to go ahead and hire Ken Untiedt when he pointed out that the Department of History already had taken my designated successor on its staff. But if one of us experienced illness, or adversity, or criticism, the other was first in line with sympathy, support, and righteous hostility. We have traveled the world together, worked together, and grown older together—he just barely sufficiently older so that often I have introduced Ab as my father—until trust and respect and even the kind of love grown men will nervously confess for each other, developed. In this centennial celebration of the Texas Folklore Society, history tells me of the role and significance of J. Frank Dobie and other directors of the Society, but for me and my generation, Frances Edward Abernethy is its personification.

Here, now, are some specific memories of Ab.

Serving on the Texas Sesquicentennial Commission in 1985, I learned of the possibility of a folklore exchange between Texas and South Australia, then celebrating its own Jubilee 150. Realizing how little I knew about folklore—remember that I have confessed that I really don't even know for certain what folklore is—I conspired to get a ticket for the trip by inviting Ab to put together the application package while I worked the "politics" of the thing in Austin. My plan worked: we were accepted and got Hazel as lagniappe for the trip. So, we three Texans spent three weeks telling our new "mates" Down Under about the ways of Texans and learning about barbees, boomerangs, and how to say "G'daiy, mate." We did twenty-four shows in twenty-one days—not bad when you consider some days were travel only. Our busiest was in Wyalla, where we visited three elementary schools, a Rotary Club, and did a TV interview on the same day. Our most memorable day was in American River on Kangaroo Island, where an insensitive hostess had scheduled us to tell the crew of the *USS Joseph Kennedy*, on shore leave, all about Texas. By show time that crew had sampled too much Australian beer to be interested in anything except more beer and girls. Ab talked the hostess into allowing us to entertain the American ambassador and his bored staff, one of whom, Colonel Walt Ford, USMC, I had taught at SFA.

The trip was grand with only minor hitches. Australia is cold in June, about thirty degrees cold, and Ab absolutely refused to take off the one pair of longjohns he had brought along. Equally bad, he acquired a turtleneck sweater, one like you see New England seafarers wear in the movies, and stubbornly refused to shed either. He demanded the co-pilot seat when we flew to Kangaroo Island, then went to sleep flying over the spectacular rocky coast of Australia as it faces Antarctica. And he almost got us into a fight by ordering us beer from New South Wales, which offended a South Australian patron of the bar in a hotel dining room. But it worked out well in the end, and we both learned that two bulls can occupy the same pen.

Some may not know that before Shakespeare and folklore, Ab's first aspiration was to become a biologist, or really a herpetologist. He loves snakes. One day after we had worked on that trail Ab made me build for him, we walked back over an area where we had been clearing privet and tie-vine impedimenta, me in front, when suddenly Ab commanded "Stop!" I did, and remained as motionless as possible. After an eternity of thirty seconds, he said, "Okay. That was a moccasin and I didn't want you to step on it and hurt it." "Thanks a lot," said I, with a mixture of equal parts gratitude for saving my life and irritation for being regarded as second in the Pecking Order of Life.

One of my finest moments in our occasional game of one-upmanship occurred in the 1970s, when I chaired SFA's Honor's Day program with Ab as the principal speaker. I gave him the glowing introduction he expected and deserved, but in the light of his well-known views about John Wayne, I concluded with, "I give you a man of True Grit, Francis Abernethy." Ab sat on the stage, stunned, lights ablazing, and tension mounting, then he rose and as he passed me on his way to the podium, said softly and without moving his lips, "You son of a bitch!" Again, my smile had to mask a deeper mirth.

Ab the Hog Hunter loaned me his trap when nocturnal visits from these feral wanderers resulted in the deep plowing of much of our lawn, and into that trap my wife eventually lured four of the critters, to their everlasting absence. It is illegal to discharge a firearm within the city limits, but Judy explains the disposition of the hogs thusly: "I don't know what happens to them; we call Ab and they go away." He told me that the shoulder of one of them was sweet meat that fed his whole family one weekend.

Ab and I dispute little, save differing opinions about John Wayne. Although I once introduced him as a man of True Grit, I think of him now in a line from the Wayne movie *Hellfighters*, that captures him so well: "He's one of a kind, the best there is at what he does."

Finally, Ab is my friend and my hero. I have decided, after all, what folklore is. As far as I am concerned, folklore is Francis Edward Abernethy.

Charlie Oden collecting folklore at the rail yard

CONFESSIONS OF A FOLKLORE JUNKIE

by Charlie Oden

I don't rightly recall just when it was that I became aware of the entity named the Texas Folklore Society, but, looking back, I realize that J. Frank Dobie began influencing my life when I began reading his works in high school. By that time, Mr. Dobie had "discovered his calling—to transmute all the richness of this life and land and culture into literature. The Texas Folklore Society was the main avenue for his new mission, and the University of Texas library with all its Texas resources was his vehicle."[1] Because he was the leading light of the Texas Folklore Society, the Society, in the person of Dobie, was also having an indirect influence on my life for many years before I was aware of its existence.

I was a frequent visitor to the school detention hall, where I read a good many books. I read everything in the school library and the hometown library that was written by J. Frank Dobie. After I began railroading, I read Mr. Dobie's books and articles in the Sunday newspaper supplements. I subscribed to the *Austin American* newspaper to read his weekly columns. In one of his columns he wrote about homemade syrup. My wife Georgia and I drove to a place I knew in East Texas to a farm where the people made syrup. It was late in the day when we turned off the main road and drove up the forward slope of a small hillock to the syrup mill. The reddish ground was covered with short Bermuda grass, and an unpainted farmhouse was in the background. A long pole was attached to the syrup mill so that a mule could pull the pole while she walked in the endless circle to power the mill. We bought two gallons, one for Mr. Dobie and one for me. I later delivered the bucket of syrup to his house in Austin, but he wasn't there. His wife accepted the syrup for him. Another time, in one of his columns, he told a hilarious story about a man in Kyle, Texas, and explained how these stories seem to move around and attach themselves to someone. I was furious. By George, that was one of *my* funny stories that I just knew to be true about a character in my home town. It was a good while before I could accept the fact that some stories we know to be true just are not.

During my working life I kept an eye out for anything by or about "Poncho" Dobie, Roy Bedichek, and Walter Prescott Webb. I made a pilgrimage to Barton Springs pool in Austin to see the bronze statue of these men. By this time I visualized the Texas Folklore Society as being a group of people possessed of great knowledge in the world of higher education, research, and understanding.

Retirement began for me in 1981. By 1985, I had joined the Houston Folklore Society, the Canadian Folk Music Society, and the Texas Folklore Society because of my addiction to folklore. During that time a compulsion to write came over me. Some of what I wrote was printed in the Houston Folklore Society's newsletter, *The Cotton Patch Rag*.

In the latter part of 1986, a circular letter came from the Texas Folklore Society asking for papers. To me it sounded a bit desperate. I had just about completed an essay on what I called "The Lingo of the Espee." I did not think that my writing skills measured up to TFS standards, but I called F. E. Abernethy and offered him what I had. He used it in *Hoein' the Short Rows*, 1987. In 1989, I contributed to *Texas Toys and Games*. I still had never gone to an annual meeting and knew no one "up front and personally" in the TFS. Georgia and I were utter greenhorns in the TFS.

Then, in the summer of 1995, I began a paper under the tutelage of Margaret Waring to be read at the Texas Folklore Society meeting the next year. In 1996, the Texas Folklore Society met at the Embassy Suites in Abilene, Texas. Georgia and I were looking forward to the Hootenanny. As the Hoot progressed, one gentleman sang a song, then, at the conclusion, remarked that there was a song that his daddy used to sing, and that he, the speaker, had forgotten the words and would like to have them if anyone could tell him what they were. The name of the song, he said, was "Turnip Greens." He then sat down on a front seat. Georgia and I

Charlie and Georgia Oden, 1985

knew the song, but we had no paper to write the words on. I scurried to the hotel registration desk, about thirty paces from where we were sitting, and got some paper. We hurriedly and excitedly wrote out the words to the song.

About that time the Hootenanny began to bog down. Jean Schnitz with her autoharp was sitting on stage trying her dead level best to coax people to come forward and do something. Georgia kept whispering to me, urging me to go "up there." I was a greenhorn, so I went hesitantly and asked Jean if I might do something. I remember her exact words: "Please do." I sang "Turnip Greens," and, when I finished, I handed the words to the gentleman who was sitting on the front seat. That night Mother Nature surprised everyone with gently falling snow, inches and inches of gently falling snow.

Charlie Oden, still sharing stories of the railroad with his folklore friends

All of us have days in our lives when nothing can go right and other days when everything goes smoothly. For Georgia and me, on our first meeting of the TFS, everything went smoothly. Thanks to Margaret Waring, I knew the material in my paper and made no blunders in presenting it. Georgia and I went about happily soaking up our first experiences during the meeting. Kent Biffle asked for a copy of my paper and used part of it in the *Dallas Morning News.*

Saturday morning, after a good breakfast, we removed the inches of snow from the windshield of the car and drove toward Austin. The snow had melted from the highways but still covered the fields, making a beautiful picture of long black lines in a white background. As we drove home we enjoyed the scenery and the car heater, and chattered back and forth about the meeting.

Since then, I have not missed but one meeting, and that was for medical reasons. I read the TFS publications, pester members for copies of papers they have presented that I especially like, buy copies of the books to give away, and buy copies for others to give them the advantage of my discount. I make photocopies of articles in the books or the papers that I have collected from TFS members and pass them on to folks whom I think would enjoy them. I started a poll of people who knew what folklore is, but that didn't get off the ground.

From high school to the present day in retirement (about seventy-three years), the TFS has materially influenced my thinking and lifestyle, both indirectly and directly. I enjoyed my ninetieth birthday on November 23, 2008, and, with any luck at all, I will be enjoying my addiction to folklore for some time to come. I'll be listening to folk music from the North Texas Irish Festival and the Houston Folklore Society, and swapping lies and being a part of the Texas Folklore Society as it faithfully searches out and records the lore of the folk.

Endnote

1. F. E. Abernethy. "Dobie, James Frank." *Handbook of Texas Online*, s.v. http://www.tshaonline.org/handbook/online/articles/DD/fdo2.html (accessed October 2008).

Mary Margaret Dougherty Campbell and son,
J. Michael Sullivan

HOOKED

by Mary Margaret Dougherty Campbell

In 1987, at the Texas/Southwest Popular Culture Association meeting, I shared ideas for possible future papers with my former Texas Tech professor, Dr. Kenneth Davis. He told me the paper topics I had in mind would be better suited for the Texas Folklore Society. Unfamiliar with the Society, I asked Dr. Davis about it. At the end of his explanation, he encouraged me to join. Shortly thereafter, I did so. For the next sixteen years, I was a sporadic member, sometimes remembering to pay my dues, intending to attend a meeting, but overall, basically inactive.

When Secretary-Editor F. E. Abernethy issued a call for papers on family lore in 2002, two family stories came immediately to mind—one about a locket, and one about a Texas Ranger. After transforming these oral legends into the written word, I submitted them, hoping Dr. Abernethy would accept one of them for publication. A few months later, I received notice that both of my stories would be in *The Family Saga* and that I should submit photos, if I had any, relevant to the stories. I sent four; he used three, a crop of one even as a chapter opener. Although now I believe Dr. Abernethy probably used all of the family stories submitted that year, I still feel honored to have our family stories published in a volume of the Publications of the Texas Folklore Society.

By that time, I had come to understand more about the Society and its rich contributions to the study of our state's folklore. I had also realized the importance of the man who was "born somewhere out there on that ranch," which is what I used to say when asked the significance of the historical marker on the farm-to-market road in southern Live Oak County where I grew up. Of course, that man was J. Frank Dobie, but growing up, I had no clue who he was, and the inscription on the marker meant little to me. I'd say, "Some famous guy was born out there in the brush."

In 2003, I decided it was time to attend a meeting. My son, J. Michael, would be spending Easter with his father; my husband, Cody, was working, and the meeting was relatively close: Kerrville. All the signs pointed me in the direction of my first TFS meeting. Prior to that meeting, my meeting/conference experiences had all been academic, consisting of concurrent sessions, attendees scattered about, a certain amount of aloofness, and no children.

Jean Schnitz attended the registration table that Thursday evening and welcomed me like I was a long lost member of a family I didn't know I had. She introduced me to her husband, Lew, and her friend Patsy Patten; these three made certain my first TFS meeting would not be my last. I had not signed up for the banquet, but they encouraged me to do so, which meant a quick trip into downtown Kerrville for a new dress, which I still enjoy wearing and reminds me of my first TFS meeting every time I wear it.

At the Thursday night Hoot, my main goal was to meet Ab and thank him for including my family stories and photos in the book. That done, I sat in the back and took it all in, observing the familiarity and congeniality among the members. I watched new arrivals greeted with warm hugs and pats on the back. And there were kids! And they were not only welcomed by all but hugged as the adults exclaimed how the children had grown since the last year's meeting. Truly, I found a familial atmosphere.

The next day, Friday, I attended every session, not wanting to miss a thing. Paper topics included "Sam Bass and the Mythmakers" presented by Nita Thurman, "Folk Art...It's Everywhere" by Karen Haile, "Walter Henry Burton's Ride from Bell County to Juarez, Mexico in 1888" by Jim Kelly, and others. Henry Wolff's "Tip to Tip: Legendary Longhorns" hit home with me since the famous Geronimo stands in his glass-fronted case on the courthouse lawn a few blocks from my home in George West. That afternoon, I eagerly called Cody to describe the papers I'd heard that day and tell him that people asked questions and offered interesting comments on the various topics. I was hooked.

The meeting in 2004 was held in Allen. J. Michael made the trip with me and also found a new set of friends in the TFS youth members. A bit reluctant at first about going to a meeting, J. Michael soon found that the kids were just as welcoming as the adults, and I barely saw him the rest of our time in Allen. He, too, was hooked.

J. Michael and I have both become involved in TFS and have attended every meeting since our first. We even drove the next year to El Paso to attend in 2005. In Galveston, the following year, J. Michael participated in the Hoot by reading a few of my poems to the group. He put together the PowerPoint presentation for my paper on souvenir plates and made sure it went smoothly. Ken Untiedt has accepted three more of my submissions for TFS publications, and I have read papers at three of the last five meetings. I have already served the Society as a councilor and am presently a member of the TFS board.

The Texas Folklore Society is like no organization in which I have ever been a part. The people, the papers, and the traditions are what make it unique. I treasure my TFS family and believe strongly in the study, documentation, and preservation of the folklore of Texas.

Sarah Greene and daughter Sally, enjoying a scenic overlook on their way to the McDonald Observatory, 1968

1968: ONE FAMILY'S FOLKLORE ODYSSEY

by Sarah Greene

In the spring of 1968, I saw a small item on a *Dallas Morning News* book page saying that the Texas Folklore Society planned its spring meeting for April 12–13 in Alpine and the Big Bend. A bus had been chartered to make the trip from Austin to Alpine. I was only vaguely aware of the Folklore Society then, but as a native Texan, I had long been looking for an excuse to visit the Big Bend. My husband, Ray Greene, agreed to stay home and mind the family newspaper, *The Gilmer Mirror*, so I could make the trip with our children, Sally and Russ (twelve and nine at the time), and my parents, Russell and Georgia Laschinger.

We boarded the bus in Austin that April, and began getting acquainted with a most congenial group. James Ward Lee, the 1968 president, was accompanied by his amusing young sons. John Q. Anderson and his wife Loraine also were among the notables on board. As we left San Antonio, John A. Lomax Jr. stood up in the front of the bus and started singing "Going Down the Road Feeling Bad," a folk song anything but representative of the passengers' sentiments.

My parents had opted for a downtown Alpine motel, where we checked in that Thursday night. The next morning we boarded a bus for the drive to Santa Helena Canyon and the Chisos Basin. On first glimpsing the Rio Grande, far below the highway on a bluff, I pointed it out to my Ontario-born father. He responded that it couldn't be; surely the Rio Bravo was a much grander stream. "Bet you ten dollars," I said. When we reached our destination and I was proved right, he said, "I should have known. Tight as you are, you'd only bet on a sure thing."

Mody Boatright in 1968, the year he was made a Fellow of the Texas Folklore Society

After we arrived at the Chisos Basin, where Mody Boatright was made a Fellow of the Texas Folklore Society, I was called to the phone in the park headquarters. By the time I got there I was panicked, quite sure some disaster had hit at home. Instead, I was told by the motel room clerk that my parents could stay on but my children and I would have to vacate our room. It had been rented out to others. This was actually no problem, as it turned out. Sul Ross State College President Brownie McNeil had offered free dormitory rooms to the TFS members at Lawrence Hall Dormitory, and he sent his college student son to transfer Sally, Russ, and me to a dorm room.

Wilson Hudson giving a paper

We enjoyed the Saturday program at the Rock Pile and went on to the McDonald Observatory, and the saengerfest that night was outstanding. Picking and singing by Brownie McNeil was one of many highlights.

I am one of many—too many now among the dear departed—who remember that 1968 meeting as uniquely wonderful. It began an association for me that has brought lifelong friendships and countless great experiences. I've missed very few of the annual meetings since then, and nothing short of hospitalization or worse will keep me from showing up each Easter weekend as I enter my ninth decade.

Rhett Rushing taking part in a Hootenanny

MY FIRST TFS MEETING

by J. Rhett Rushing

It was the fall of 1982. I was an undergraduate Aggie looking at my chemistry grades and slowly coming to the realization that veterinary medicine was probably not my career path. I was good at English, I loved history, and the Boy Scout in me had a passion for anything about cowboys and Indians and Texas in general.

I was the kid that would cut class to go fishing and secretly cooked squirrel stew in an illegal crock pot in my dorm room. I knew all about making homemade wine from Mustang grapes, and on more than one occasion had hung deer to skin and butcher in the communal shower of my dorm.

What I wanted to be was Fred Gipson's "hound dog man," but there was little in the way of financial security or gushing approval from professional parents in the direction I was heading. Like most nineteen-year-olds, I craved legitimacy and a little respect, but that sort of stuff required either phenomenal athletic prowess or years and years of hard work.

So, I wound up in an Intro Folklore course taught by Tom Green. Suddenly I found myself reading all the time. Evidently, folks before me had gone to the trouble of collecting all these tales and recipes and customs and written them down in books. All my English and history and anthropology courses suddenly became useful as I devoured folklore, text after text after text. Hell, I could even find use for all that chemistry and biology and math stuff, as well.

In the spring I took Mexican American Folklore from Joe Graham, and the whole world changed. Joe recognized my enthusiasm and started carefully pointing me in different directions—probably as much to keep me out of his office as to allow me to explore new ground—folk art, folk architecture, folk medicine (all the stuff I liked and had interests in suddenly became legitimate, if I just put "folk" in front of it), folk foodways, etc. And that's when the circus came to town.

Joe Graham was the program chair for the 1983 TFS meeting, and that year it was going to be held in College Station—about 125 yards from my dorm room/taxidermy/butcher shop that was quickly becoming a respectable little folklore library. Joe figured that if I wanted to get my feet wet and see what folklore really smelled like, then I should volunteer myself to assist with the meeting arrangements. I worked the registration table, I fetched water, I moved chairs and hauled boxes and stuffed goody bags from the Chamber of Commerce, and I got to eyeball folks coming from all over and beyond just to talk about Texas folklore. I was quickly overwhelmed, and it was just getting started.

I was not entirely aware of what one did at a "Hoot," so I sat back and listened. Someone had provided free beer, so I figured I could tolerate just about anything after that. The room started filling up with people—people with name tags. I started recognizing the names on the name tags because they were on the backs of the books in my room and on the articles I kept getting in class and at the library. I was the kid in the candy store.

And then folks started picking and singing—songs I had grown up with, songs that I seemed to know intuitively like they were genetically imprinted in some deep East Texas part of my brain. These were songs about stuff my family knew: railroads and sawmill towns and the army and cowboys and church and food—there were a lot of songs about food.

As the tall guy that everybody called "Ab" led the Hoot on through the night and into the morning, only a dozen or so diehards remained, among them my professor Joe Graham and a really funny guy named John O. West who was talking to Elmer Kelton (a name tag I recognized and kept trying to introduce myself to but never got up the courage). You couldn't have pried me out of there with a crowbar, but I went heartsick when the hotel manager stuck his head in and said it was time for us to leave. Evidently this was not a problem for experienced TFS "Hooters," because Rosemary Killam announced that we would be moving the party to her hotel room. There was no question that I'd been included in the invitation, though none of these folks knew me from Adam's off ox.

When we got to the room people arranged themselves in a loose circle on the floor, though one fella named John Graves (I realized that he was the *Goodbye to a River* and *Hardscrabble* John Graves) draped himself across the bed and leaned in from there. Don Swadley said the rules were simple—as the huge bottle of Weller bourbon in a paper sack made its way around—you were to take a drink and come up with a song for everyone to play and sing. To my wide eyes this was a great game, and as it went from round to round I realized that I really belonged in that room and in that circle. I knew most of the songs they were singing, but more importantly, I knew most of the words to those songs.

After one particularly lengthy version of "Buffalo Gals," John Graves pointed straight at greenhorn me and said "Ab, is this boy one of yours?" To which Ab replied without hesitation, "Nope, but I'll take him."

Of course, my feet didn't touch the ground for the rest of that weekend, but if there was any way to measure how welcome Ab's comment made me feel—right there in a room full of my heroes—it would border on the numinous. Twenty-six years later, I've never been associated with such a loose herd that made me feel any more welcome. Pass the bottle.

Carol, Pete, and Erik Hanson

LOOKING BACK WITH THE HANSONS

by Carol Hanson

The Texas Folklore Society has a rich history, with some larger-than-life folks birthing the Society into existence and guiding its earliest years of infancy and beyond. There have also been those who contributed monumental amounts of time, sweat, ink, and tears before they left us. There have been many who have "been there" to nurture and encourage, and to provide smiles and laughter. And there have been many who have coordinated all the endless details of the meetings, banquets, publications, communications, finances, and everything else that needs to be done to keep the Society running from day to day.

And then, there are those of us who participate just by being in attendance at the meetings—from Thursday's Hoot to Saturday's Business Session and check-out at noon. We soak up the annual camaraderie, the familiar faces and stimulating culture, and welcome opportunities to buy more books (or at least consider buying them), sometimes bringing new folks along and helping the TFS wherever we can, perhaps by creating our own smaller traditions within the larger group. This article is an account of how our family became involved with the Texas Folklore Society and what it has meant to us. It began with me.

I'm a native Texan, born in the 1950s to a very blue-collar family in Dallas County that, while appreciating the need for education, never expected me or my siblings to go much further than getting a high school diploma. No doubt it surprised my parents that I persisted in efforts towards a college degree. After finally completing a master's degree in Library Science, I began working at Dallas Public Library in 1979, in the Texas/Dallas History Division.

In the early 1980s, I joined the Dallas Westerners' Corral because of encouragement from our division's manager at Dallas Public Library. After my involvement in that organization for a couple of years, several members who were also members of the Texas Folklore Society began "educating" me about the TFS. They included Dean and Olivia Nichols, Milton and Deurelle McAffee, Charles and Ernestine Linck, and my boss, Ruth Lambert, who had become a good friend. I finally succumbed to their urgings and agreed to accompany Ruth to my first TFS meeting in 1985. So, in April of 1985, I drove Ruth and myself to Abilene to the Kiva Inn, which was a very nice hotel—but it was the people involved in that TFS meeting who created the welcoming atmosphere.

It didn't take long to be hooked. What wasn't to like? There were interesting, friendly people with Texas roots, and with an appealing open-mindedness about the cultures that co-exist in Texas, as well as a sincere, healthy curiosity about almost everything in our society. Like many others, I suspect, the Hootenanny (Hoot) was instantly my favorite part of the TFS experience—because of the music, fun, and relaxed vibes, I suppose. At that meeting, I met some very interesting folks, including Martha Emmons and John O. West, who sang a duet of their "Rum" song, which I later learned had been an annual event for many years. (I know the song has another name, but I don't recall it.) Well, I kept returning to TFS meetings: in 1986 at Jefferson, in 1987 at Galveston, in 1988 at Lubbock, and in 1989 at Uvalde. Each one seemed to be better than the one before.

Pete and I had begun dating at the end of 1987, and by March of 1989 we were engaged—so he came with me for the first time to the Uvalde meeting. And then he was hooked as well! We were married in June 1989. Unfortunately, we missed the 1990 meeting because a very good friend was getting married that same weekend. However, by then I was pregnant, and in 1991 it was the Hanson *family* attending, with four-month old Erik in tow to the TFS meeting in San Marcos.

And so, our family has come to anticipate attending Texas Folklore Society meetings as a springtime tradition; because of them, we have managed to see places in Texas we would never have visited otherwise: San Angelo, Victoria, Midland, Uvalde, Nacog-

Baby Erik was a hit with members at the 1991 meeting

doches and, of course, El Paso—we *definitely* would have never made it there if not for the Texas Folklore Society! By the time he was four or five, Erik's first question when we told him we had arrived at the TFS hotel was usually, "Are the girls here?" (meaning Acayla and Sierra Haile). He's grown up with those two at these meetings, from crawling around the pallets that Karen and I put down to running and playing tag in later years. For him, it's almost like another set of cousins he gets to see once or twice a year.

Now, the serious part of TFS meetings—the papers all day Fridays and on Saturday mornings—has always been enlightening and enjoyable to Pete and myself each year. I've always been delighted with the variety of topics covered, and being part of an organization that explores so many facets of our society and the culture of everyday people has especially intrigued me. But, I'm afraid the benefits of those sessions were usually lost on Erik, for the most part. He was always more interested in the other children who attended. So, he made friends with the Haile girls, the Untiedt children, the

TFS kids playing together at a meeting

Deans' grandsons, and later J. Michael Sullivan and Taylor Lang and several others. He usually enjoyed the Hootenanny, including the times he was in the middle of it. (Once when Erik was about three, we arrived just as the Hoot was getting kicked off by John O. West and before we knew it, Erik was there on stage with John singing "Froggie Went a Courtin'" to Erik on his knee. When he was much older, he played a snare drum solo that he had learned that year for his band at one of the Hoots.)

Some of our favorite Hootenanny memories have been:

- Ab playing either the guitar or the bass fiddle, and especially him singing (or getting some audience participation on) "The Strawberry Roan"
- Lee Haile singing the "Home-Grown Tomato" song
- Joyce Roach playing her fiddle (and why haven't we seen her do that in recent years?)

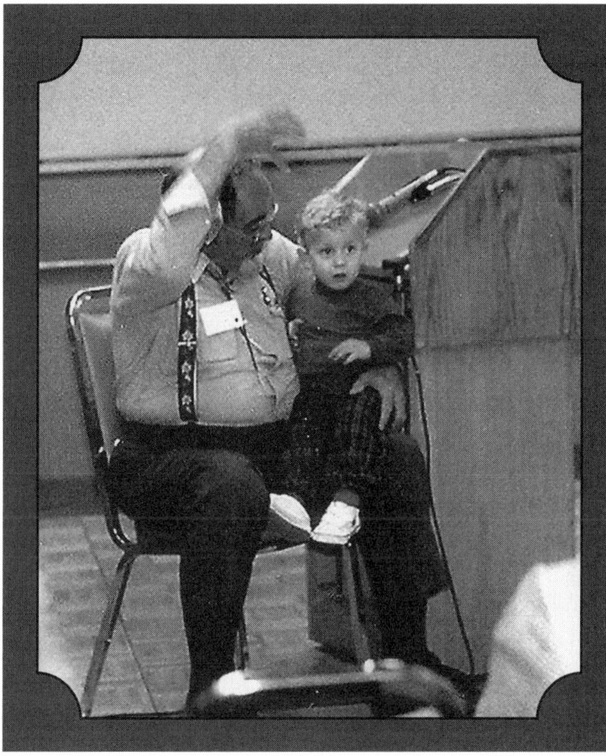

A very young Erik Hanson with John O. West at a Hoot

- Acayla and Sierra Haile (with their parents) singing either "Battle of New Orleans" (with appropriate actions) or "Grandma's Featherbed"
- Brenda Black White reciting any of her own delightful, very emotional poems
- Jean Schnitz playing any song on her hammer dulcimer
- I don't recall the fellow's name (he only came to TFS two or three times—but he was very crafty and a hilarious wordsmith in songwriting. He brought his very own

curiously designed, hinged wooden guitar that would fold up, and a *hilarious* song he wrote and sang with a rather crusty voice about all the things about his body he'd lost as he aged—his hair, his eye-sight, his energy, his hearing—and then the great punch-line (if I recall it correctly): "of all the things I've lost, I miss my mind the most!" (Pete and I both *really* enjoyed that fellow and his song.)

It's been an honor and blessing to make the acquaintance of such wonderful, learned, talented, good-hearted people who make the Texas Folklore Society what it is—Ab and Hazel Abernethy, Kenneth Davis, George Ewing, John O. and Lucy West, Jean Schnitz, Lu Mitchell, Joyce Roach, R. G. Dean, Lee and Karen Haile, Ken and Tierney Untiedt, and many others have been among the people we've always looked forward to seeing each year.

Among the most memorable papers that I recall over the years would be these:

- Joyce Roach and Robert Flynn's unusual duet presentation of "Holier than Thou"—(It would be great to have a reprisal of that one)
- James Ward Lee's "Pie" was great fun and has inspired me to not be afraid to make a good pie, especially any meringue pie
- George Ewing's presentation about walking sticks he had made with examples, which he also later sold—we bought one that day, letting Erik pick one out; it was, of course, the *tallest* stick George had!
- The Kid's Folklore Session which Karen Haile chaired in 2002; a major feature was talking about and demonstrating folk-toys, which Lee has become an expert on, and he demonstrated several. Back in 1999, on a vacation, when we stopped at the St. Louis Arch, we bought Erik a Jacob's Ladder toy and he later learned all the tricks on

Erik demonstrating his Jacob's Ladder skills

the instructions, so at the TFS Kids' Session, Erik demonstrated some of the tricks he had mastered.

In addition to the scholarly learning and the fellowship with the other TFS members, we've always enjoyed visiting new places in Texas, and learning about them. The tours arranged by the Local Arrangers are always especially satisfying, because we're usually provided with the BEST tour guides for the site and really get the "straight skinny" on the subject. Some of the most memorable tours have included:

- The horses at the Chaparrosa Ranch, which were directed into their places with no corral or bridles, only hand signals along with popping lariats and whips—it was utterly amazing how the cowboys did that! (Uvalde, 1989)
- The fantastic Fort Chadbourne tour, where among the many intriguing sights of the fort's remains and fascinating artifacts and inscriptions found there, Pete *and* Erik got to see a real live Horny toad and learned how fast they can be [Pete *is* a Yankee, you know, and Horny toads never made it to Illinois] (San Angelo, 2001)
- A personal tour of the TFS office in Nacogdoches in 2000—that was a great treat, and Erik discovered some of Ab's best "toys" from the far corners of the earth.

It's always difficult explaining to anyone outside this organization why the meetings are so special and why we *really* have to attend each year. I know others have described them as being similar to a family reunion, and that is sort of true. But when I leave the TFS meeting on Saturday each year, I often feel that my mind has been stretched and I have discovered new twists on topics I thought I already understood, and that rarely happens at a family reunion. There have been occasions when I have laughed so hard I was almost crying while listening to a well-crafted story, song, or even a "scholarly" paper; that also has rarely happened at any of the professional meetings I've attended. And frequently, as we depart the TFS meeting, I vow that I'm going to find some topic to work into a paper for next year—except, so far, that has never happened.

However, over the years, the Texas Folklore Society has influenced our family in various subtle ways. It was at the first meeting that I learned of Hank the Cowdog—because John Erickson was the Banquet speaker and did all of the voices for a chapter of one of his first Hank books. I've loved that series ever since. And my son Erik (who wasn't yet born) learned to love Hank later, too. As a

Pete Hanson building a snowman at Easter, with the help of son Erik, and Acayla and Sierra Haile

librarian, I've become a big booster for Hanks' stories; whenever youngsters between the ages of eight and twelve were looking for a good book or series to read, I have often pointed them towards Hank. The Texas Folklore Society has influenced my library career overall, having made me more conscious of books with folklore value. I've ordered materials for my library's collection on occasion because of that sort of topic, and sometimes I've ordered some of the TFS publications. Also, after hearing Lu Mitchell perform, I've been lucky enough to get her to provide an adult program for my library a couple of times, since we live in the same big-city area.

The meetings are mini-vacations for us. One of the early Folklore meetings we attended when Erik was young was the April meeting in Abilene when it snowed all day on Friday. Erik, Acayla, and Sierra got to build a snowman that day, with Pete's assistance. Ab later said that was the first snowman built (that he knew of) at a TFS meeting, and we sent a picture of it for the archives. We had been told about the Buffalo Gap history park and had planned on checking it out on Saturday before leaving. Well, the snow had closed it down, which was a disappointment. But, a couple of years later, we drove through Abilene as part of our summer vacation trip to Colorado and took an afternoon break there, which was really good because there was a little playground with old-fashioned sturdy play equipment, which helped use up some of Erik's energy for the remainder of that day's traveling.

In recent years, we've also attended the Texas Folklife Festival in San Antonio in June, which provided more fun with the Haile family, Jean Schnitz, Kay Arnold, and a few others. Erik especially enjoyed helping out at the Hailes' folk-toy booth, where he picked up skills with tops and the bull-roarer. I also assisted for three or four years there at the TFS table as well, along with Jean and Kay. In 2004 and 2005, the Texas Folklore Society experimented with a summer camp for kids of the Society; the camp was at Treetops in the Forest, run by Chris Kalstrom and located in the Davy Crockett National Forest. Erik participated both years and truly enjoyed the experience, which gave him a different perspective of folklore, nature, and the ways of learning about both.

The Texas Folklore Society has, in short, become an intrinsic part of our family's life and traditions, and has affected how we see the "outside" world. Obviously, as evidenced in this paper, our enjoyment has also centered on our son's experiences, which I believe is typical of most parents that I know in the Society. He is, after all, the center of *our* universe. We appreciate the enriching experiences, the fun opportunities to learn new things, and the personal relationships we have enjoyed because of this organization, and we look forward to many more ahead. We hope the friendships we all have developed will last for a long time. I am *so* glad that I attended that first meeting in Abilene way back in 1985.

Jack Duncan

UNDER THE INFLUENCE

by Robert J. (Jack) Duncan

In myriad ways, both directly and peripherally, my life has been immeasurably enriched and informed by my long association with the Texas Folklore Society (TFS) and its diverse members. At North Texas State University (now the University of North Texas) as an undergraduate, I had taken the Life and Literature of the Southwest course under Professor George D. Hendricks. Later, I took his graduate course on folklore and wrote my term paper on chain letters. Professor Hendricks suggested that I submit my paper for possible presentation at one of the annual TFS meetings, and he invited me to the 1970 meeting at Wimberley.

My wife Elizabeth and I attended the Wimberley meeting, but we missed the 1971 San Antonio meeting because the birth of our second child was imminent. But after that, our exposure to the TFS at Wimberley apparently "took," because since 1972, I somehow have been fortunate enough to be able to attend every annual meeting (and Elizabeth has missed only one of those meetings). Over the decades I have been influenced by writers and other fully actualized folks that I have come in contact with at the annual TFS meetings or, one way or another, as a result of my TFS membership.

* * *

At Wimberley, Elizabeth and I were amazed at the quality and diversity of the presentations. Three, in particular, were especially impressive and remain vivid and memorable nearly four decades later. Sylvia Grider's paper about a horrendous Depression-era dust storm in the Texas Panhandle was graphic, and James Ward Lee's talk about attending a fundamentalist brush arbor revival as a child in Alabama was hilarious and insightful. Our overall favorite, though, was Sid Cox's beautifully textured saga of his family's home place. Sid humbly prefaced his presentation by saying that fifteen or twenty minutes of the audience's time represented "high wages" for him and a profound honor. Then he proceeded to blow the audience away. His paper was so good that he was asked to repeat it between sessions for anyone who had missed it or who felt compelled to hear it repeated. Those three papers and others "hooked" us, and we knew we would be back.

We also were very impressed by John Lomax's *a capella* singing of religious and folk songs. Later we would learn that John was a son of John Avery Lomax, who traveled the South in the 1930s, recording songs by prison inmates, such as folk and blues musician "Lead Belly" (Huddie William Ledbetter). John (Jr.) also was the brother of Alan Lomax, who directed the Library of Congress's archive of folksong recordings.

Also among those present at the Wimberley meeting were Bertha Dobie (J. Frank Dobie's widow), Martha Emmons, and Mody Boatright. As a fundraiser, the Society raffled off a commemorative quilt made by Loraine Anderson. Sylvia Grider won it, and folksinger/novelist/attorney Hermes Nye asked Sylvia if that was the first time she had ever taken a chance on a quilt.

* * *

We joined the Texas Folklore Society at just about the time that Wilson Hudson turned over the Secretary-Editor duties to Francis Edward (Ab) Abernethy and the TFS headquarters moved from the University of Texas (at Austin) to Stephen F. Austin State University, in Nacogdoches. As I recall, that also more or less coincided with our change in publishers from the SMU Press to Bill Wittliff's Encino Press.

Our two children, Brad and Robert Christopher, were born in 1968 and 1971, respectively. They still keenly remember attending TFS meetings with us in the 1970s and 1980s. By the age of four or five, Brad was no trouble whatsoever at TFS meetings. He would attend the sessions and listen attentively, the same as the adults in the audience. At about that age, he also sometimes accompanied me when I interviewed people for TFS articles and papers I was writing.

During the 1970s, I often made audiotapes of the presentations and hootenannies. In 1979, when I was program chairman, I enlisted the help of friend and fellow member Wayne Lambert. Wayne recorded the entire meeting on large reel-to-reel tapes. I still have those tapes.

* * *

J. Mason Brewer was the banquet speaker at the 1972 meeting in College Station. Brewer was a scholarly author, a distinguished university professor, and a dignified elder gentleman of color. A beautiful young woman had sat next to him at the sessions earlier that day. I assumed that she was his daughter, or perhaps even a granddaughter. But no, she was his wife.

J. Mason Brewer speaking at a TFS meeting

Brewer rose to make his banquet address. The title of his presentation was "I Knew Them All," wherein he told of his acquaintance and association with all the early TFS folklorists. After he had spoken for perhaps a couple of minutes, it dawned on me that Brewer was speaking in rhymed verse, yet the content of his talk seemed as natural as an unrestrained casual conversation. And as far as I could tell, he was using no notes at all. His talk of perhaps half an hour was a virtuoso performance by a master wordsmith, and an awe-inspiring thing to behold.

* * *

Ed Offield and I worked together for many years in the central laboratory of St. Regis Paper Company's Flexible Packaging Division in Dallas. Ed was an avid reader, and he was interested in Texas and western history. I knew that if I could get Ed to just one of the TFS meetings, he would be "hooked." That happened in 1973, and his addiction to it was just as I had predicted.

In 1973, Elizabeth and I flew from Dallas to Laredo for the Easter weekend meeting and rode back with Ed. Elizabeth had never flown before. The first leg of the trip was from Dallas to San Antonio on a new carrier, Southwest Airlines. On that flight, there were tornadoes below us, and we weathered a lot of turbulence. During the landing approach, at literally the last minute when we were just a few dozen feet above the runway, a big gust of wind caused one of the wings to suddenly dip dangerously. I was clutching the armrests for dear life. In those days I frequently traveled on business, but this was by far the scariest flight I had ever been on. As soon as we were safely on the tarmac, one of the flight attendants blurted out on the plane's speaker system, "Thank God, we made it!" Elizabeth, who blissfully had no flight experience, and hence no frame of reference, looked at me and asked, "Was there something unusual about this flight?" A couple of days later, on our road trip back with Ed, we would witness the extensive damage that the tornadoes and high winds had caused.

While in Laredo for the meeting, the three of us crossed the border to do a little shopping. We agreed that, to try to avoid "Montezuma's revenge," we would not drink any water in Mexico. Soon after crossing the border we visited the Cadillac Bar (or one of its competitors). Ed and I each ordered a bottle of beer. Elizabeth ordered a Coke. Ed and I were intently discussing something when I noticed that Elizabeth was drinking her Coke from an ice-filled glass. I reminded her of our resolution to avoid the water, and she replied that she was drinking Coke, not water. I gave up. Fortunately, she didn't get sick.

At the Friday night banquet, we happened to meet and share a table with artist Ben Carlton Mead and his wife, Maida. Ben, who had illustrated several of Dobie's books, including his landmark and breakthrough book *Coronado's Children*, had been a TFS member in the 1930s but had not attended for decades until Ab extended a special invitation to him to attend the Laredo meeting. The Meads lived in North Dallas, and Elizabeth and I lived not far away, in Mesquite. Maida died in 1975. Ben became a close friend of our family. In late 1976, Ben and David Weber worked to organize the Dallas Corral of Westerners International, a group that still meets monthly for dinner and presentations by guest speakers. I tried to contact and invite all the TFS members in the Dallas area to the first meeting. From the beginning of the Dallas Corral, there were several members of that organization who were also TFS members.[1]

* * *

From 1971 until 1978, the Encino Press, in Austin, was the Society's publisher. William D. Wittliff, owner of the small press, didn't attend TFS meetings, but I became acquainted with him anyway. On our family vacation in September of 1974, we stopped by the Encino Press on Austin's Baylor Street one Saturday to visit briefly with Bill. Elizabeth took Brad and Robert across the street to play under the historic Treaty Oak (this was decades before it was maliciously poisoned.) An acorn fell from high in the old tree and thumped Brad on

Jack and Brad Duncan outside the Encino Press with Bill Wittliff

the head. He began to cry, but then he became mesmerized when Elizabeth explained to him that it might have been a good omen. In the color snapshot that Elizabeth took of Bill, Brad, and me a few minutes later on the front porch of the Encino Press, if you look closely, you can see that Brad's eyes are still a bit red.

Bill Wittliff and his Encino Press published approximately 250 books and other items and won more than 100 awards. But eventually he retired the Encino colophon and segued into a very successful film career. Wittliff still owns, and has his office in, the Morley mansion on Baylor Street in Austin, a house that William Sydney Porter once occupied before he became the famous short story writer O. Henry. An extremely creative and multi-talented person, Wittliff began taking still photographs for movie studios. Soon he was writing screenplays, directing, and producing films. In one capacity or another (or more), he has been deeply involved in the films *Raggedy Man*, *The Red Headed Stranger*, *Country*, *The Cowboy Way*, *Barbarosa*, *Honeysuckle Rose*, *Ned Blessing*, *Legends of the Fall*, *The Perfect Storm*, and others, as well as the landmark and classic television mini-series *Lonesome Dove*. In 1985, Bill served on the board of trustees for Robert Redford's Sundance Institute for Film and Television. In the 1980s, Bill obtained many of J. Frank Dobie's papers at an estate sale. Soon, he and his wife Sally founded the Southwestern Writers Collection at Southwest Texas State University (now Texas State University).

Bill had worked as sales manager for SMU Press shortly after graduating from college. Before long he and Sally had moved to Austin and founded the Encino Press in their garage and small house. A few years later, they bought the Morley house at 510 Baylor Street. On the day of my visit in 1974, Bill told me that he had bought the house from an opera diva. He said that a few days after they had the formal legal closing, he heard a noise coming from one of the outside doors. He said that the opera singer, screwdriver in hand, was in the process of removing one of the hand-painted ceramic doorknobs. She told Bill that she had forgotten to mention that she intended to remove the antique doorknobs before the sale. The last time I looked, those doorknobs were still on the doors.

* * *

During my years of employment as a packaging scientist at St. Regis Paper Company, I often made trips to the company's production plant in Middletown, Ohio. On one of those trips in 1975, after my flight arrived at the Cincinnati airport, which is actually across the Ohio River in Covington, Kentucky, I drove my rental car into Indiana and visited Stith Thompson, who had been the first TFS Secretary-Editor. Thompson is known to folklore scholars worldwide as the author of the six-volume masterwork entitled *Motif Index of Folk Literature: A Classification of Narrative Elements in Folktales, Ballads, Myths, Medieval Romances, Exempla, Fabliaux, Jest-books, and Local Legends*. I had called him a few days earlier to ask if I might drop by to meet him. When I arrived, I was surprised to see that the building located at the address he had given me was that of a nursing home.

I visited with him for a while and asked him to sign a couple of books for me. As I recall, he was ninety years old. He was quite hard of hearing. He seemed glad to have a TFS visitor. Thompson said that his doctor had limited him to several cigars a day—six, I think—and he was enjoying number six that evening while we visited. At the next annual TFS meeting, I was scheduled to read a paper, and I used a few minutes of my allotted time to convey greetings from Stith Thompson to the members and to report on my visit with him. He died the following year.

* * *

In 1977, Ed Offield and I had planned to drive from Dallas to El Paso to attend the annual meeting. We considered renting a van and providing roundtrip rides for a fee. We advertised our intentions, but only two riders signed up: Martha Emmons and Loraine Anderson. So, we rented a car rather than a van and, thankfully, got it with unlimited mileage. Martha came up from Waco via bus, and Loraine came to Dallas from Louisiana. Ed and I took turns driving and the two older ladies rode in the backseat. It was about a twelve-hour trip. What Ed and I didn't know was that the two women had a personality conflict, and an extreme one. By the time we arrived in El Paso the next morning, we were painfully aware of that fact, and we still had the return trip in store.

The meeting itself was great, though. It was a joint meeting with the New Mexico Folklore Society. Ben Mead showed slides of his sketches and paintings to illustrate his talk about some of his sketching trips in the 1930s. Also, eminent New Mexico folklorist T. M. Pearce, a professor at the University of New Mexico, gave a great paper about hand signals and signs. A young Hispanic fellow was using a new technological device—a video camera—to record the presentations. I visited with him and asked him about his taping. "I am recording the program for the school children of Cuba," he told me. I was very surprised until I realized that he had been sent to the El Paso meeting by the superintendent of the public school system of Cuba, New Mexico.

* * *

In the final session[2] of the 1978 meeting at Nacogdoches, Martha Anne Turner, who was an English professor at Sam Houston State University, in Huntsville, and the author of many books, grossly exceeded her allotted time of fifteen to twenty minutes. Her typescript appeared to be a thick sheaf of papers. I was tape recording the presentations. After the first forty-five minutes of her talk, my cassette ran out of tape. She talked for *at least* fifty or fifty-five minutes, probably more. Glen Lich chaired the session. I was sitting on the first or second row. I could see the concern on Glen's face, and I felt his frustration.

After Martha Anne had talked for somewhat more than twenty minutes, she said (in an aside to Glen) something like, "I want to be sure to not talk too long, Glen, so please hold up your hand so I can see it after I have spoken for fifteen minutes. Then I can use the next two or three minutes to wrap up." When she said that, Glen immediately raised his hand, and Martha Anne almost simultaneously looked down at her notes. To this bystander it almost looked as though she was intentionally avoiding looking in Glen's direction. Five or ten minutes later, Glen, in despair, repeated the hand signal, and Martha Anne again immediately looked down.

Members of the audience were leaving in droves to check out of the hotel by the noon deadline. But many were then returning to hear Jim Lee's presentation, always a highlight of any TFS program in which he participates. Finally, Martha Anne concluded her talk and sat down. When Glen introduced Jim Lee, Jim said what a hard act Ms. Turner was to follow. In fact, he said, she was *so* hard to follow that, if he was ever again scheduled to follow her, he would just pass. She dabbed at her eyes some with a tissue, but in my judgment the emotion she showed was not remorse.

The next year, I was program chairman. Ms. Turner submitted to me a typescript of her paper that looked to be at least as thick as the one she had been reading from at the Nacogdoches meeting. I wrote back, praising the paper (which was excellent) but saying that I would need to see a shorter version before I could assign her a place on the program, especially in light of what had happened in

Nacogdoches. She answered my letter, saying that she was very busy, what with book promotions, television interviews, and such—too busy, in fact, to submit a shortened version of her paper, but she assured me that her presentation would take no longer than twenty minutes. I wrote her again to make sure that there would be no misunderstanding, stating that she would *not* be on the program. She wrote back, saying that she was *astounded.*

* * *

Martha Emmons was the grand elder lady of the TFS. In 1924, Martha, a young public school teacher, wrote to Dobie and sent him a one-dollar bill to join the Society and pay her dues. He wrote back, saying that if she would send a second dollar, she would receive the TFS book for that year. She did so and remained a member for most of the next sixty-six years, until her death in 1990.

During our trip to El Paso in 1977, at one point Martha and I were alone in the car for a few moments. She told me that many TFS members considered her a staunch Baptist to whom strong drink was anathema. However, she said, she grew up in an Irish family, and her father always kept whiskey in their home. She also confided in me that, although many TFS folks frequently called her "Miss Martha," she disliked the designation. I asked her why. She replied that the title "Miss" just called undue attention to the fact that she was "an old maid." Martha's death was a great loss to the members of the Society.

At the 1970 Wimberley meeting, I had seen Mody Boatright. I could have bought one of his handmade wooden paisanos at that meeting for a five-dollar donation to the TFS. But I didn't have an extra five dollars at the time.

At the 1981 TFS banquet in Denton, John O. West auctioned off one of the Boatright paisanos that had been given back to the Society to make it available for the purpose of fundraising. Our twelve-year-old son, Brad, was sitting next to Martha Emmons. He told her that our family desperately wanted that paisano. I bought it in the auction that evening for $200. Martha had an

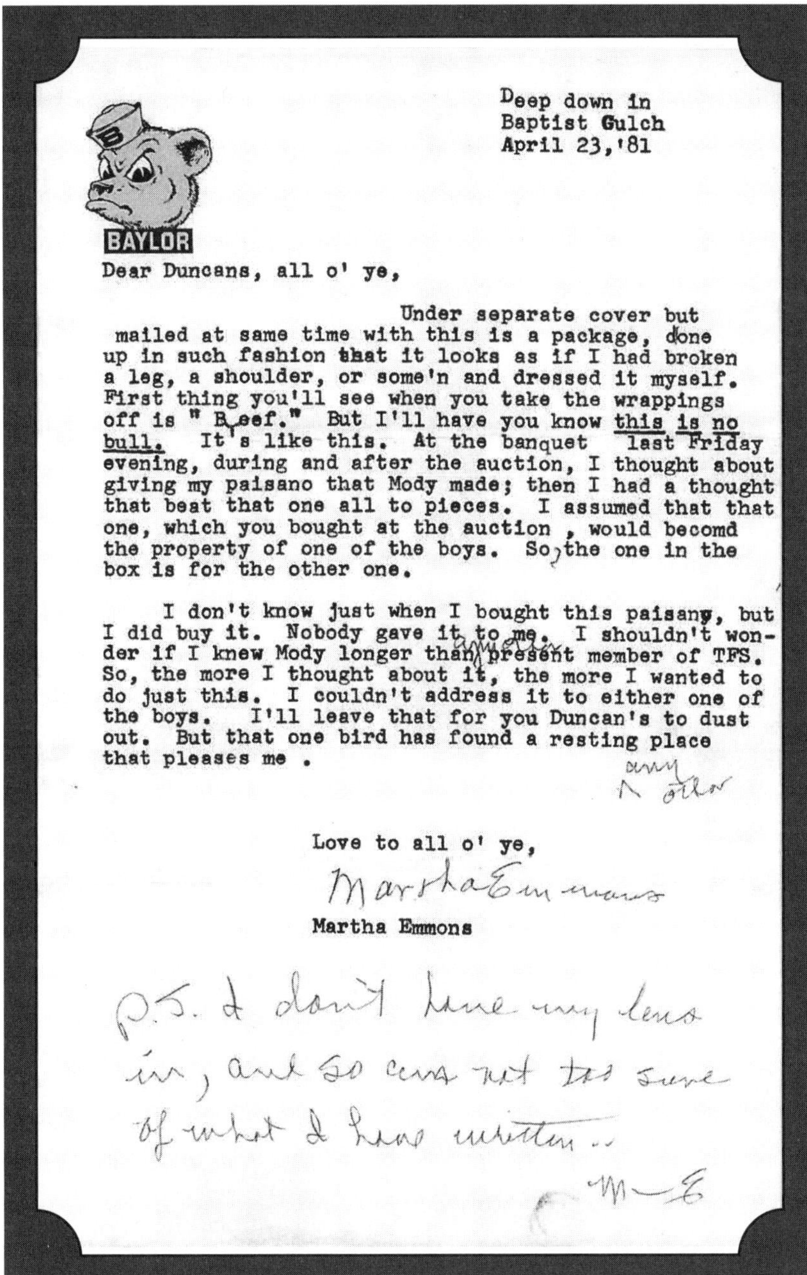

Deep down in
Baptist Gulch
April 23,'81

Dear Duncans, all o' ye,

Under separate cover but mailed at same time with this is a package, done up in such fashion that it looks as if I had broken a leg, a shoulder, or some'n and dressed it myself. First thing you'll see when you take the wrappings off is " Beef." But I'll have you know this is no bull. It's like this. At the banquet last Friday evening, during and after the auction, I thought about giving my paisano that Mody made; then I had a thought that beat that one all to pieces. I assumed that that one, which you bought at the auction , would becomd the property of one of the boys. So, the one in the box is for the other one.

I don't know just when I bought this paisano, but I did buy it. Nobody gave it to me. I shouldn't wonder if I knew Mody longer than any other present member of TFS. So, the more I thought about it, the more I wanted to do just this. I couldn't address it to either one of the boys. I'll leave that for you Duncan's to dust out. But that one bird has found a resting place that pleases me .

Love to all o' ye,

Martha Emmons

Martha Emmons

P.S. I don't have my lens in, and so am not too sure of what I have written..

M—E

The letter from Martha Emmons, explaining why she was giving her Mody Boatright paisano to the Duncans extra Boatright paisano that she had contemplated donating for a future TFS auction. But she wrote me that next week, saying that she had had an epiphany that evening and was sending us her extra paisano:

> At the banquet last Friday evening, during and after the auction, I thought about giving my paisano that Mody made; then I had a thought that beat that one all to pieces. I assumed that that one, which you bought at the auction, would [eventually] become the property of one of the boys. So, the one in the box is for the other one. . . . So, the more I thought about it, the more I wanted to do just this. I couldn't address it to either one of the boys. I'll leave that for you Duncans to dust out. But that one bird has found a resting place that pleases me.[3]

After the banquet and hoot that Friday night, John O. West told me that he didn't have a place to stay that night. Oh, he had a room that he was sharing with a fellow trans-Pecos professor, but the fellow professor needed the room to entertain a newly-acquired girlfriend. My family and I were staying at my father's house in Denton, so I told John to follow me there, where he could sleep on the living room couch. We arrived at Dad's house so late that everyone already was asleep. We located a blanket and a pillow and gave them to John, and he slept on the couch, unbeknownst to Dad and his family. The next morning I cringed when John poured a couple of big dollops of whiskey into his mug of coffee and set the bottle on the kitchen table. My stepmother was a teetotaler, but fortunately John stowed his bottle before she woke up.

* * *

The weather was strange for the 1988 meeting in Lubbock. Within twenty-four hours we experienced thunder, lightning, and rain. Not so unusual, you say? Then add to that a dust storm, tornadoes, hail, high wind, sleet, and snow. Ed and Mae Offield were flying in for the meeting. Their flight from Dallas was delayed; their plane was put in a circling, holding pattern and was eventually diverted to El Paso or somewhere similarly remote. When they finally arrived on Friday, Ed said he would never fly again. It wasn't clear to me whether he meant just to TFS meetings, or if he was swearing off airplanes altogether. But he was touchy about it, so I didn't press him to be more specific.

Lawrence Clayton had arranged to have John Erickson entertain at the banquet. John, author of the popular Hank the Cowdog series of humorous (actually more aptly described as hilarious) books, used ten or twelve different characters' voices to dramatize his stories. I had the unsettling feeling that John was looking directly at me during much of his presentation. Just my imagination, I told myself. Afterwards, I bought a couple of his books and stood in line to have them signed. When it was my turn to get his autograph, John said, "Don't I know you?" No, we had never met. But it turned out that he and I had both written some guest columns called "Southwest Letters" for the *Dallas Times Herald* in the early 1980s. Our photos ran with our columns. I had read John's columns, but it never occurred to me that he had read mine. He was one of *my* readers. Small world!

* * *

After we arrived in Abilene for the 1996 meeting, it started to rain. Later, the rain turned to snow. That Easter weekend Abilene got 9 ? inches of snow. Austin freelance writer Gene Fowler read a paper at the meeting. He told me that he rented a car for just twenty-four hours to drive from Austin to Abilene, give his paper, and drive back to Austin. He said that as he drove out of Austin, the sun was shining. The closer he got to Abilene, the worse the weather got. He drove through ice and snow, both coming and going, but by the time he was back in Austin, the weather was fine. Gene said it was a surreal experience. He gave a good paper, though.

* * *

There are a great number of people that I haven't mentioned because they were not central to any of the vignettes I've included, and I didn't set out to be a namedropper. But in closing I can't resist mentioning several of them. They include many dear friends who have been very active in the Society, friends such as Dean and Olivia Nichols, Orlan Sawey, Jim Byrd, Fran Vick, Robert and Jean Flynn, Charles and Lou Rodenberger, Elmer and Ann Kelton, Jim and Mary Harris, Tom and Mary Crum, Milton and Deurelle McAfee, Jim and Liz Vause, Ted and Maisie Paulissen, John Lightfoot and Patsy Patten, Charles Linck and Ernestine Sewell, Jerry Lincecum and Peggy Redshaw, Faye Leeper, Art and Margie Hendrix, Al and Darlyne Lowman, Hazel Abernethy, Ernest Speck, Margaret Waring, Ken Davis, Melvin Mason, Chris Waring, Brenda Black White, Kent Biffle, Joyce Roach, Ruth Lambert, Paul Patterson, Bill Stokes, and on and on.

As I said, I'm under the influence of strong spirits, even when I'm stone-cold sober. I have personally benefited greatly from the scholarship, fellowship, and friendship of this motley group of very diverse and wonderful individuals. I am thankful to one and all for enriching my mind and soul.

Endnotes

1. Ben K. Green and A. C. Greene earlier had planned to form a Dallas Corral, but it did not materialize.
2. The official program for that meeting shows that Martha Anne Turner's presentation was scheduled for the previous session. But the order of the papers must have been rearranged, because Martha Anne's presentation was definitely in the final session, chaired by Glen Lich, and immediately before Jim Lee's presentation.
3. Letter from Martha Emmons, "Deep Down in Baptist Gulch" [Waco] to "Dear Duncans, all o' ye," dated April 23, 1981.

Contributors' Vitas

Meredith E. Abarca earned a B.A. in English/American Literature from the University of California at Santa Cruz and a Ph.D. in Comparative Literature from the University of California at Davis. She is an associate professor of English at the University of Texas-El Paso. Her courses generally include Chicana/o Literature, Mexican-American Folklore, Film and Literature of the Americas, Critical Theory, and Women Philosophers in the Kitchen. She is the author of *Voices in the Kitchen: Views of Food and the World from Working-Class Mexican and Mexican American Women*, published by Texas A&M University Press, 2006. Some of her articles have appeared in *Food & Foodways*. Her work has also been published in edited collections and encyclopedias. She has given a number of international lectures in Mexico, Poland, Scotland, Australia, and Italy.

Francis Edward Abernethy, Distinguished Regents Professor Emeritus of English at Stephen F. Austin State University, was Secretary-Editor of the Texas Folklore Society from 1971 to 2004, editing or co-editing over twenty volumes of TFS publications in his thirty-three years of leading the organization. He is the Curator of Exhibits for the East Texas Historical Association and a member of the Texas Institute of Letters. He has written and published poetry, short stories, a folk music book entitled *Singin' Texas*, a book of legends entitled *Legends of Texas' Heroic Age*, and a history of the Texas Folklore Society in three volumes. He has lectured widely, both popularly and academically. He is a World War II veteran, he explored the caves of Mexico and the Yucatan for over twenty years, he built the La Nana Creek Trail in Nacogdoches, he is a world traveler and a scuba diver, he soloed in a Cessna and skydived with his son and grandson, and he plays the bass fiddle in the East Texas String Ensemble of Nacogdoches. He was born in Altus,

Oklahoma, December 3, 1925, grew up in the Panhandle and East Texas, has been married to Hazel Shelton Abernethy since 1948, and has five children and six grandchildren, whom he loves dearly.

Dr. Len Ainsworth is Emeritus Professor and Vice-Provost for Academic Affairs of Texas Tech University. He is a charter board member of the National Cowboy Symposium and Celebration and a long-time member of the National Ranching Heritage Center, both located in Lubbock. In retirement he owns the Adobe Book Collection and deals in collectible and rare books on Texas and the West.

Scott Hill Bumgardner is a small-scale rancher, real estate consultant, retired Houston cop, grandpa, and professional storyteller. He has served several terms as president of the Houston Storytellers Guild and has been a member of the Houston Rodeo Speakers Committee since 1991. Scott has been active for many years keeping the legends and folklore of the West alive. His cowboy poetry has been featured in anthologies, and he has produced three audio CDs. Folks enjoy his tales and rhymes about bad horses, cattle, and even the adventures of "Snappy the Amazing Pet Gator." His historical tales and cowboy poetry sometimes take a turn for the outlandish; funny, far-fetched tales keep falling out of his head. Though he has been honored with nominations as a top cowboy poet, the lighter side of his nature keeps the audience on the edge of their seats as his fun, high-action tales come roaring by.

Mary Margaret Dougherty Campbell holds a B.A. and an M.A. in English from Texas Tech University, and an M.S. in Educational Administration from Texas A&M University, Corpus Christi. She has had articles published in *English in Texas*, *South Texas Traveler*, *South Texas Catholic*, and *Cowboy Magazine*, as well as essays in three TFS publications: *The Family Saga*, *Folklore: In All of Us, In All We Do*, and *Death Lore: Texas Rituals, Superstitions, and Legends of the Hereafter*. Her poems have appeared in *English in Texas*, *American Cowboy*, *Rope Burn*, four volumes of the *Texas Poetry*

Calendar, and *Big Land, Big Sky, Big Hair: The Best of the Texas Poetry Calendar*. She is the Executive Director of George West Storyfest and currently serves the TFS as Vice-President.

Charles Chupp is a retired Senior Right-of-Way agent, author, artist, and hometown philosopher. He has authored six previous books and has written a weekly newspaper column for better than fifty years. He still composes his tales on a lined pad with a Scripto pencil. Information about his books, and hundreds of his "I Got NO REASON TO LIE" columns are available at www.CharlesChupp.com. He called the area outside of De Leon, Texas, where he grew up, "Poverty Knob." He now lives in-town—within the "Poverty Sink" addition. Recently widowed, he brags on his daughter Tracy, his son Ace, three grandchildren Audrey, Mercedes, and Taylor Ann, and two great-grandchildren Angel and Ilia.

Kenneth W. Davis, a past president of the Texas Folklore Society, is Professor Emeritus of English, Texas Tech University. He is also active in the West Texas Historical Association, the Texas State Historical Association, and the local chapter of Westerner's International. He is an active member of Western Writers of America. He remains much interested in traditional oral narration and folkways of his fellow native Texans. He resides in Lubbock with Babe the Wonder Dogge, a Cairn terrier whose latest efforts are to learn how to drive a Ford Explorer.

Charles C. Doyle was born in Marlin, Texas (to immigrants from Arkansas), but moved to Weimar, Texas, as an infant. He attended The University of Texas (B.A. 1964, Ph.D. 1969). Since 1974, he has taught folklore, Renaissance literature, and linguistics in the English department at the University of Georgia. His principal folklore specialty is proverbs. He has belonged to the TFS since the early 1970s. He used to play the trombone in the Longhorn Band. Now he plays the trombone in the Classic City Band of Athens, Georgia.

Robert J. (Jack) Duncan has lived in McKinney most of his life. Jack is a writer/editor/researcher for Retractable Technologies, Inc., a manufacturer of safety needle medical devices in Little Elm. He is also a widely published freelance writer, in both scholarly and popular publications. He has taught at Collin College and Grayson County College, and has worked in other capacities for two community colleges. Jack was TFS president once upon a time, and has been a participating member for nearly four decades. He continues to take graduate courses at UNT in a variety of disciplines. He is married to his high school sweetheart, the former Elizabeth Ann Harris; they have two sons and five grandsons.

Clarence Jay Faulkner is a third generation Texan born in Waco and raised, for the most part, by his grandmother Pearl Grusendorf Whitlock. During the 1950s and early '60s, he logged many miles on Greyhound buses between Waco and Fresno, California, where his parents had gone to seek their fortune. Along the way he often listened in on stories being told at the cafes or on the county courthouse squares where he lingered drinking a soda pop or just stretching. He loved the sight of the oilfield pumping units and ranch windmills. Later on, he worked as a computer programmer for a number of oil production operators throughout the Permian Basin, and came to love the rugged beauty of Far West Texas. He also took a liking to J. Frank Dobie's stories, cowboy poetry, and Texas folklore. Through short story writing and attaining Toastmaster's ATM-Gold certification, he found an audience for his "Hooked on Texas" tales and stories. He hopes to retire to Alpine, Marfa, or Fort Davis to spend his sunset years as a campfire storyteller under the stars.

Sue M. Friday, a native of Houston, lives on a farm outside Charlotte, North Carolina. Her husband Tom, also a native Texan, died in December 2008. In April 2009, cousins and friends gathered at the Hemphill dogtrot for a memorial luncheon. Tom would have enjoyed the stories told on him. Most were true.

Bruce A. Glasrud is Professor Emeritus of History, California State University, East Bay; retired Dean, School of Arts and Sciences, Sul Ross State University; and a Fellow of the Texas State Historical Association. He resides in Seguin, Texas. Born and raised in Minnesota, Bruce received his Ph.D. in history from Texas Tech University—one of the early products of the "Texas Tech School of Black History." He has published thirteen books and sixty-plus articles in scholarly works. He is co-editor of *The African American West: A Century of Short Stories* (Colorado, 2000), *Buffalo Soldiers in the West: A Black Soldiers Anthology* (Texas A&M, 2007), *The African American Experience in Texas* (Texas Tech, 2007), and *Black Women in Texas History* (Texas A&M, 2008).

Sarah L. Greene has lived most of her life in Gilmer, where she was the third-generation publisher of the semi-weekly *Gilmer Mirror*, a family-owned newspaper now in the hands of a fourth generation. After attending Stephens College in Columbia, Missouri, she received a bachelor of Journalism degree from the University of Texas–Austin in 1949. She worked as a reporter for the *Dallas Morning News* for three years before she and her husband, the late Ray H. Greene, moved to Gilmer to join the *Mirror* staff. She was a writer and editor from 1953 to 1982, when she became publisher. She retired in 2007 but continues to write a regular column. She has been president of the Texas Folklore Society, the Texas Press Association, and the North and East Texas Press Association. She served on the Texas Commission on the Arts, and was a founding director of Historic Upshur Museum in Gilmer and the Upshur County Arts Council. She is an Ambassador of the Texas Folklife Festival in San Antonio, and she has presented papers for the Texas State Historical Association and the East Texas Historical Association.

Lee Haile lives in Bandera County near Tarpley in the beautiful hill country of Texas with his family. He has a sawmill and a woodshop, and is a professional storyteller/musician. He is currently involved in building their house, "doing all the work myself, using all native materials from our land and surrounding ranches, without borrowing any money."

Carol Hanson was born and raised in Dallas, Texas, the child of August and Mary Helen Stanglin. She has four brothers and one sister—two of her brothers, Phil and David, accompanied her on the Sesquicentennial Wagon Train in May of 1986. Carol received her Masters of Library & Information Sciences degree from North Texas State University in Denton in December 1979. She has been a librarian at Dallas Public Library, Zula B. Wylie Library in Cedar Hill, and the Betty Warmack Branch Library of Grand Prairie. In 2004, she returned to Dallas Public Library to be Assistant Manager at the Kleberg-Rylie Branch Library. On June 17, 1989, she married Pete Hanson in Cedar Hill, Texas, where they still live with their son, Erik. Carol joined the Texas Folklore Society in 1985, after being a member of the Dallas corral of the Westerners organization and being encouraged by some to attend a TFS meeting. Carol attended the 1985 meeting with Ruth Lambert, and has been hooked ever since. Most anything associated with history interests her, which explains her dabbling with her family's genealogy for twenty-plus years, and is considered to be the family historian for the Stanglins. She also has interest in photography, scrap-booking, and gardening—and of course, reading. Erik was born in December 1990, and is currently a senior at Cedar Hill High School, where he has been very involved in playing percussion in the school band since his sixth grade year.

L. Patrick Hughes is a Professor of History at Austin Community College, where he has served on the faculty since 1977. A graduate of the University of Texas, he is also a guest lecturer for UT's Elderhostel and Road Scholar programs. He is an active member of numerous state and regional organizations, and he is the 2008–2009 president of the Texas Folklore Society.

Elmer Kelton had his introduction to folklore as a boy, listening to his father and other cowboys telling stories. Born on an Andrews County ranch in 1926, he attended school in Crane, Texas. One of his teachers, and a lifelong influence, was Paul Patterson. He majored in journalism at the University of Texas and broke into fiction writing via the Western pulp magazines in the late 1940s. He was an agricultural journalist forty-two years, continuing a fiction writing career in parallel to his job. He has published about fifty novels, including *The Time It Never Rained*, *The Good Old Boys*, and a series based on the Texas Rangers. He lives in San Angelo, Texas.

James Ward Lee is Emeritus Professor of English at the University of North Texas. He joined the Texas Folklore Society in 1958, and read his first paper before the Society in 1959. He was president of the Texas Folklore Society in 1967–68, and was elected a Fellow of the Society in 2005. He is author of many articles in Society publications, as well as numerous books and articles on literature and folklore. His most recent books are *Literary Fort Worth* (with Judy Alter), *Adventures with a Texas Humanist*, and *Texas Country Singers* (with Phil Fry).

Jerry B. Lincecum, a sixth-generation Texan, is Emeritus Professor of English at Austin College. He holds a B.A. in English from Texas A&M University, and M.A. and Ph.D. degrees from Duke University. A past president of the Texas Folklore Society, he has presented many papers at annual meetings of the Society, and he co-edited *The Family Saga: A Collection of Texas Family Legends* for the TFS in 2003. Since 1990, he and Dr. Peggy Redshaw have directed "Telling Our Stories," a humanities project at Austin College that aids older adults in writing their autobiographies and family histories. He also directs the Legacy program for Home Hospice of Grayson County, which collects the life stories of Hospice patients and publishes them in booklet form.

Al Lowman, in business since 1935, is now retired but marches on as Stringtown's foremost sedentary lifestyle activist. He is a past president of the Texas Folklore Society, the Book Club of Texas, and the Texas State Historical Association. Most recently he is founder and honorary curator of the Al Lowman Printing Arts Collection in the Cushing Library at Texas A&M University.

Archie P. McDonald has taught history at Stephen F. Austin State University for forty-four years, and served as director of the East Texas Historical Association and editor of the association's *Journal* for thirty-seven years. He is a past president of the Texas State Historical Association, past vice-chair of the Texas Historical Commission, and author/editor of more than twenty books on historical topics—and one book of humor titled *Helpful Cooking Hints for HouseHusbands of Uppity Women*. Along with teaching, Archie currently serves Stephen F. Austin State University as the University/Community Liaison.

Charlie Oden is an old fellow who lives with a daughter and her family in Irving, Texas, and who was born to pioneer parents and inherited their pioneer values, including a love for listening to and telling stories, and in finding and writing stories. The music he listens to as he drives along is the music of singer/songwriters who are selling their CDs at their performances. Their songs are recordings of the lore of the people today. He enjoys the music of Pete Seeger, Woodie Guthrie, Wayne King, and Johann Strauss. Charlie grew up on a truck farm, served in the military, worked for over forty years for "The friendly Espee" (Southern Pacific) Railroad. Along the way he accumulated ninety semester hours toward a degree in accounting. When he passed an Internal Revenue Service examination for enrolled agent, he and his wife Georgia operated what they called a "moonlighting" business in which they guided clients along the labyrinth of Federal and State tax laws. He enjoys being a member of the TFS and being in contact with the other members.

Peggy A. Redshaw, a native of Central Illinois, is a member of the Biology Department at Austin College in Sherman, Texas. She has been a member of the Society for fifteen years, has presented four papers at the TFS meetings, has an article in PTFS LVIII, served as a Councilor, and helped organize the 82nd meeting of the TFS at Sherman in 1998. She has also presented papers in Folklore sessions at the East Texas Historical Association and the Texas State Historical Association.

Joyce Gibson Roach is a Fellow of the Texas Folklore Society, a Fellow of the Texas State Historical Association and of the Clements Center for Southwest Studies at SMU, and a member of the Texas Institute of Letters and the Philosophical Society of Texas. She also holds Lifetime Memberships in the West Texas Historical Association, the East Texas Historical Association, and the Horned Lizard Conservation Society, of which she is currently national president.

Vicky Rose grew up in Central Texas listening to her grandparents' tales of outlaw relatives and her great-great-grandmother's escape from Santa Anna in the Runaway Scrape. Since then, she has lived in East Texas, West Texas, and the Houston metropolitan area. She has worked as a cashier in grocery and convenience stores, a receptionist for attorneys and a car dealership, a door-to-door surveyor, a bookkeeper at a brickyard, a general flunky in a dry cleaning establishment, and has owned and operated her own barbershop. At age fifty-two she earned a B.A. degree in journalism from Angelo State University. Her articles have appeared in *Roundup*, *Country Line Magazine*, *The Tombstone Times*, *Backwoods Home*, and *Ranch & Rural Living* among others. She currently resides once again in Central Texas.

J. Rhett Rushing is the staff Folklorist and Oral History Program Director for UTSA's Institute of Texan Cultures. A Native Texan and proud Aggie, husband, and father, Rhett has been a TFS member for twenty-six years, a past president, and has contributed a number of articles and papers to the Society's publications.

Jean Granberry Schnitz was born in Spur, Texas. She graduated from Raymondville High School in 1948, and from Texas College of Arts and Industries (now Texas A&M University-Kingsville) in 1952. She and Lew Schnitz were married in 1953, and have three sons and four grandchildren. A retired legal secretary, Jean lives near Boerne. She became a Director on the Board of the Texas Folklore Society in 2002, and was elected Vice-President for 2005–2006. She presided as President at the 91st annual meeting of the Texas Folklore Society in San Antonio in April of 2007. She was a participant in the Texas Folklife Festival in San Antonio for the 28th year in 2009. She has presented nine papers before the TFS since 1990.

Tim Tingle is an enrolled member of the Choctaw Nation of Oklahoma and a frequent speaker at tribal events. Author of six books, including the award-winning *Crossing Bok Chitto*, Tim performed Choctaw traditional stories at the Native American wing of the Smithsonian Institute in 2006 and 2007. At the 2008 American Library Association Conference in Anaheim, California, he spoke at the multi-ethnic concert "Many Voices, One Nation" and in 2007 served on an ALA panel of ethnic folklorists and writers, "Voices from the Inside."

Kenneth L. Untiedt grew up in DeWitt, Iowa, where he met his wife Tierney. He moved to Lubbock, Texas, where he served in the U. S. Air Force. After his enlistment, he became a police officer on the Lubbock Police Department, where he worked for nearly thirteen years while he earned his B.A., M.A., and Ph.D. from Texas Tech University. He became the Secretary-Editor of the Texas Folklore Society in 2004, and he is currently an associate professor of English at Stephen F. Austin State University. He and his wife live in Nacogdoches with their four children, Miché, Brody, Ashland, and Autumn.

Frances Brannen Vick was born in Trinity County in East Texas, where the E-Heart cattle roamed and where the old family land is still intact, currently held in sacred trust by her three children. She has spent her lifetime pursuing fun, and was fortunate enough to find it in the jobs she held—in teaching and in various types of publishing, including Official Publications at the University of Texas at one time. Her retirement has been equally fun so far, culminating in writing some books—*Petra's Legacy* and *Literary Dallas*—and thinking about others she might write. Her three children, her six grandchildren, and her five great-grandchildren have contributed mightily to her fun and continue to do so. She has also been fortunate enough to find friends who have contributed enormously to the pursuit of fun. And she has had fun with the Texas Institute of Letters, the Texas State Historical Association, the Philosophical Society of Texas, and the most fun group of all, the Texas Folklore Society.

Lucy Fischer West grew up in El Paso, the daughter of a Mexican mother and a German father. Her memoir, *Child of Many Rivers: Journeys to and from the Rio Grande*, was published in 2005 by Texas Tech University Press. It received a Border Regional Library Association Southwest Book Award, a WILLA Literary Finalist Award from Women Writing the West, and a Violet Crown Special Citation from the Writers' League of Texas. Previously, her essays have appeared in *BorderSenses*, *Password*, and two Texas Folklore Society publications: *The Family Saga* and *Both Sides of the Border*. She is featured in *The Best of Texas Folklore Volume 2*, from Writer's AudioShop, and the upcoming volume of *Literary El Paso*. A career educator, she currently teaches world history at Cathedral High School, and is President of the Texas Folklore Society.

INDEX

B

C

D

E

G

I

J

K

L

M

N

O

S

T

U